THE ED PONSI FOREX PLAYBOOK

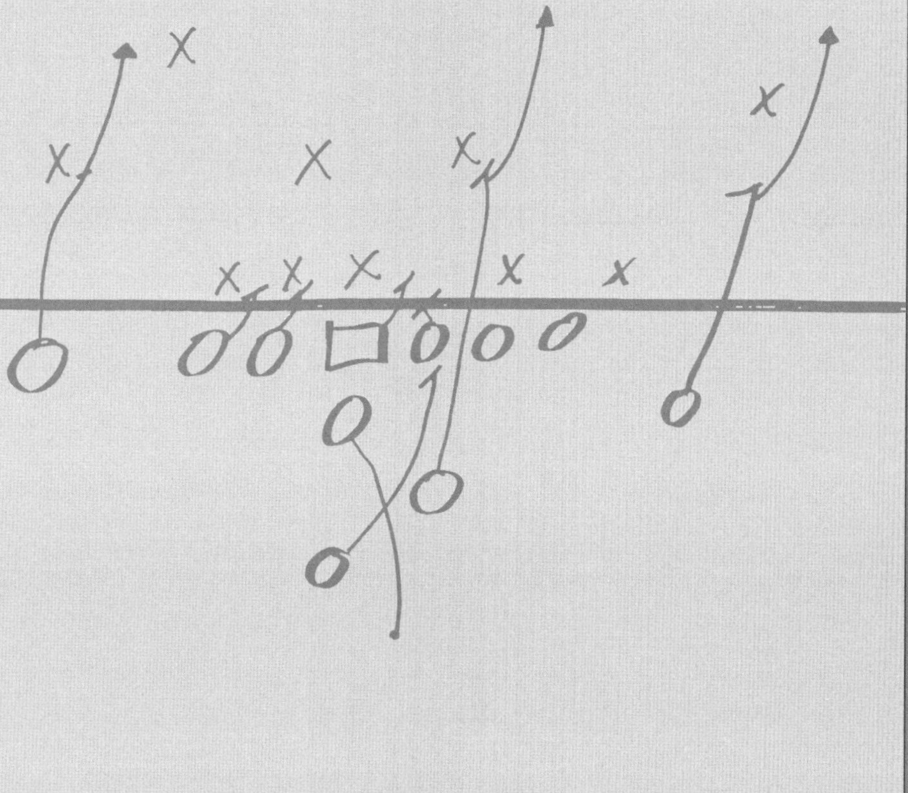

Founded in 1807, John Wiley & Sons is the oldest independent publishing company in the United States. With offices in North America, Europe, Australia, and Asia, Wiley is globally committed to developing and marketing print and electronic products and services for our customers' professional and personal knowledge and understanding.

The Wiley Trading series features books by traders who have survived the market's ever-changing temperament and have prospered—some by reinventing systems, others by getting back to basics. Whether you are a novice trader, a professional, or somewhere in between, these books will provide the advice and strategies needed to prosper today and well into the future.

For a list of available titles, please visit our web site at www.WileyFinance.com.

THE ED PONSI FOREX PLAYBOOK

Strategies and Trade Set-Ups

ED PONSI

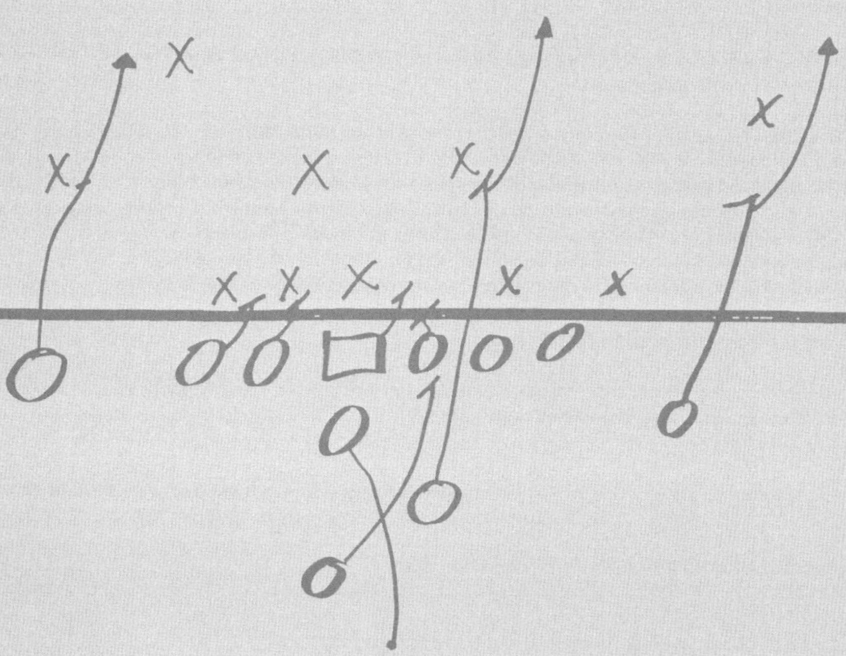

WILEY

John Wiley & Sons, Inc.

Published by John Wiley & Sons, Inc., Hoboken, New Jersey.
Published simultaneously in Canada.

For general information on our other products and services or for technical support, please contact our Customer Care Department within the United States at (800) 762-2974, outside the United States at (317) 572-3993 or fax (317) 572-4002.

Wiley also publishes its books in a variety of electronic formats. Some content that appears in print may not be available in electronic books. For more information about Wiley products, visit our web site at www.wiley.com.

Library of Congress Cataloging-in-Publication Data:

Ponsi, Ed, 1961–
The Ed Ponsi Forex playbook : strategies and trade set-ups / Ed Ponsi.
p. cm.
Includes index.
ISBN 978-0-470-50998-2 (pbk.)
1. Foreign exchange market. 2. Speculation. I. Title.
HG3851.P648 2010
332.4′5–dc22

2010004715

Printed in the United States of America.

10 9 8 7 6 5 4 3 2 1

This book is dedicated to the two loves of my life, Renata and Renee

CONTENTS

PREFACE

"Sports is human life in microcosm."
—Howard Cosell

A couple of years ago, I received an e-mail from a person who claimed to be a publisher. He'd heard me speak at a conference and wanted to know if I'd be interested in writing a book. My first thought was that this was a practical joke; after all, real writers work hard all their lives for such an opportunity, and here it was, unsolicited, knocking on my door. The eventual result of this conversation was my first book, *Forex Patterns and Probabilities* (John Wiley & Sons, 2007), one of the most popular books written to date on the subject of currency trading.

As I write now nearly three years after the first book's release, "FPAP" is still going strong and so are sales of the FXEducator DVDs, and I am constantly amazed at the reaction they have received. The book's success is even more incredible because unlike many of the other titles on the subject of Forex, there are no market makers or Forex brokers pushing it to their clients. I credit the success of "FPAP" to word of mouth: People love the book and tell their friends, who also love it. I have received many e-mails and letters from readers expressing their appreciation for "FPAP," and I just want to humbly and sincerely thank all of you for your kind support.

I've always thought of trading as a sport, and like many of my readers, I've played on amateur sports teams (my favorites are baseball, American football, and ice hockey) and I'm a sports fan. I'm sure many of you have noted the similarities between sports and trading, and it does seem that many traders are former athletes or at least athletically inclined.

One of the main differences between sports and trading is that most of us do not have a trading "coach." Trading is often a solitary occupation, and there is no designated person to lead us through the wilderness and on to victory.

This book is organized into five parts: Part I, "Training Camp," contains basic but vital information to lay the groundwork for your success. The next part, "Scoring Points," delves into more advanced trading concepts. Then Part III, "Winning the Championship," deals with specific techniques that will give your trading an edge. Part IV, "Commitment to Excellence," presents more advanced money-making trading concepts, and in the final section, "Staying in Shape," the reader learns which situations to avoid in order to enjoy a long and successful trading career.

By the time you have finished reading this book, you'll have an arsenal of trading strategies at your disposal. You'll also understand many diverse trading topics such as:

- Placing winning Forex trades using observation and analysis
- Trading like a hedge fund
- Interpreting the comments of a central bank
- Using a COT report
- Using Fed Funds futures and STIRs
- Understanding quantitative easing

Better still, you'll learn not just the meaning of the preceding terms, but how to use these situations as opportunities to make money.

If all of that sounds complicated, don't worry—it's not. None of these topics is complicated, and you'd understand them clearly and forever if only someone would explain them to you in a way that makes sense. Allow me to be that person.

The purpose of this book is to cover as much ground and as many useful concepts as possible, and to do so as efficiently as possible. With that in mind, I've written a book that is as much visual as it is verbal. That way, I won't sound like a robot, and you won't feel as if your head were about to explode.

After all, the purpose of any book is not for the author to impress you with his or her mental power or verbal dexterity. The purpose should be to give as much useful information as possible, and to give it as clearly as possible, so that the greatest amount of readers will understand (and fewer of them will be bored to tears). It is intended to be a reference guide that is also fun and easy to read.

Just like a pro athlete in a big game, pro traders sometimes make mistakes. Remember, when I write about the mistakes that traders make, I'm not looking down on them. I understand what they are going through because I've already made those mistakes (at least once, probably twice) and lived to tell the tale. I'm not some ivory-tower intellectual giving proclamations about the markets, but a guy from the trenches of the trading battlefield who has survived the wars and can offer some guidance and assistance to those who are taking up the fight.

What is the real connection between trading and sports? At the heart of it, I believe we follow sports because we want to emulate the positive things that we see, like scoring the big goal or making the impossible save. From our involvement in sports, we can also learn what not to do: Nobody wants to be the player who drops the ball, or shoots and misses at an open net.

More deeply, we want to feel the thrills and joys that a winner feels and avoid the feelings of losing and of loss. We can all relate to either scenario, because we have all been winners and losers at various times.

There is an undeniable, underlying logic to trading, but so often we are blinded by the brilliance of the prizes that we take our collective eye off the ball and lose sight of the facts. Who wouldn't be excited by the prospect of earning large sums of money, of being able to afford anything we want at the drop of a hat? Who wouldn't want to provide a fantastic lifestyle for themselves or their loved ones? The pull of trading becomes inescapable when we consider that anyone armed with the proper mind-set, some sensible strategies, and a keen sense of risk management can win at this game.

All of this is true, but how we ultimately arrive at winning may not be via the method or the means that we initially had in mind; in fact, we usually need to unlearn our misconceptions before we can succeed. This book will challenge many of those misconceptions.

Here is another similarity between trading and the sports world—trading is often a meritocracy. If an athlete wants to earn more money, the way to do it is through superior performance. Make the right decisions, do the right things, and you win the game and collect the prize. The problem for so many traders is that we don't know how to make the right decisions, and the idea of winning these incredible prizes causes us to take leave of our senses—right in the middle of the big game!

Here is the core problem with what most traders are doing—we are trying to make the right decisions based on the wrong things. Then when the decision turns out to be the wrong one, we don't understand what happened. In order to get you to make the right decisions, we will have to master the process that leads up to the decision.

"Knowing is not enough; we must apply."
—Bruce Lee

PART I

TRAINING CAMP

CHAPTER 1

WE PRACTICE LIKE WE PLAY

"When I was young, I never wanted to leave the court until I got things exactly correct. My dream was to become a pro."

—Larry Bird, 3-time Most Valuable Player,
National Basketball Association

One day during football practice, I was goofing around instead of playing hard. After all, it was only practice. My coach pulled me aside. "Ed," he said, "You have the potential to be a good player, but if you develop bad habits in practice you're likely to carry those habits onto the playing field. When you practice, you have to practice like you play. Because in the end, when the pressure is on, you're going to play the way you practiced."

He was right. Normally, it was my job to catch passes while on offense and prevent receivers from catching the ball while on defense. During our next game, I found myself playing an unfamiliar position (defensive linebacker) due to a teammate's injury.

We were in the heat of battle and the other team was advancing down the field, when I was suddenly caught out of position. At a crucial moment, I didn't know what I was supposed to do and I wasn't quite sure where I was supposed to be. If only I had paid closer attention in practice, perhaps I could have made the transition seamlessly. Instead, I found myself confused and out of position, and the opposing team scored as a result. I had let my teammates down due to my inattentiveness during practice.

"The more you sweat in practice, the less you bleed in battle."

—Author Unknown

Can you think of any great professional athlete who doesn't practice? Pro athletes spend many, many hours honing their craft. Basketball Hall of Famer Larry Bird was so proficient at making foul shots (his career average was .886, making him one of the most accurate ever from the foul line) that when he had to miss a shot on purpose (while filming a commercial), he found it difficult to fail. Bird had so conditioned himself to succeed through hours of practice that *it took him 10 attempts to succeed at missing the shot!*

What was it that made "Larry Legend" such a master at his craft? He did not possess an imposing physical presence; at 6 ft. 9 in., he wasn't a short man, but he wasn't tall by NBA standards (7-foot tall NBA basketball players are not uncommon). He couldn't jump very high and he wasn't particularly fast.

The key to Bird's success was this—nobody worked harder than Larry Bird. He was a perfectionist who would practice for hours. Bird was such a fanatic, he was even known to practice shots *with his eyes closed*! So what was it about him that made Larry Bird a winner? Better still, how would Bird himself *define* the term "winner"?

> "A winner is someone who recognizes his God-given talents, works his tail off to develop them into skills, and uses these skills to accomplish his goals."
>
> —*Larry Bird*

Just like Larry Bird, as well as every other great athlete, we also must condition ourselves to succeed through practice. Everyone reading this book needs to open a demo account. This goes for experienced traders too; any time you learn a new trading technique, you have to practice it in a demo account first. And when you trade in a demo account, I want you to treat it as if it were *all the money in the world*, because that's the way you're going to feel when you're trading in a live account.

I realize there are those who will say that demo trading doesn't help, that it doesn't feel the same as real trading. It doesn't *feel* the same because you're not *treating* it the same way that you treat real trading. Treat practice—in this case demo trading—as if it were real, and it will help your live trading. All the practice in the world will do you no good if you treat it like a joke. It's all in your head. We practice like we play.

A SERIES OF HABITS

Make a habit of doing things the right way. Trading is nothing but a series of habits, and if you form bad habits while practicing, those habits will resurface at the most inopportune moments. Practice good techniques and habits in the demo account, and when you find yourself in the heat of battle, you'll carry those good habits with you onto the Forex playing field.

If you are new to trading, you should trade a demo account for at least three months. When you open the account, you'll see that the demo will expire, usually after 30 days, but don't worry—you can always open another demo account. A good rule of thumb would be for you to trade successfully for at least three months in a demo account before attempting to trade live.

This part is important—when I say "trade successfully," that doesn't mean that you should place random trades or hold on to losing trades in the hope that they will become winners. That is not successful trading; in fact, if you are hanging on to losers, please understand that this could ultimately result in the demise of your account and the end of your trading career, because a person who does this will eventually hold a loser that will not come back. We will mention some hard-and-fast risk management rules during the course of this book, and those rules must never be broken.

RULES TO LIVE BY

Let's get some rules straight right now, so there is no doubt in your mind. In fact, you might want to write these down and stick them to your computer monitor, so that you'll never forget. Make it part of your routine to review these rules daily, and try to ingrain them into your thought process. Here are some rules to live by:

Rule #1: Holding Losses Is Not Allowed
Rule #2: Adding to Losses Is Not Allowed
Rule #3: You Must Use a Stop on Every Trade
Rule #4: Always Tighten Stops, Never Loosen Stops

Rules #1 through #3 seem fairly self-evident, but Rule #4 might require an explanation. In trading, when we say "tighten," this means to move the stop closer to the current price, thus reducing risk. Whenever we move a stop, we must tighten it. This means that we raise a stop when we are in a long position, or we lower a stop when we are in a short position.

On the other hand, "loosening" a stop is prohibited, because it increases risk. An example of loosening would be to lower the stop on a long position, or to raise the stop on a short position. In either case, the risk is increased—so loosening a stop is considered unacceptable. Traders who loosen stops have a tendency to cease using them, thus opening the door to a huge and unrecoverable loss.

FROM THE MINORS TO THE MAJORS

> "Practice does not make perfect. Only perfect practice makes perfect."
> —*Vince Lombardi, Pro Football Hall of Fame Coach*

If you can trade successfully for at least three consecutive months in a demo account, and if you are doing everything correctly (notice that I didn't say "if you feel confident"; confidence can be a wonderful thing, but confidence alone will not make you into a winning trader), then feel free to progress to live trading. My recommendation is that your first live account should be a "micro" account, one that allows you to trade live, but at the same time allows for little risk.

Trading in a micro account is the equivalent of playing "penny poker." It's a real game with real money, but it's difficult (but not impossible) to get hurt when you're trading EUR/USD for 10 cents per pip. If you continue to trade well in your micro account, move up to a "mini" account, one where EUR/USD has a value of $1 per pip.

Think of this progression as you would consider an athlete rising through a minor league system; for example, before making it to the "big leagues," a baseball player must advance through level A, then level AA, and finally the highest minor league level, AAA. Think of demo trading as level A, micro trading as level AA, and mini trading as level AAA. If you can proceed successfully through these levels, spending at least three months trading successfully at each level, you just might be ready for the major leagues—in this case, a standard account (one in which EUR/USD has a pip value of $10).

By now, these questions might be on your mind: "How long will it take to learn how to trade?" or "How long will it take me to progress to the top level of trading?" The answer really depends upon the individual. We have laid the groundwork for your rise through the minor league ranks, but everyone learns at their own pace, so if you're not ready to advance, be patient. After all, how long does it take to learn how to play the piano, or to ice skate? The answer depends on the student and their level of motivation.

Try not to worry about the length of time involved; instead, focus on doing things correctly. The market will still be there when you're ready. If you do things the right way, you'll get there faster.

> "If you don't have time to do it right, when will you have time to do it over?"
>
> —*John Wooden, Player and Coach, Basketball Hall of Fame*

There is also a question of aptitude; we have all heard of the player who would've been great, except for a flaw in his game that he just couldn't seem to correct. Think of the tennis pro who could've won Wimbledon but for her weak first serve, or the baseball player who couldn't make it in the majors because he never learned to hit a curveball.

In similar fashion, traders have to work the flaws out of their game. Some people take to trading quickly, and others may never get the hang of it. Try not to worry about how long it takes to become a good trader; instead, concern yourself with mastering the skills and perfecting the processes of trading. When you have accomplished this, you will be a good trader. First comes the work, and then come the rewards.

MONEY ON MY MIND

I frequently hear the question, "How much money will I make?" When we ask this question, we are looking at trading in the wrong way. Try to think of it this way: You are not trying to "make money," but instead you are trying to master a process.

> "An athlete cannot run with money in his pockets. He must run with hope in his heart and dreams in his head."
>
> —*Emil Zatopek, Runner, Olympic Gold Medalist*

Ask yourself this question: What does a concert pianist focus on when he is practicing? Most likely, he is concerned with the task at hand—"Are my dynamics correct? Am I hitting the keys too hard or too soft?" What does a brilliant hockey player like Alexander Ovechkin think about when he is blazing a path around the other team's defense and toward the net? I sincerely doubt that Alex the Great is thinking about money; he is probably calculating how sharply he can turn on his skates at his current speed without losing an edge. When Michelangelo applied his artistry to the ceiling of the Sistine Chapel, I somehow doubt that he was calculating his hourly pay for the project.

> "When I go out on the ice, I just think about my skating. I forget it is a competition."
>
> —*Katarina Witt, Figure Skater, Olympic Gold Medalist*

Anyone who does excellent work of any kind is probably focused on that work alone, and when the mind begins to wander toward the payoff, the work is likely to suffer. Focus instead on excellence, on performing the task flawlessly, and the money will follow.

I know this might sound crazy, but try not to think about money while you are trading. Money is an emotional topic, and when we think about money while trading, it tends to cloud our judgment. Our minds wander toward the things we could buy with that money, and away from the task at hand.

So, whether you are practicing in a demo account or trading in a live account, try thinking in terms of playing a game, as opposed to trading for money. You are playing a game, and the object is to collect points or pips. This might help to protect you from the emotional ramifications of thinking about money while you are trading.

Finally, whether you are practicing or playing, you must acquire an attitude of persistence. Consider the following quote, attributed to a heavyweight boxing champion.

> "Fight one more round. When your feet are so tired that you have to shuffle back to the center of the ring, fight one more round. When your arms are so tired that you can hardly lift your hands to come on guard, fight one more round. When your nose is bleeding and your eyes are black and you are so tired that you wish your opponent would crack you one on the jaw and put you to sleep, fight one more round—remembering that the man who always fights one more round is never whipped."
>
> *—James J. "Gentleman Jim" Corbett, Heavyweight Boxing Champ*

It's just like my American football coach always used to say, "We practice like we play." This means that, even though it's only practice, you run until your lungs feel they are about to burst—and then run harder. Even though that guy on the other side of the line of scrimmage is your good friend, you are going to hit him as hard as you possibly can on the next play. In other words, play like you mean it.

In the heat of battle, when you must react in a split second and have no time to think, your reaction will depend on the habits you've formed. The habits we take with us onto the field of play are created on the practice field. But winning doesn't take place when we step on to the field; we win or lose long before we press the key and place the trade. We win or lose based on our preparation for the game, or for the trade. In closing, consider the following statement from a book that has been lionized by traders for decades:

> "The victorious strategist only seeks battle after victory has been won; whereas he who is destined to defeat first fights and afterwards looks for victory."
>
> *—Sun Tzu, from* The Art of War

CHAPTER 2

THE PLAYING FIELD

"Whenever I get to a low point, I go back to the basics. I ask myself, 'Why am I doing this?' It comes down to passion."

—Lyn St. James, Professional Race Car Driver

Most traders will tell you they're passionate about trading, and if we really want to succeed, we're going to need that passion. We need passion to make the commitment to learn all we can about trading, and then we must put in the time and effort to follow up on that commitment.

We are going to cover a few basics here relating to the Forex playing field. This is essential stuff if you are new to currency trading, but if you're experienced, don't turn the page just yet—I'll bet that most of the experienced traders will learn something new in this chapter, something that just might come in handy someday as you stand on the playing field in the heat of the battle. Allow your passion to succeed to be greater than your desire to rush through and flip ahead to the next chapter!

TWO OF A KIND

When I first began trading, I had difficulty with the concept of a "currency pair." Every currency trade involves at least two currencies, because that is the only possible way to trade. If someone tells you that he or she is short the U.S. dollar, then by definition, that person must be long something—perhaps euros, or Japanese yen, or maybe even a basket of currencies.

You see, you can't trade one currency. Just try it sometime. Take 20 U.S. dollars and see if you can find someone who will give you $21 USD for it—not at some point in the future, but right now, on the *spot.* Unless you're a regular Artful Dodger, it's not going to happen. Someone might offer you $19, but that trade is a guaranteed loss; you'd be a fool to accept less than $20 for a $20 note.

TABLE 2.1 Major Currencies and Corresponding Central Banks

Currency	Symbol	Central Bank
Euro	EUR	European Central Bank, ECB
U.S. Dollar	USD	Federal Reserve, Fed
Swiss Franc	CHF	Swiss National Bank, SNB
Japanese Yen	JPY	Bank of Japan, BoJ
British Pound	GBP	Bank of England, BoE
Canadian Dollar	CAD	Bank of Canada, BoC
Australian Dollar	AUD	Reserve Bank of Australia, RBA
New Zealand Dollar	NZD	Reserve Bank of New Zealand, RBNZ

One currency alone doesn't fluctuate, so if you leave $20 on the nightstand, it will still be worth $20 when you wake up. The *buying power* of $20 may fluctuate, but the face value of the note will never be more—or less—than $20. However, the value of a currency fluctuates constantly when measured against other currencies.

Every time you visit a foreign country, you exchange one currency for another. In many cases, this rate of exchange, or exchange rate, is not fixed and fluctuates freely. This exchange rate between a pair of currencies is what Forex traders actually trade. With that in mind, let's familiarize ourselves with some of the most widely traded currencies and their corresponding central banks (see Table 2.1).

Perhaps you've heard some of the colorful nicknames of these currencies. It's important to know them because at some point, you'll be reading an article about the Forex market, and the author will use the nickname instead of the official name of the currency. It's vital that when you encounter these nicknames, you understand which currency is being discussed (see Table 2.2).

Some of the nicknames have colorful origins. For example, the terms "kiwi" and "loonie" refer to the images of birds that appear on the dollar coins of New Zealand and Canada, respectively. "Single currency" refers to the fact that the euro is a single currency that is used by many individual countries.

TABLE 2.2 Major Currencies and Corresponding Nicknames

Currency	Symbol	Nickname
Euro	EUR	Single Currency
U.S. Dollar	USD	Greenback, Buck
Swiss Franc	CHF	Swissy, Chef
Japanese Yen	JPY	Yen
British Pound	GBP	Sterling
Canadian Dollar	CAD	Loonie
Australian Dollar	AUD	Aussie
New Zealand Dollar	NZD	Kiwi

THE MANAGER

> "A baseball manager is a necessary evil."
>
> —*Sparky Anderson, Baseball Manager, Hall of Fame*

Nearly every team has a manager or a coach who is responsible for managing the players. It's the manager's job to create rules and policies that are beneficial to the team, and to make sure that the components of the team are functioning as one.

When it comes to Forex trading, nearly every currency has a manager who performs a similar task. If we pay close attention to these "managers" and their policies, they will reveal their "game plan" to us, allowing traders to profit from their actions. In fact, they often reveal these plans intentionally, as we independent traders are often a component of those plans!

A central bank is the "manager" responsible for monetary policy. The central bank manipulates interest rates and the money supply to influence economic activity. For instance, a central bank might lower short-term interest rates, making it cheaper to borrow money and therefore easier to open a business or buy a house. This should have the effect of stimulating the economy.

Stimulus can also be achieved by increasing the money supply; one way a central bank can accomplish this is by injecting capital directly into banks. According to this theory, if banks are flush with cash, they will be more likely to loan money to businesses and individuals. Conversely, a central bank can raise interest rates or decrease the supply of money, either of which will slow economic activity.

The stated mission of most central banks is to promote steady, sustainable economic growth while keeping inflation low. In the case of most developed countries, this means annual GDP growth of about 3 percent to 5 percent, with inflation targeted at 3 percent or below.

UNDER MY THUMB

Some central banks, such as the ECB and the Fed, are independent; that is, they are not under the thumbs of their respective governments. This is important because politicians usually desire lower interest rates—even when it is not the right move for their country's economy or future.

Perhaps you have heard it said that people "vote with their pocketbooks." This means that an incumbent politician stands a better chance at reelection if the economy is strong, and faces a tougher battle if the voting populace is unhappy with their current economic situation. This is true despite the fact that an incumbent politician's actions may not have impacted the economy at all. Not every economic success or failure lies in the hands of politicians, most of whom are experts in law as opposed to economics.

If a politician seeking reelection feels that he can influence a central bank to cut interest rates, he will usually do so and worry about the consequences at a later time. Those consequences include inflation, which often occurs when economic growth is left unchecked and when interest rates are left too low for too long.

Meanwhile, an independent central bank can take actions to control inflation (such as raising interest rates or reducing the money supply) without having to worry about the political ramifications. But even in situations where the central bank is independent, the leaders of that central bank may try to curry favor with politicians—and thus seek reappointment—by keeping interest rates lower than necessary.

THE COACHING STAFF

Nearly every central bank has within it a special body—a sort of "coaching staff"—responsible for making decisions on interest rates, money supply, and other aspects of monetary policy. For example, the ECB has a Governing Council, which consists of six members of an executive board, plus the governors of the national central banks of the euro area countries.

The U.S. Federal Open Market Committee has 12 members, and the Bank of England's Monetary Policy Committee has nine. Despite having a Monetary Policy Committee, the Reserve Bank of New Zealand is a little unusual in that just one person, the governor of the RBNZ, is responsible for the bulk of the decisions. Table 2.3 shows the decision-making bodies and the benchmark interest rates for the major currencies.

TABLE 2.3 Major Central Banks and Key Interest Rates

Central Bank	Decision-Making Body	Key Interest Rate
European Central Bank (ECB)	The Governing Council	Minimum Bid Rate
Federal Reserve (Fed)	Federal Open Market Committee (FOMC)	Fed Funds Rate
Swiss National Bank (SNB)	The Directorate	Swiss 3-Month LIBOR
Bank of Japan (BoJ)	The Policy Board	Overnight Call Rate
Bank of England (BoE)	Monetary Policy Committee (MPC)	Official Bank Rate
Bank of Canada (BoC)	The Governing Council	Overnight Rate
Reserve Bank of Australia (RBA)	Reserve Bank Board	Cash Rate
Reserve Bank of New Zealand (RBNZ)	Governor of the RBNZ	Official Cash Rate

A TEAM WITHOUT A MANAGER

It's interesting to note that not all countries have a central bank. For example, Singapore has a Monetary Authority, the MAS. The MAS differs from most central banks in that it does not directly manipulate interest rates to achieve a desired result, choosing instead to influence exchange rates.

For example, if concerned about inflation, the MAS might strengthen the Singapore dollar vs. the U.S. dollar directly, instead of raising interest rates. Conversely, the MAS could weaken the Singapore dollar if deflation were to become a concern.

Panama has no central bank, yet until recently it enjoyed a history of low inflation. Over the past several decades, Panama's economy has been considerably more stable than that of many of its Latin American neighbors.

Another country that lacked a central bank was the United States. That's right; the United States actually had no central bank during various points in its history. The current U.S. Federal Reserve was created in 1913.

OTHER NOTABLE CURRENCIES

In addition to the majors, there are many other currencies, some of which are less liquid. Don't ignore these currencies; sometimes, the best opportunities occur in places where many traders won't even look (see Table 2.4).

COMMONLY TRADED CURRENCY PAIRS

Most combinations created from the eight major currencies (USD, EUR, GBP, JPY, CHF, CAD, AUD, NZD) result in a liquid, tradable pair. Table 2.5 shows the most commonly traded pairs.

OTHER NOTABLE CURRENCY PAIRS

There are many additional currency pairs beyond the majors. Pairs that contain only one major currency tend to be less liquid, and not every Forex broker offers them, but occasionally they present superior opportunities (see Table 2.6).

WHO DECIDES?

The ISO (International Organization for Standardization) determines the symbol for a currency and the order of currencies in each pair. The ISO, which refers to itself as the

TABLE 2.4 Less Widely Traded Currencies

Country	Name	Symbol	Country	Name	Symbol
Argentina	Peso	ARS	Mexico	Peso	MXN
Belize	Dollar	BZD	Norway	Krone	NOK
Belarus	Ruble	BYR	Peru	Nuevo Sole	PEN
Brazil	Real	BRL	Poland	Zloty	PLN
Chile	Peso	CLP	Russia	Ruble	RUB
China	Yuan	CNY	Rwanda	Franc	RWF
Colombia	Peso	COP	Singapore	Dollar	SGD
Czech Republic	Koruna	CZK	South Africa	Rand	ZAR
Denmark	Krone	DKK	Sweden	Krona	SEK
Estonia	Kroon	EEK	Saudi Arabia	Riyal	SAR
Egypt	Pound	EGP	Somalia	Shilling	SOS
Georgia	Lari	GEL	Tanzania	Shilling	TZS
Hong Kong	Dollar	HKD	Thailand	Baht	THB
Hungary	Forint	HUF	Tunisia	Dinar	TND
India	Rupee	INR	Turkey	Lira	TRY
Indonesia	Rupiah	IDR	Uganda	Shilling	UGX
Israel	New Shekel	ILS	Ukraine	Hryvnia	UAH
Jordan	Dinar	KWD	Uruguay	Peso	UYU
South Korea	Won	KRW	Uzbekistan	Sum	UZS
Kuwait	Dinar	KWD	Viet Nam	Dong	VND
Malaysia	Ringgit	MYR	Zimbabwe	Dollar	ZWD

TABLE 2.5 Widely Traded Currency Pairs

Symbol	Description
EUR/USD	Euro/U.S. Dollar
GBP/USD	British Pound/U.S. Dollar
USD/JPY	U.S. Dollar/Japanese Yen
USD/CHF	U.S. Dollar/Swiss Franc
EUR/JPY	Euro/Japanese Yen
EUR/GBP	Euro/British Pound
EUR/CHF	Euro/Swiss Franc
GBP/JPY	British Pound/Japanese Yen
GBP/CHF	British Pound/Swiss Franc
NZD/USD	New Zealand Dollar/U.S. Dollar
AUD/USD	Australian Dollar/U.S. Dollar
USD/CAD	U.S. Dollar/Canadian Dollar
AUD/JPY	Australian Dollar/Japanese Yen
NZD/JPY	New Zealand Dollar/Japanese Yen

TABLE 2.6 Less Widely Traded Currency Pairs

Symbol	Description
EUR/DKK	Euro/Danish Krone
USD/SEK	U.S. Dollar/Swedish Krone
USD/SGD	U.S. Dollar/Singapore Dollar
EUR/RUB	Euro/Russian Ruble
EUR/SEK	Euro/Swedish Krone
CAD/CHF	Canadian Dollar/Swiss Franc
NZD/CAD	New Zealand Dollar/Canadian Dollar
USD/HKD	U.S. Dollar/Hong Kong Dollar
USD/CNY	U.S. Dollar/Chinese Yuan
USD/DKK	U.S. Dollar/Danish Krone
USD/BRL	U.S. Dollar/Brazilian Real
USD/MXN	U.S. Dollar/Mexican Peso
USD/RUB	U.S. Dollar/Russian Ruble
GBP/NZD	British Pound/New Zealand Dollar

"world's largest developer and publisher of International Standards," is a network of the national standards institutes of 157 countries.

When trading in the spot currency market, the order of the currencies in any given pair is fixed. In other words, EUR/USD is the official order of the two currencies contained in that pair; however, this does not prevent various entities from providing an inverse quote, such as USD/EUR. If you do happen to see a quote for USD/EUR, you are probably looking at an inverse quote, which simply measures the current value of one USD in terms of euros. The official order of the pair when trading in the spot market is always EUR/USD, as determined by the ISO.

METHOD TO THE MADNESS

While the order of the currencies in each pair may appear to be somewhat random, there are some general rules at work here. For example, in every currency pair in which it is a member, EUR is listed first (EUR/USD, EUR/JPY). GBP is also listed first (GBP/USD, GBP/JPY), unless it is matched against the euro (EUR/GBP).

AUD and NZD are always listed first, except when they are matched against EUR or GBP. JPY is usually listed as the second member of the pair (USD/JPY, AUD/JPY). USD can be listed first (USD/CAD, USD/CHF) or last (AUD/USD, NZD/USD). Remember, the order of a currency pair never changes, regardless of which currency is the stronger of the two.

The first currency of any currency pair is called the *base currency*. The second member of any currency pair is called the *counter currency* or *quote currency*.

SPOT AND FUTURES MARKETS

There are numerous ways to trade currencies, and this can cause quite a bit of confusion. One key distinction is the difference between the Forex spot market, also known as the cash market, and the Forex futures market.

What is the spot or cash market? Suppose that you are thirsty; you walk into a store and purchase water. You give *cash* to the person behind the counter, and he gives you water, right now, on the *spot.*

The cash or spot Forex market refers to the exchange rate *right now*. The trade occurs immediately, *on the spot.*

What is the futures market? Suppose that you are not thirsty now, but you believe that you will be thirsty next week. You want water delivered to your door next week, which is in the future. You enter into a *contract* with the store owner to deliver water to you in the *future* at a specified price.

The Forex futures market refers to the exchange rate in the future. The difference between these two examples is the essential difference between the Forex spot and futures markets.

LET'S GET PHYSICAL

In the world of futures trading, a trader who holds a contract to maturity may be forced to deliver or take delivery of the commodity listed in the contract. This is referred to as *physical delivery*, or *physical settlement.*

For example, suppose a cereal company wants to buy a specific quantity of wheat (accept delivery of wheat) on a specific date in order to manufacture more of its products. At the same time, a farmer wants to sell (deliver) wheat after his crops are harvested. The farmer and the cereal company enter into a futures contract; this way, the company knows it will have the wheat it needs, and the price that it will pay. The farmer knows he will have a buyer for his wheat, and the price he will receive.

The benefit to both parties is that they achieve the certainty they need to operate their respective businesses. The cereal company now knows how much it will have to pay for the wheat, the quantity it will receive, and the date it will receive it; the farmer now knows if he can afford that new tractor he's had his eye on, because he knows how much money he will receive for his crops when they are harvested. He also knows the date, the time, and the location to which he must deliver the commodity.

CONTINUAL LINKED SETTLEMENT

A similar situation can occur in the currency futures market; situations can and do occur where a trader may be forced to deliver Swiss francs (or U.S. dollars, or British pounds) or accept delivery of euros (or another currency). This is undesirable for most currency traders, who simply want to speculate on the ups and downs of the market and do not wish to possess any actual foreign currencies.

In the world of spot Forex, when you trade the spot market with a Forex broker you will never have to take delivery of a foreign currency. In other words, if you put U.S. dollars into your Forex account and trade nothing but the EUR/CHF currency pair, you will never be forced to take delivery of either euros or Swiss francs.

This is because unlike futures contracts, the spot contracts never really mature; settlement on most spot Forex contracts is achieved through a system called continual linked settlement, or CLS. With most brokers, open positions are automatically rolled over to the next settlement date at a predetermined time, usually 17:00 New York time. This allows traders to speculate on movements in currency exchange rates without having to deal with issues of delivery.

When you withdraw funds from the account, you will receive the currency you initially deposited. Whatever currency you put into your trading account is the same one you will withdraw, unless the currency broker is providing an exchange service on your behalf.

Many currency brokers do not provide this type of service due to money laundering regulations and concerns. Plus, it would be a nightmare for brokers if they were saddled with delivery; imagine the extra work and expense involved in the tracking and delivery of myriad physical currencies.

Some Forex brokers do provide currency delivery services for their customers who want to take physical possession of a currency, but such services are not free, so if you are interested in delivery, be sure to check with your broker beforehand.

CHAPTER 3

CALCULATIONS AND STANDARDIZATIONS

"You are never really playing an opponent. You are playing yourself, your own highest standards, and when you reach your limits, that is real joy."

—Arthur Ashe, Champion Tennis Player

He was a great tennis player, but he was so much more than that. With his unwavering commitment to social justice, Arthur Ashe was much more than a tennis champion; he was and continues to be an inspiration to millions of people around the world. Mr. Ashe's quote about an athlete playing against himself also translates to trading; although many of us believe that we are trading against an individual, an institution, or even our broker, the truth is that in the world of trading, our greatest ally—and our greatest enemy—is ourselves.

Like Arthur Ashe, many athletes and entertainers use their fame and fortune to further a worthy cause. Famous traders like George Soros and Bruce Kovner also use their fortunes to champion the causes in which they believe. The question is this: if you can succeed as a trader, will you do something, even some small thing, to make the world a better place? Money can be a strong motivator, but once you've obtained money, what will be your motivation? It's never too early to start thinking about this.

Let's continue with some important concepts; if you don't understand every one of the following concepts, then you're not prepared to trade!

LOT SIZE

Simply put, one lot is the unit of measurement (in terms of size) for a currency pair. Just as 100 shares of stock equals one lot in the equity markets, 100,000 units of currency equals one standard lot in the retail Forex market. You could say that one lot is the standard unit size of a Forex transaction. In recent years, mini, micro, and even so-called "nano" accounts have been introduced to allow individual traders greater flexibility and to lower the barriers to participation in the Forex markets.

One Standard Lot = 100,000 Units of the Base Currency
One Mini Lot = 10,000 Units of Currency
One Micro Lot = 1,000 Units of Currency
One Nano Lot = 100 Units of Currency

PIP VALUE

One pip is the unit of measurement (in terms of price or value) for a currency pair.

One pip EUR/USD (Standard Account) = $10 USD
One pip EUR/USD (Mini Account) = $1 USD
One pip EUR/USD (Micro Account) = 10 cents USD
One pip EUR/USD (Nano Account) = 1 cent USD

The value of a pip is determined by the second member of the currency pair, known as the *counter* or *quote* currency, and has a fixed value in that currency. For example, every currency pair that ends in USD (GBP/USD, AUD/USD, etc.) has a fixed value of $10 per pip in a standard account. However, a currency pair that ends in GBP (such as EUR/GBP) has a fixed value of 10 British pounds per pip in a standard account, and a currency pair that ends in CHF (such as USD/CHF) has a constant value of 10 Swiss francs in the same account. If you're an American and you're trading a USD-based account, the value of 10 British pounds or 10 Swiss francs—as measured in U.S. dollars—fluctuates constantly. Therefore, when they are measured in USD, the pip values of EUR/GBP and USD/CHF are constantly changing.

Conversely, to a trader in the United Kingdom who is using a British pound-based account, the pip value of EUR/GBP never fluctuates—it has a constant value of 10 pounds per pip in a standard account because the quote (second) currency is GBP. However, in a pound-based account, the pip values of EUR/USD and GBP/USD are constantly changing, because these pairs are quoted in USD (the second member of the pair), and the value of the greenback fluctuates constantly against the British pound.

Fortunately, nearly every currency trading platform comes equipped with a pip calculator, which can be used to determine the current pip value of any currency pair. Or just type the words "pip calculator" into a search engine and you'll see dozens of free calculators are available online. But what is the actual calculation that is being performed by the pip calculator?

PIP CALCULATION

Here is the calculation for the value of 1 pip of EUR/USD:

In a standard account: EUR/USD pip = 0.0001 × 100,000 = USD \$10.00 per pip
In a mini account: EUR/USD pip = 0.0001 × 10,000 = USD \$1.00 per pip
In a micro account: EUR/USD pip = 0.0001 × 1,000 = USD \$0.10 per pip
In a nano account: EUR/USD pip = 0.0001 × 100 = USD \$0.01 per pip

That was easy; the calculation becomes more difficult when the counter or quote currency is not USD. Now let's try the same calculation to determine the value of 1 pip of USD/CHF:

In a standard account: USD/CHF pip = 0.0001 × 100,000 = CHF 10.00 per pip
In a mini account: USD/CHF pip = 0.0001 × 10,000 = CHF 1.00 per pip
In a micro account: USD/CHF pip = 0.0001 × 1,000 = CHF 0.10 per pip
In a nano account: USD/CHF pip = 0.0001 × 100 = CHF 0.01 per pip

If you live in the United States, you might be asking yourself, "What good is it to know that USD/CHF is worth 10 CHF per pip in my standard account? I need to know the pip value of USD/CHF in U.S. dollars." In this case, you want to know what one pip is worth in terms of the first currency in the pair, also known as the *base currency.*

For example, suppose you have a USD-based account, and you are trading USD/CHF in a standard account. You know that one pip of USD/CHF is worth 10 CHF, but since you are trading in USD, you really need to know the value of one pip USD/CHF in terms of USD.

All the trader needs to do in this case is divide the 10 CHF by the exchange rate of USD/CHF. For example, if the USD/CHF exchange rate is 1.1500: 10 divided by 1.1500 = \$8.69 USD per pip; and if the USD/CHF exchange rate is 1.1000: 10 divided by 1.1000 = \$9.09 USD per pip.

As you can see, the pip value of USD/CHF fluctuates when it is calculated in terms of the base currency, in this case U.S. dollars. Note that the pip value in this case rises as the two currencies approach parity. If USD and CHF were to achieve parity—in other words, if one USD had a value equal to exactly one CHF—the exchange rate of USD/CHF would be 1.0000, and the value of one pip of USD/CHF in a standard account would be exactly \$10.

FIRST CURRENCY = 1

Here's a little trick to help you understand what the exchange rate is really telling you.

Whenever you look at a currency quote, think of the first member of the currency pair as the number 1. For example, if you see that the quote for EUR/USD is 1.4525, it means

FIGURE 3.1 EUR/USD chart indicating an exchange rate of 1.4343. At that time, one euro = 1.4343 USD, or about $1.43.
Source: Created with TradeStation.

that 1 euro equals 1.4525 U.S. dollars, or about $1.45. If USD/CAD is trading at 1.0500, then 1 U.S. dollar is worth 1.05 Canadian dollars. If the GBP/JPY exchange rate is 145.00, that means the value of 1 British pound is equal to 145 Japanese yen (see Figure 3.1).

If GBP/USD exchange rate is 1.6050, then 1 GBP = 1.605 USD
If USD/JPY exchange rate is 106.50, then 1 USD = 106.5 JPY
If EUR/CHF exchange rate is 1.5000, then 1 EUR = 1.5 CHF
If AUD/NZD exchange rate is 1.2750, then 1 AUD = 1.275 NZD

POSITION: LONG, SHORT, OR FLAT

As a trader, your position will always be long, short, or flat.

Long = a position that will benefit if the exchange rate rises
Short = a position that will benefit if the exchange rate falls
Flat = absence of a long or short position

Why do traders use the terms "long and short" instead of "buy and sell"? *Long* and *short* are more precise terms. Consider this. Suppose you ask for my opinion on the USD/CHF currency pair, and in reply I tell you that I'm selling USD/CHF.

This could mean (1) that I believe the exchange rate of USD/CHF is going to fall, so I am selling the pair short, or (2) that I went long USD/CHF earlier and now I'm selling to close the position and (hopefully) take a profit.

Those are two very different meanings that can be attributed to the same phrase. But if I were to tell you that I am short USD/CHF, that can only mean one thing; it can only mean that I'm in a trade that will become profitable if USD/CHF falls. If USD/CHF falls, I will win and if USD/CHF rises, I will lose. It's that simple. In this case, you could say that I have a "short position" in USD/CHF.

Similarly, if I tell you that I am buying EUR/CHF, it could mean that (a) I'm buying to open a long position because I believe the EUR/CHF is going to move higher, or (b) I'm already short EUR/CHF and I'm buying to cover (close) that position, hopefully at a profit.

However, if I were to say that I have a long position in EUR/CHF, it can only mean that I'll make money if EUR/CHF rises, and I'll lose money if it falls. Traders use the more precise terms of *long and short* instead of *buy and sell* to more accurately convey their intended meaning.

What is the difference between a trade and a position? Let's begin with the assumption that I have no open trades. If I then place a trade to buy 10 lots of EUR/USD, and then an hour later I place another separate trade to buy 5 more lots, this would result in a cumulative long position of 15 lots of EUR/USD.

In this example, there were two trades, but only one position. In other words, your current position—whether it is long, short, or flat—is the end result of the trades you have placed.

LONG ONE, SHORT THE OTHER

In every currency trade, the trader is short one currency and long another. He or she is favoring one currency to rise, and the other to fall in relation to it. Any time a Forex trader "goes long" a currency pair, he or she is long the first member (base currency) of the pair and short the second member (counter or quote currency) of the pair:

Long EUR/USD	Trader is long the EUR and short the USD
Long GBP/CHF	Trader is long the GBP and short the CHF
Long USD/CAD	Trader is long the USD and short the CAD

Conversely, when a trader shorts a currency pair, he or she is short the first currency (base currency) of the pair and long the second (counter or quote currency):

Short AUD/JPY	Trader is short the AUD and long the JPY
Short NZD/USD	Trader is short the NZD and long the USD
Short USD/CHF	Trader is short the USD and long the CHF

Even though there are two currencies in every pair, it might be helpful to think of each currency pair as a single unit, similar to how we perceive a stock. For example, if a trader believes that the fictional stock XYZ is going to rise in price, then he or she would open a long position in XYZ. Similarly, if a trader believes that the *exchange rate* of fictional currency pair ABC/XYZ is going to rise, then he or she would open a long position in ABC/XYZ. In this case, the trader is long currency ABC *and* short currency XYZ.

Remember, an individual currency doesn't rise and fall on its own, but it constantly fluctuates in relation to other currencies. You will often hear traders refer to the *price* of a currency pair, but in reality it is the *exchange rate* between two currencies that we are trading in the Forex market. The use of the word "price" to describe the exchange rate is common slang among Forex traders.

THE CHART TRACKS THE BASE CURRENCY

When you are reading a chart, please keep in mind that the direction of the exchange rate is based on the first member of the pair, the base currency. Therefore, if the chart is moving up, the base currency is gaining vs. the quote, or counter, currency (see Figure 3.2).

The chart illustrates the GBP/USD currency pair. On left side of the chart, the exchange rate is moving higher, which indicates that the British pound (base currency) is

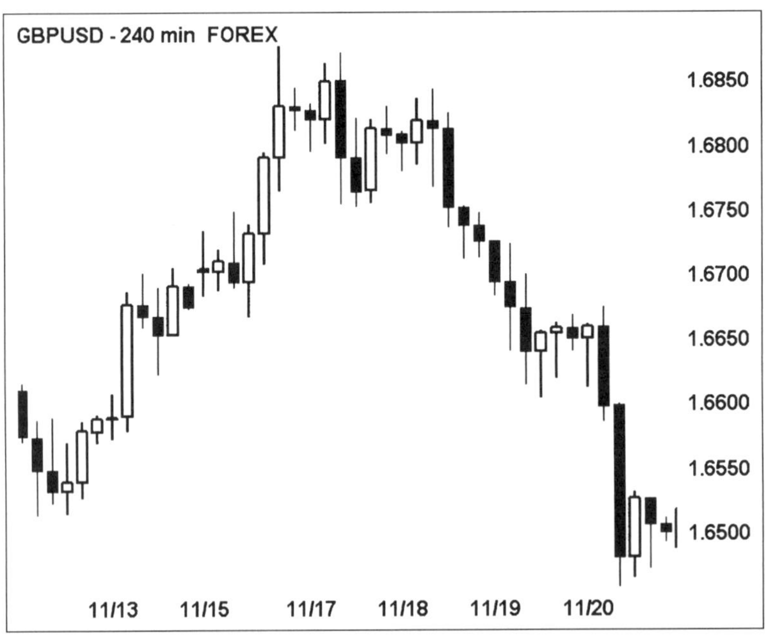

FIGURE 3.2 British pound is rising vs. the U.S. dollar on the left side of the chart, and falling vs. the USD on the right.
Source: Created with TradeStation. © TradeStation Technologies, Inc. All rights reserved.

rising vs. the U.S. dollar. This could also be correctly interpreted to mean that the U.S. dollar (counter currency) is falling vs. the British pound.

The right side of the chart illustrates a falling exchange rate for the GBP/USD pair. This means that the British pound (base currency) is falling vs. the USD. It also means that the U.S. dollar (counter currency) is rising vs. the British pound.

MARGIN REQUIREMENTS

Margin is the deposit that is required to open or maintain a position. Margin can be described as either "usable" or "used."

Used margin: the amount that is being used to maintain or open a position
Usable margin: the amount available to open new positions or add to existing positions

Does a trader need $100,000 to trade one standard lot of currency? No, in fact, with a $1,000 margin balance in your account and a 1 percent margin requirement to open a position, you can buy or sell a position worth up to $100,000. This allows a trader to leverage his or her account by up to 100 times, a leverage ratio of 100:1.

In the stock market, if a trader's account falls below the minimum amount required to maintain an open position, he will receive a "margin call" from the broker, requiring him to either add more money into the account or close the open position. Unlike stock brokers, most Forex brokers will *automatically* close a trader's open positions when the margin balance falls below the amount required to keep the positions open.

Why the difference in procedure? Suppose that you live in the United States and have a stock trading account with a U.S. broker. It's entirely possible that due to over-leveraging of the account, a trader could lose more than the total amount of money in the account.

When this happens, a representative from the broker then calls the trader, asking him to deposit funds just to bring the account back up to zero. If the trader fails to comply, the broker can turn the debt over to a collection agent, or initiate procedures that could damage the credit rating of the stock trader. This is easily accomplished because both the broker and the trader are located in the same country.

But the world of Forex is different; because of the international nature of this market, it can be difficult for a broker to collect funds that are owed to it. For example, suppose a broker is located in Switzerland, and a client of the broker lives in Costa Rica. If the trader in Costa Rica fails to send funds owed to the broker in Switzerland, the broker may find it difficult to collect that money. In fact, that Swiss broker may have clients in 100 different countries, and the time and effort involved in chasing them around the world to collect funds would be too great.

This is why many Forex accounts will automatically close all open trades before all of the funds are drained from an account. This way, the currency broker can avoid being forced into assuming the role of a collection agent. It also allows Forex brokers to operate with a lean staff relative to that of a stock brokerage.

Of course, you will never find yourself in the sad situation of receiving a margin call or of having your positions closed against your wishes if you use good risk management techniques, such as never allowing a loss to run against you, and never adding to a losing position.

LEVERAGE

I got my start in the trading world as a stock trader, and I still trade stocks when the occasion is right. I speak frequently to stock traders, and many of them are very concerned about the amount of leverage that is used in the currency markets. Often, the conversations go something like this:

"Ed," they tell me, "you must be insane to use leverage of 100 to 1. If I used that type of leverage, I would blow up my stock trading account in 15 seconds."

By the way, they're right; stock traders leverage their equity at much lower rates than currency traders, usually between 2-to-1 and 10-to-1. But as we will see, there is a good and practical reason for the high degree of leverage used by Forex traders. The conversation continues:

"You see, currencies are much, much less volatile than stocks. That's why we use so much leverage," I explain.

"Nonsense!" is the usual reply. "Forex trading is extremely volatile! Just the other day I saw the EUR/USD currency pair move about 100 pips in just five minutes!"

"True, but have you ever thought about what that really means? When EUR/USD moved 100 pips in five minutes, that's about the same as saying it moved one penny. Would you get excited about a stock because it moved one penny in five minutes? Would you consider it extremely volatile? Would you be afraid to trade it? You probably wouldn't trade that stock because the movement was too slow."

You see, comparing leverage in the stock market and the Forex market is not an apples-to-apples comparison. To illustrate this, consider the rally in the EUR/USD pair that took place from early 2006 until the middle of 2008. During that time, the exchange rate rose from beneath 1.2000 to 1.6000, which counts as a massive move in the currency markets. This constitutes a move of over 4,000 pips.

But in reality it also constitutes a total move of 40 cents. Think about it: during that massive, $2^1/_2$ year rally, the euro rose from approximately \$1.20 to \$1.60, a grand total of 40 cents. How would you feel about a stock that moved a total of 40 cents over a $2^1/_2$ year period? My guess is you probably wouldn't be thrilled with it, and you probably wouldn't trade it.

The volatility of many currency pairs is in reality equal to about one to two cents per day. Would you trade a stock that made an average move of one or two cents per day? Good luck with that.

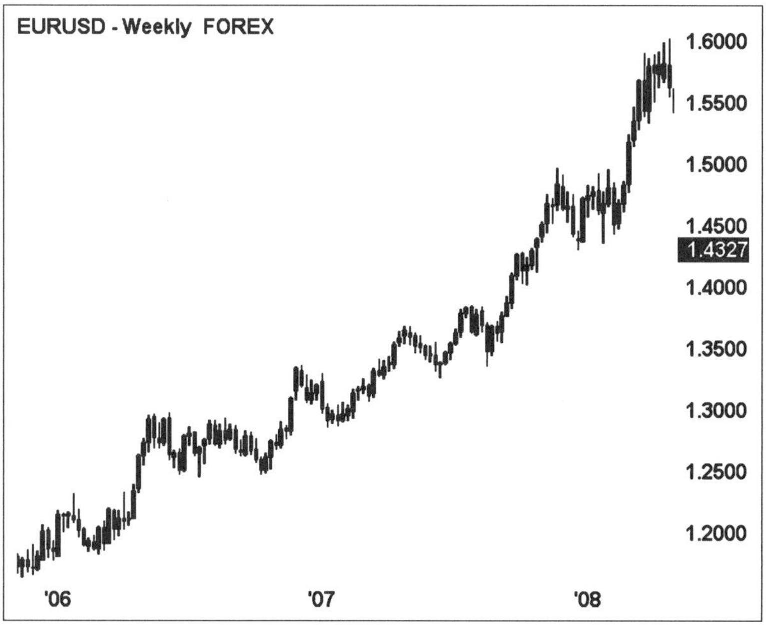

FIGURE 3.3 A big rally in the EUR/USD pair from 2006–2008 is actually a move of 40 cents.
Source: Created with TradeStation.

But with the use of leverage, a move of just 1/100 of a penny can result in a profit or a loss. Leverage turns Forex into a tradable market for the average person and allows us to stand on the same playing field as banks and hedge funds. We can see that without the use of massive leverage, the currency market is hardly worth the effort of trading (see Figure 3.3).

We have seen that the use of a high degree of leverage is a necessity in the Forex market in order to make speculation viable. One side effect of this massive leverage is that a trader's buying power will normally be much higher than his or her equity. In order to avoid problems that can be caused by this high degree of buying power, a Forex trader's main concern should not be how large of a position he or she can afford to take, but instead how much actual money is at risk.

Don't ever enter a trade or increase the size of a trade just because you have sufficient buying power to do so. Never base any trading decision on your buying power. Think of buying power as the amount of rope a broker is willing to give you to hang yourself. You have the option of simply saying, "No thanks!"

CHAPTER 4

FOLLOW THE MONEY

"The dictionary is the only place that success comes before work. Hard work is the price we must pay for success. I think you can accomplish anything if you're willing to pay the price."

—Vince Lombardi, Pro Football Hall of Fame

Here is a simple yet overlooked method for understanding the forces that move the currency markets. Many in the currency industry refer to this as "capital flow," the phenomenon of money flowing out of one country and into another. This flow of capital leaves a trail, and traders who want to gain clues as to which currencies will take off next—and which ones are set to sink—will simply "follow the money."

Capital flow is simply another way of looking at supply and demand. If many people want one item, the price of that item rises, but in the currency world this concept goes much deeper. Since there are two currencies involved in every Forex transaction, we are searching for situations where investors will sell one currency and purchase another in order to obtain something specific.

That specific item could be shares of a hot stock, or a quantity of precious metal, or a prized parcel of real estate, or even a government bond. We're searching for anything that has a strong enough attraction to capital that it can create a flow of money out of one country and into another. If the money is merely being redistributed within the borders of one country, this will not be sufficient to move the currency markets.

HOT STOCKS

Here's an example. Back in the late 1990s, the U.S. stock markets were on fire—especially tech stocks. In fact, for the year 1999, the NASDAQ composite index gained more than

85 percent! According to the *New York Times*, in the year 1999 the NASDAQ experienced the largest calendar year gain ever for any broad U.S. equity index.

Other equity indexes around the world scaled new heights as well, and many believed the rise of U.S. technology companies like Cisco Systems, Intel, Microsoft, and others heralded the dawning of a new age. Something special was happening in the United States, and investors around the world wanted a piece of the action. But how would overseas traders participate in the great U.S. tech bull? What would they have to do in order to own a piece of the hottest stock market in the world?

SMALL SCALE

To understand the "hot market" phenomenon, let's look at an example. Suppose a person lives in Switzerland and wants to buy hypothetical tech stock ABCD that trades only on the NASDAQ in the United States. Since ABCD is priced in U.S. dollars, he is going to need greenbacks to purchase the shares. So, he withdraws some Swiss francs from the bank, exchanges the francs for U.S. dollars, and then opens his U.S. stock trading account and purchases the shares.

In order to facilitate the stock transaction, the trader sold CHF and purchased USD. His actions alone will not move either currency, but what if traders all over Switzerland have the same idea at about the same time? The result would be a stream of capital pouring out of Switzerland and into the United States to purchase stock ABCD.

The "hot market" phenomenon was in full effect in 1999 as capital flowed into the United States from around the world to participate in the tech rally. Although there were many other factors at work that year, the U.S. dollar did have a very good year vs. the Swiss franc in 1999 (see Figure 4.1).

LARGE SCALE

Now consider that investors all around the world want to participate in the tech rally and own stock ABCD; those traders are going to pull money out of various countries, exchange their currencies for U.S. dollars, and purchase shares of stock. Imagine that you are a hedge fund manager investing in various markets around the world; if you believe there is a superior opportunity out there, you are going to sell shares from one market and move that money to another market.

So, if I believe that Latin American stocks represent the greatest opportunity in the equities markets, and at the same time I am less enamored with my holdings in, say, Europe, I might sell my European stocks. In return for those shares, I will receive euros, and then perhaps I'll exchange those euros for another currency. Perhaps I'll exchange my euros for Brazilian real so that I can invest in the Bovespa—the largest equity market in Latin America.

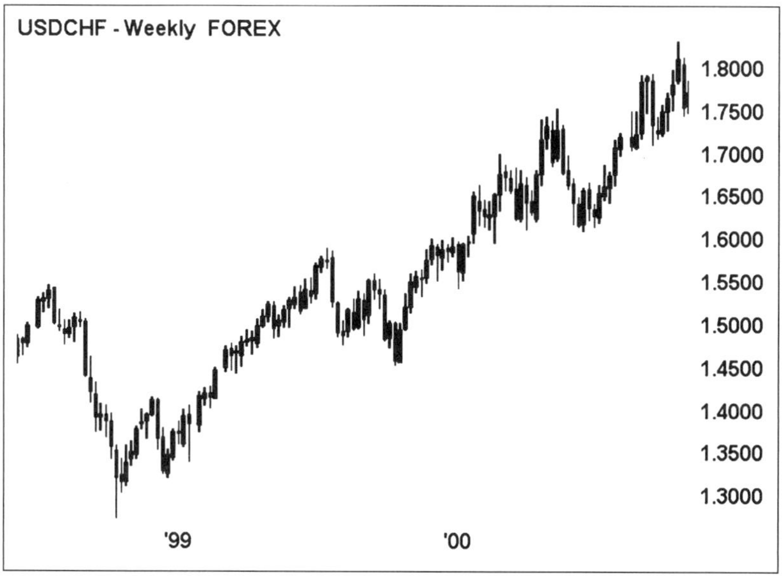

FIGURE 4.1 Capital flow was a factor as the U.S. dollar crushed the Swiss franc during 1999–2000.
Source: Created with TradeStation.

If just one fund manager is taking this action, the results will be inconsequential, but if many fund managers start taking the same trade simultaneously (as they often do), the result is going to be a flow of capital out of Europe and into Brazil. Under such circumstances, one would not be surprised to see the Brazilian real begin to climb against the euro.

HOT COMMODITIES

We can see how a hot stock market can influence exchange rates, and the same can be said about a variety of markets. For example, if commodities prices are rising, countries that produce these commodities could experience an inflow of capital.

For example, Canada and Australia are big commodities producers; Australia is the world's fourth biggest producer of gold, while Canada is the seventh biggest (Canada also exports a significant amount of oil, while Australia does not). If the price of gold suddenly takes off, people around the world will need to send more capital to these countries to purchase the same amount of gold. The rising price of gold (and rising metals prices in general) creates buying pressure for the Australian dollar and the Canadian dollar.

Because many commodities are priced in USD, there is a magnified effect at work here; gold and the USD move in opposite directions most of the time, so the effect of rising metals prices on commodity currencies is magnified when we measure those currencies vs. the U.S. dollar (see Figure 4.2).

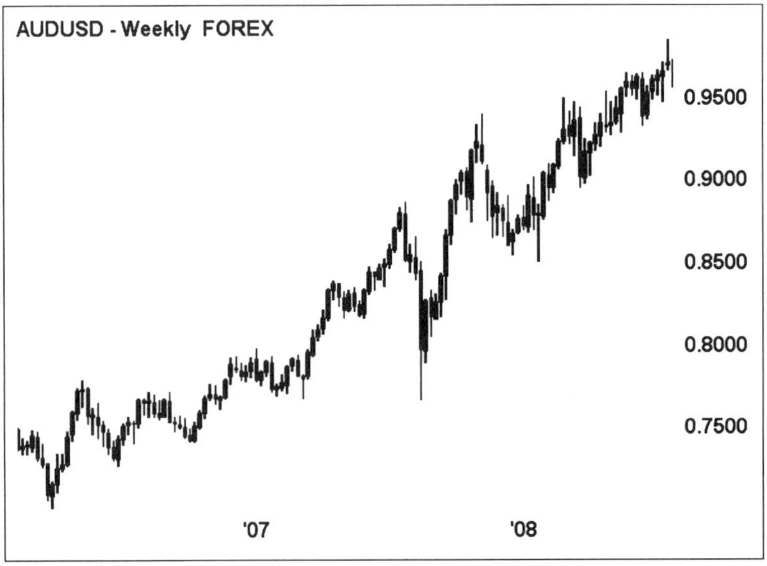

FIGURE 4.2 During the commodity rally of 2007 and early 2008, the Australian dollar rocketed vs. the USD.
Source: Created with TradeStation.

HOT REAL ESTATE

We've examined the effect of rising stock prices and of rising commodities prices on currencies, but the cause of a capital flow can be something less obvious. For example, what if real estate investors in Great Britain determined that they just had to own Japanese real estate?

Perhaps they felt that those Japanese properties were undervalued and due for a big rise in value. They might sell shopping malls in Great Britain and exchange those British pounds for Japanese yen, so that they could purchase apartment buildings in Tokyo. If this occurred on a large scale, the result would be a flow of capital out of Great Britain and into Japan, and the effect of this could influence the exchange rate of the GBP/JPY pair.

DIFFERENTIALS MAKE THE DIFFERENCE

Now that we understand how capital flows can influence currency exchange rates, I want to introduce you to the ultimate in our "follow the money" philosophy: the flow of capital that is created by interest rate differentials in various countries. Don't be intimidated; it's easier than it sounds.

Let's suppose that you have some money in your pocket and you want to place it in a savings account. You travel to the center of your town, where you find several different banks, each willing to accept your deposit. The banks are all reputable, and they all offer the same approximate degree of safety. Which bank should you choose for your investment? If all other things are equal, you're going to choose the bank that offers the highest return. Most people would come to the same conclusion.

If more savers are attracted by the rates at one bank, we could say that bank is getting stronger. It is feasting on deposits, the "mother's milk" of banks, and it will probably lend that money out to borrowers at a higher rate of interest than it is paying to you, the depositor.

Meanwhile, the bank across the street is offering a much lower savings rate, and people are pulling their money out of that bank and investing it in the bank that offers the higher yield. You could say the bank across the street is getting weaker as capital is flowing from the low-yield bank to the high-yield bank.

The preceding scenario is not terribly different from what occurs in the Forex market: central banks raise and lower interest rates, and this causes capital to flow in and out of countries, making some currencies stronger and some weaker. If a person borrows money from Japan at a very low rate of interest and invests it "down the block" in a New Zealand bank, he or she is literally taking capital from Japan and sending it to New Zealand. If enough people do this, the effect will be to weaken the yen and strengthen the New Zealand dollar as money flows from the former to the latter.

This is exactly what Japan wants, because the flow of capital out of Japan will weaken the yen. A weak currency is important to Japan because the Japanese economy is almost entirely driven by exports; therefore, a falling JPY is good for the sales of companies like Sony and Toyota.

"MRS. WATANABE"

Currency trading has become something of a phenomenon around the world, and today we can "follow the money" not just by watching stock and commodity prices, but by observing the actions of independent traders. This is especially true in Japan, where many individuals, particularly women, have become active in the currency markets.

Collectively known as "Mrs. Watanabe," Japanese women have had a profound effect on high-yielding currencies such as the New Zealand dollar and the less-liquid Turkish lira. Mrs. Watanabe's strategy often involves shorting the Japanese yen in favor of a high-yielding currency. For example, when the Reserve Bank of New Zealand attempted to weaken the high-yielding kiwi in 2007, individual Japanese investors took the other side of the trade en masse, and they are credited with thwarting the RBNZ's efforts. An August 3, 2007, *Times Online* article entitled "The Kimono Traders" had this to say:

> *Turkey's nightmare is that the Japanese housewives will lose interest and pull out of the lira, causing it to plunge. And it is not just the Turkish government that is petrified by the Japanese housewives' spectacular assault on its currency. Two months ago, when the New Zealand government tried to intervene in currency markets by selling the dollar, its efforts were immediately and completely consumed by Japanese investors with virtually no effect on the exchange rate.*

The influence of Mrs. Watanabe on the Japanese yen was profound, as every rally was met with selling pressure from individual investors:

> *Because the housewives are endless sellers of the yen, any upward pressure on the Japanese currency is almost entirely absorbed by the online traders. For months now, the yen has fallen against most global currencies at every turn.*

While many of these individual traders made huge sums of money, they had a tendency to be JPY "perma-bears." This aspect of their trading style did not serve them well when the yen underwent a severe reversal in 2008, and those who didn't have an exit strategy were punished. In trading, there is no such thing as a permanent or irreversible trend.

The phenomenon of Mrs. Watanabe was also chronicled by the *New York Times* and the *Financial Times*, among others. As online currency trading continues to expand, expect the individual to play an even larger role in determining capital flows and exchange rates in the future.

In summary, capital flows have a huge impact on currency exchange rates. There is an incredible amount of money out there just searching for a hot stock, or a hot commodity, or even a bit more yield. Shifts in interest rates and in the perceived values of stocks, commodities, real estate, and other items can send a flood of capital into one country and out of another.

PART II

SCORING POINTS

CHAPTER 5

USING THE U.S. DOLLAR INDEX

"I want to be remembered as the guy who gave his all whenever he was on the field."

—Walter Payton, NFL MVP and Super Bowl Champion

Let's keep the intensity level up, gang! Maybe you know what the U.S. Dollar Index is or maybe you don't, but have you ever used it to place a currency trade? Let's take a look at ways to use this tool to set up some good trades—and avoid some bad ones.

When the general public wants to get an idea of how the U.S. stock market is doing, they turn to the S&P 500 or the Dow Jones Industrial Average. When they want to know what's going on with commodities prices, they look to the Reuters-CRB Index. Where can they turn when they want to know what's happening with the U.S. dollar? The best place to look for a general indication of the health and strength of the greenback is the U.S. Dollar Index.

The U.S. Dollar Index measures the value of the U.S. dollar against a basket of currencies. The symbol is $DXY (hence the origin of its nickname, *Dixie*), and the index trades on the ICE Futures Exchange (formerly known in the U.S. as the New York Board of Trade, or NYBOT). The USD index is updated 24 hours a day, seven days a week.

The index can be used to diversify trades involving the U.S. dollar, and it can also be used to hedge USD spot positions. Forex traders often use the U.S. Dollar Index to confirm USD trades vs. individual currencies, especially against the euro. The index basket consists of the euro (EUR, 57.6 percent), Japanese yen (JPY, 13.6 percent), British pound (GBP, 11.9 percent), Canadian dollar (CAD, 9.1 percent), Swedish krona (SEK, 4.2 percent), and Swiss franc (CHF, 3.6 percent) (see Figure 5.1).

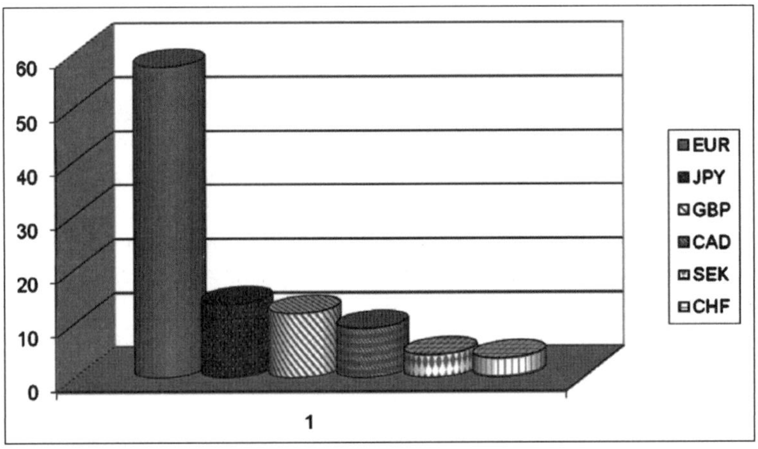

FIGURE 5.1 Components of the U.S. Dollar Index.

ORIGIN AND HISTORY

The USD index was started in 1973, soon after the demise of the Bretton Woods agreement. At Bretton Woods, New Hampshire, representatives from many of the world's largest economies met in July 1944 to deal with post–World War II economic realities. These nations agreed to fix their exchange rates to the greenback, which in turn was fixed to gold at $35 per ounce.

The exchange rates were "pegged" in order to provide the stability needed to rebuild the world's economies after the devastation and confusion that reigned in Europe after the Second World War. Accordingly, any charts of currency pairs that depict exchange rates during the Bretton Woods era are less than meaningful, because any price movements that occurred during that time are not a pure reflection of free-market trading.

After Bretton Woods finally collapsed in the early 1970s, ushering in an era of free-floating exchange rates for much of the world, the need grew for a "measuring stick" to chronicle the ups and downs of the world's dominant currency, the U.S. dollar, vs. its chief counterparts. This need led to the introduction of the U.S. Dollar Index in 1973.

The USD index was initiated with a base value of 100 and its current value is relative to this base. For example, if the U.S. Dollar Index were to rise to 110, this would mean that the U.S. dollar has gained 10 percent vs. the other currencies in the basket since the inception of the index. On the other hand, if the U.S. Dollar Index were to fall to 50, that would mean that the U.S. dollar has lost half of its value vs. the other currencies in the basket since the inception of the index.

In its original form, the U.S. Dollar Index contained the German mark, French franc, Italian lira, and other European currencies. With the inception of the euro in 1999, these and other European currencies were combined into one currency. This partially explains why the euro makes up such a large portion of the USD index.

MAKING MONEY

Since the USD index is a futures contract, it can be traded independently as a stand-alone entity, but how else can currency traders use it to make money? Because the euro accounts for more than half of the index, the $DXY is especially helpful when used in conjunction with the EUR/USD pair.

When you look at a U.S. Dollar Index chart, remember, the direction of the index is based on the U.S. dollar (the chart goes up when the USD goes up), while the direction of the EUR/USD currency pair is based on the euro (the chart goes down when the USD goes up), so these two trading vehicles generally move in opposite directions. Let's look at one way traders can use the USD index to confirm trades in the EUR/USD pair.

CONFIRMATION

Take a look at the chart of the USD index in Figure 5.2. After a steep drop, the Dixie found significant support at the 76.75 area; once the index was finally able to break through support, that same area near 76.75 began to act as resistance. This is not unusual, as support levels that break often act as resistance levels, and vice versa. The price crept up toward 76.75 once again on the evening of October 28, 2009 (see Figure 5.2).

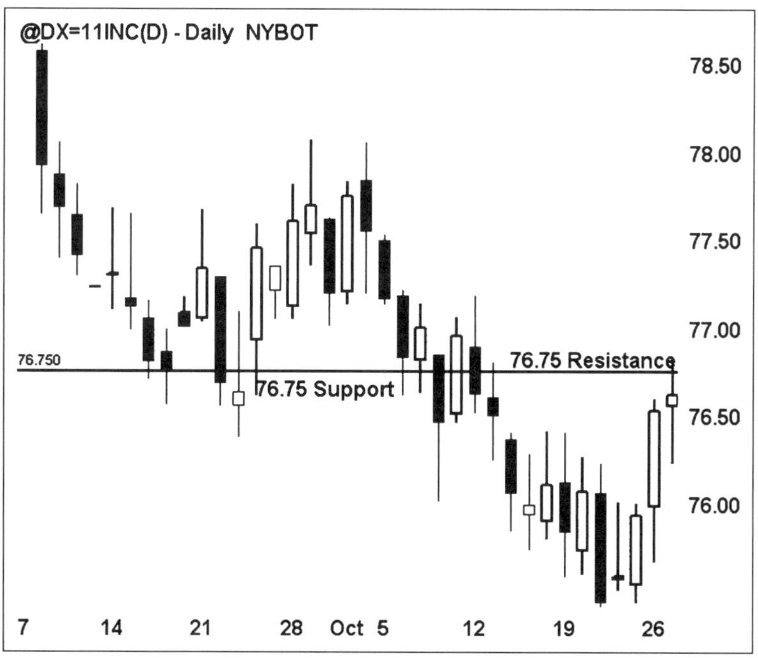

FIGURE 5.2 Support becomes resistance on the USD Index.
Source: Created with TradeStation.

At the same time that the price was hitting resistance on the USD index, the EUR/USD currency pair was drifting lower, toward the round number of 1.4700, an area of possible psychological support. In addition, the area near 1.4700 had acted as support several weeks earlier (see Figure 5.3).

Here we have a near-perfect scenario: The EUR/USD exchange rate had fallen to an area of prior support, which also happened to be a round number. It's human nature to place orders on round numbers, so there was a good chance that buy orders might be located in that area.

Let's think about that for a minute. At any time in your life, have you ever said to yourself, "I'm going to buy that stock when it hits 20," or "I'm going to sell that stock when it reaches 100"? People place orders on round numbers all the time, and this tendency of human behavior improves the odds that the price might bounce when it reaches the round number of 1.4700.

In addition to these two bits of evidence, let's add to the mix the fact that the USD index is simultaneously hitting resistance. This is also bullish for the euro, because if the greenback is hitting resistance, the chance of a euro bounce increases. Now we have three reasons to buy the euro at 1.4700 (EUR support, EUR/USD round number, $DXY resistance), but we're not finished yet.

Of course, everything that occurs on the intraday chart should be viewed within the context of a longer term chart, so let's take a look at the daily chart for EUR/USD. The chart shows an uptrend that had been in effect for the better part of a year, beginning in March of 2009.

In other words, if we buy euros at 1.4700 due to the plethora of evidence mentioned above, our trade will exist in harmony with a longer-term trend—yet another factor in

FIGURE 5.3 EUR/USD drifts toward old support at 1.4700.
Source: Created with TradeStation.

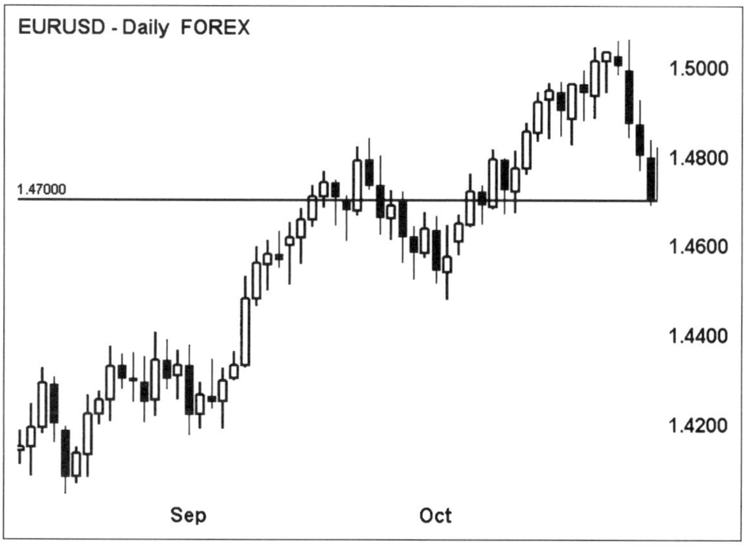

FIGURE 5.4 Drop to 1.4700 is a pullback within an uptrend.
Source: Created with TradeStation. © TradeStation Technologies, Inc. All rights reserved.

our favor. By looking at the big picture, we can see that a drop to 1.4700 would represent a mere pullback within a dominant trend (see Figure 5.4).

Let's review. We have (1) a long-term uptrend in euros, (2) prior support at 1.4700, (3) round number support at 1.4700, and (4) simultaneous resistance on the U.S. Dollar Index at 76.75. With all of these factors in our favor, should we go long EUR/USD at 1.4700? (See Figure 5.5.)

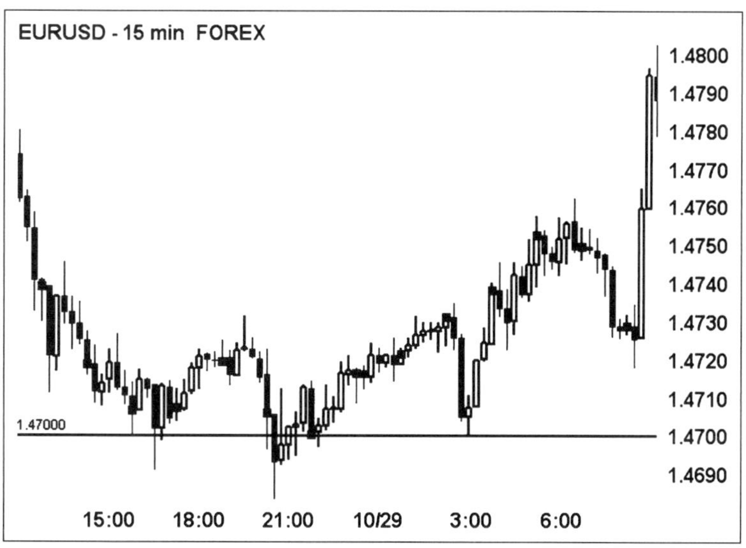

FIGURE 5.5 EUR/USD bounces repeatedly off 1.4700.
Source: Created with TradeStation. © TradeStation Technologies, Inc. All rights reserved.

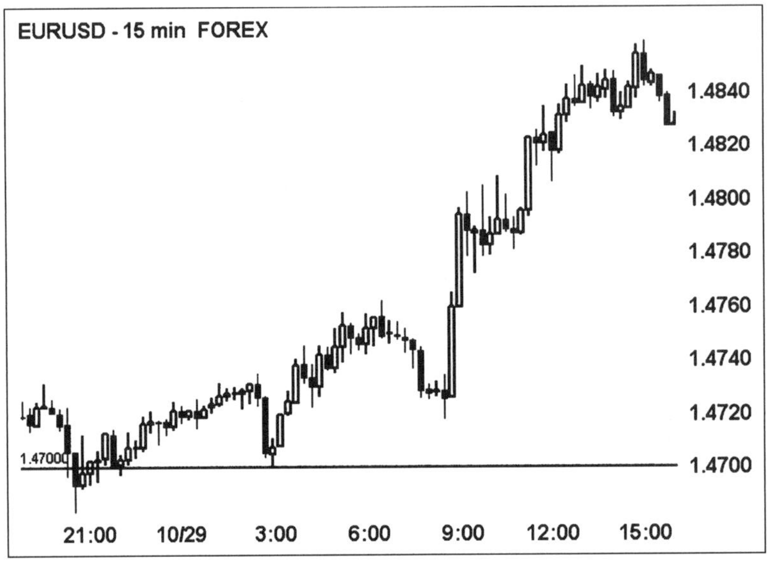

FIGURE 5.6 EUR/USD bounces 150 pips higher from support.
Source: Created with TradeStation.

Here on the 15-minute chart, we can see that the answer is a resounding "yes." On the night of the 28th and on the morning of the 29th, the price bounced several times off the 1.4700 area before rocketing above 1.4800.

The fact that EUR/USD never fell as much as 20 pips below the 1.4700 figure on any of these bounces speaks volumes about the quality of support at that level. By the afternoon of the 29th, the pair traded up to 1.4850, a bounce of 150 pips from support (see Figure 5.6).

This is a near-perfect example of how to use the U.S. Dollar Index to confirm trades on the EUR/USD currency pair.

On the longer term charts, 1.4700 also turned out to be a significant level; the price bounced repeatedly off that area during the next six daily candles before rebounding to 1.5000 (see Figure 5.7).

CONTRADICTION

Now that we understand how to confirm EUR/USD trades using the USD index, what should we do if we fail to receive that confirmation? Should we go ahead with the trade, or pause? Let's take a look at a scenario where the charts of the $DXY and EUR/USD contradict, instead of confirm, each other.

Here's an example. In June 2009, the EUR/USD pair appeared to be on the verge of a breakdown after forming a head and shoulders pattern on the daily chart, which

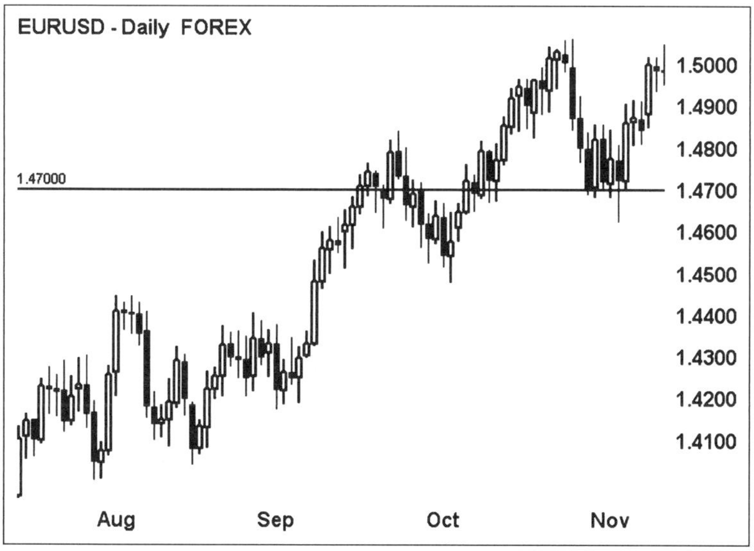

FIGURE 5.7 EUR/USD also found long-term support at 1.4700.
Source: Created with TradeStation.

is considered bearish for the euro and bullish for the greenback. Undoubtedly, this formation excited some dollar bulls, who stood to profit if the head and shoulders were to decisively break major support, which was located near 1.3800 (see Figure 5.8).

Ah, but perhaps those dollars bulls would have pulled in their horns if they had checked the weekly chart of the U.S. Dollar Index. If they had, they'd realize that the

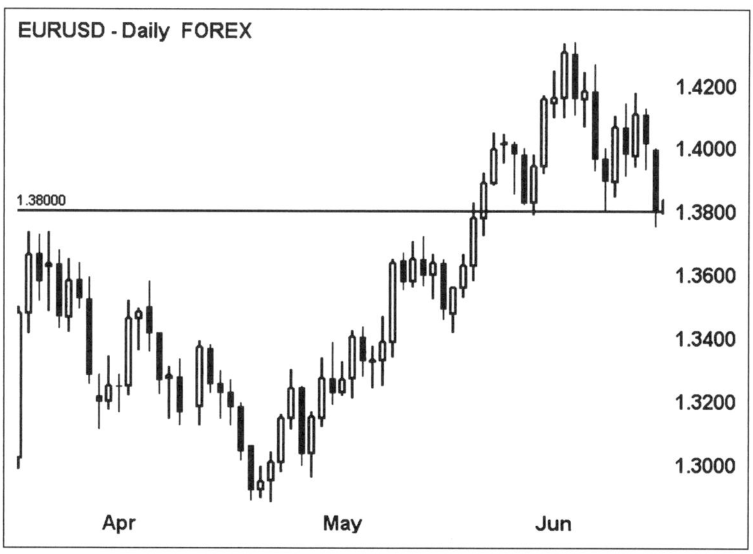

FIGURE 5.8 EUR/USD daily chart indicates a bearish head and shoulders pattern.
Source: Created with TradeStation.

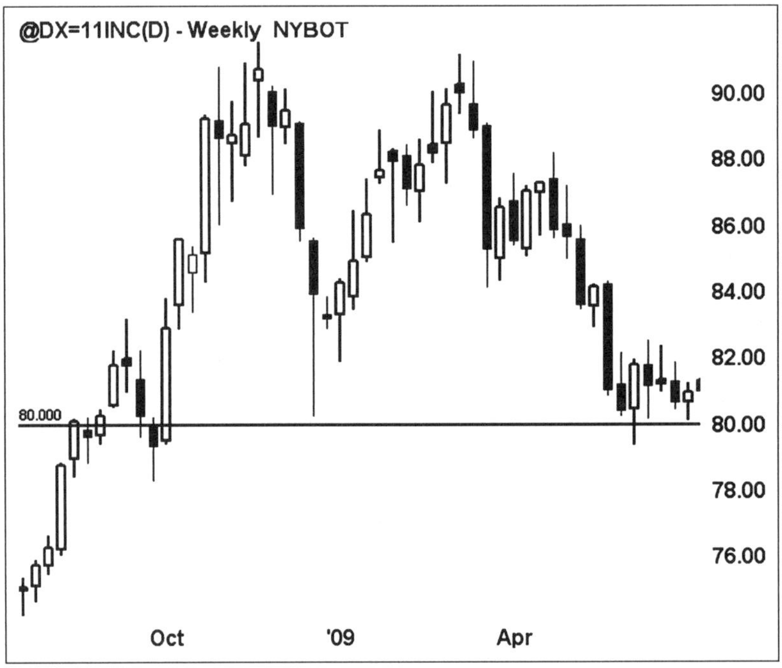

FIGURE 5.9 USD index weekly chart teeters on support near 80.00.
Source: Created with TradeStation. © TradeStation Technologies, Inc. All rights reserved.

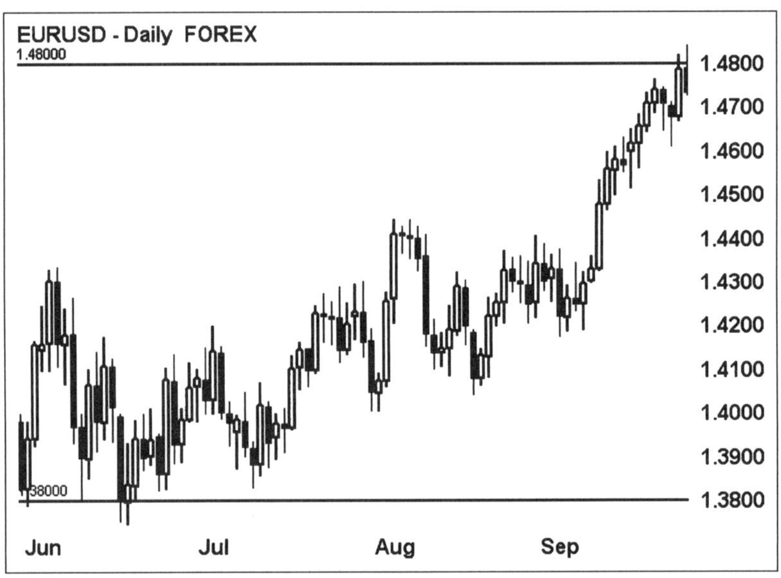

FIGURE 5.10 EUR/USD fails to break support at 1.38, rallies to 1.48.
Source: Created with TradeStation. © TradeStation Technologies, Inc. All rights reserved.

index also sported an ominous topping formation. The USD index was teetering on support at 80.00, and a break of that level would mean bad news for dollar bulls (see Figure 5.9).

Clearly, the EUR/USD daily chart was bullish for the dollar, while the USD index weekly chart was bearish for the greenback. So what is the correct action to take in a situation where the charts contradict each other in this manner? Perhaps the best response is to use the index as a filter to keep us out of bad trades in the EUR/USD pair.

If you grew up in a major city as I did, perhaps you recall your parents telling you to look both ways before crossing the street. Another admonishment was that you should "look before you leap." Well, we could also apply that concept to trading; before leaping into that head and shoulders breakdown in EUR/USD, the trader should "look both ways" and check the USD index to see if a contradictory signal is being given.

In this case, the proper course of action would be to stay out of the EUR/USD short trade, since the two charts contradict each other, and instead wait for opportunities where the charts provide confirmation instead of contradiction. As it turned out, the head and shoulders on EUR/USD failed to break down, as presaged by the USD index weekly chart. The neckline of 1.3800 held firm, and several months later, EUR/USD traded 1,000 pips higher, at 1.4800 (see Figure 5.10).

CHAPTER 6

CONTRARIAN INDICATORS AND THE COT REPORT

"Most of the money you'll win at poker comes not from the brilliance of your own play, but from the ineptitude of your opponents."

—Lou Krieger, Poker Player and Author

Have you ever known someone who was consistently wrong? I think most of us have met or known someone who just seemed to be wrong all the time. I'm talking about the kind of person who, if he said, "The sky is blue and the grass is green," you'd look out the window just to be sure that the sky really was blue and the grass really was green.

On an episode of the popular 1990s sitcom, *Seinfeld*, one of the show's protagonists realizes that his actions are consistently wrong. Unhappy with the direction his life is taking, he decides to do the exact opposite of every instinct that occurs to him. After all, if all of his instincts are wrong, then the exact opposite must be right.

He sees a beautiful woman sitting at the counter in a restaurant. Instead of telling lies to impress her, he tells her that he's unemployed and living with his parents. She immediately becomes enamored with him, and they begin a relationship.

By chance he meets the owner of a professional baseball team. Instead of kissing up to him, he rants about how the owner's bad decisions have ruined his favorite team. Immediately, the owner responds by offering him a job working in the team's front office.

It seems that every time our protagonist goes against his instincts, he ends up making the right choice. But what does this have to do with trading?

THE SUCKER AT THE TABLE

There is a saying among poker players: If you don't know after 20 minutes who the "sucker" at the poker table is, then the sucker is probably you. By using contrarian indicators, we can essentially see who the sucker is, and more—we can actually see which cards he is holding and which way he is betting. Traders use contrarian indicators as an example of what *not* to do—and then they do the opposite.

Most of us have acted as a contrarian indicator at one time or another in our trading careers, and just like the sucker in the poker game, we probably didn't even realize it. For example, early in my trading career, I noticed that many of the more experienced traders were very friendly toward me and the other new traders—maybe *too* friendly. At first I thought, "Well, they are probably just a nice bunch of guys and gals."

But if you've ever worked on a trading floor or in a trading room with professionals in New York City, London, or any of the world's trading capitals, you realize that this is a joke. At that level, traders tend to have Type A personalities (if there were such a thing as "Type A Plus," I'm sure some of them would qualify). Some can even be ruthless; let's just say they are not known for their cuddliness and warmth. So why would this hard-bitten, tough-as-nails group shower the new hires with warmth and attention?

SIFTING THROUGH THE NEWBIES

Simply put, they were searching for the contrarian indicator—they were trying to locate the trader or traders among the newbies who was likely to be wrong most of the time. Once the contrarian indicator (CI) has been identified, the experienced trader simply takes the opposite side of the CI's trades. This is done with the belief that if the CI is nearly always wrong, then the person who does the opposite will nearly always be right.

This will continue until the CI loses his or her job for being wrong so often, but never fear, there are always new recruits arriving to take the place of the fallen. Then the experienced traders must sift through a new batch of traders to identify the next CI, and so on.

I know all of this sounds incredibly cruel, but that's the way it is. We see examples of contrarian indicators in all levels of trading and in every trading market.

For example, in the equity markets, an "odd lot" trade is any stock trade that consists of less than 100 shares (a round lot consists of 100 shares). Many stock traders analyze the positions taken by these odd lot traders because they assume that these traders are not very good at their craft. The thought process behind this is that if these folks were any good at trading, they would be able to afford at least 100 shares or more of stock.

In this example, it is the odd lot trader that serves as the contrarian indicator. According to odd lot theory, if the odd lot traders are all buying a particular stock, it might be a good idea to short that stock. In the futures and Forex markets, there exists another time-tested form of contrarian indicator.

COMMITMENT OF TRADERS REPORT

When it comes to the currency markets, a favorite contrarian indicator is the Commitment of Traders report, popularly known as the COT report. This is a weekly report that was created in 1962 and is published by the Commodity Futures Trading Commission (CFTC) with a stated goal of "providing the public with current and basic data on futures market operations."

The report was originally intended to reveal information about open positions in agricultural commodities, but over the years it has been expanded to include many areas of trading, including Forex futures. It compiles statistics for markets in which 20 or more traders hold positions equal to or above the reporting levels established by the CFTC.

For the purposes of this report, the CFTC classifies traders into three different groups: commercial traders (big companies), noncommercial traders (large speculators), and small speculators (small traders). Let's take a closer look at these categories.

COMMERCIALS, NONCOMMERCIALS, AND SMALL SPECULATORS

Commercials include some of the biggest and most influential players in the markets; they are exempt from position limits and are subject to less stringent margin requirements than most speculators. Commercials include farming companies, mining companies, and companies that create and market food products.

The main focus of a commercial trader is to minimize risk by hedging and by locking in prices for the raw materials that the company needs to create its products. Commercial traders are not speculators; they participate in the futures markets out of necessity.

Noncommercials are also big and influential players in the commodities markets, but unlike the commercials, they are mainly involved in speculation rather than production. Many hedge funds fall into this category. Since they make their living by trading the markets, you might be tempted to think of the noncommercial traders as the "smart money." But are the noncommercial traders really all that smart?

The *small speculators* category includes all traders with positions below reportable levels. In our earlier example of odd lot theory, small stock speculators were used as a contrarian indicator, meaning that they are often on the wrong side of the trade. Although this assumption is not always true, its genesis is based on the idea that if these small speculators were good traders, they would eventually become bigger traders.

Rightly or wrongly, the "small speculators" subset of traders is often referred to as the "dumb money," and like it or not, all of us at one time or another have fallen into this category. But are the small speculators really that dumb? The answer might surprise you.

REPORTABLE VS. NONREPORTABLE POSITIONS

All of the currencies listed on the COT report are analyzed vs. the U.S. dollar, with USD as the second member of each "pair." To gain a better understanding of the

Japanese Yen - Chicago Mercantile Exchange

Commitments of Traders - Futures Only, June 23, 2009

Code-097741

Reportable Positions							Nonreportable Positions	
Noncommercial			Commercial		Total			
Long	Short	Spreading	Long	Short	Long	Short	Long	Short
22,186	26,193	294	31,454	30,287	53,934	56,774	19,863	17,023

Contracts of JPY 12,500,000

FIGURE 6.1 This COT report shows a difference of opinion between large and small speculators.
Source: Chicago Mercantile Exchange.

information contained in the report, let's take a look at a slice of statistical information relating to Japanese yen futures contracts from the COT report of June 23, 2009 (see Figure 6.1).

The section titled "Reportable Positions" deals with the noncommercial and commercial traders, while the "Nonreportable Positions" segment refers to the small speculators. The Reportable Positions section includes a category called "spreading," but since a spread is neither a net long nor a net short position, we will disregard those transactions.

The report indicates that noncommercial traders (big speculators like hedge funds and institutional traders) are long 22,186 contracts and short 26,193 contracts; in other words, big speculators are "net short" the yen. Commercial traders (big companies that are affected by fluctuations in the Japanese yen) are long 31,454 contracts and short 30,287 contracts; they are "net long" the yen, if only slightly. The size of each contract is listed as 12,500,000 Japanese yen.

COMMERCIAL MOTIVATIONS

On the surface, the noncommercial and the commercial traders seem to be at odds with one another, but let's remember one very important point: The noncommercials are speculators; they make their living by trading the markets. Meanwhile, generally speaking, the commercial traders earn their living via commerce and are not necessarily trading in the futures market to turn a profit. A commercial trader is much more likely to be involved in this market in order to protect company interests against potentially damaging fluctuations in the Japanese yen.

For example, suppose that an export company based in Japan needs to protect itself against the possibility of a strengthening yen. This company might open a long position in yen futures, so that any business losses due to a strong JPY will be offset by a gain in the company's futures position. This is an example of the true meaning of hedging *(many retail Forex traders define hedging as the holding of simultaneous long and short positions of equal size in the same currency pair).*

Meanwhile, an American company that ships a significant quantity of exports to Japan may seek protection against the possibility of a weaker Japanese currency, because this could lead to fewer purchases of U.S. exports by Japanese buyers. A short JPY futures position could be used by the American company to offset any damage it might suffer due to a weak Japanese yen.

NONCOMMERCIALS VS. SMALL SPECULATORS

Because of the major difference in the motivations of noncommercial and commercial traders, we will focus our attention on the noncommercials. Since they are big professional traders (remember, in order to reach the classification of a noncommercial trader, they must be trading futures contracts in a large, "reportable" size), they have access to the best analysis and research that is available.

Now that we have determined that the noncommercials (big specs) are short the yen, please turn your attention to the small speculators, which are located under the "Nonreportable Positions" section. According to the data, the small specs are long 19,863 contracts and short 17,023 contracts; in this case, we could say that the small specs are "net long" the Japanese yen.

To summarize, the noncommercials are net short the JPY, the positions of the commercials are irrelevant, and the small speculators are net long. At this point we have to ask ourselves, "Which side is most likely to be correct?" Is it the big noncommercial speculators, who manage large positions on a full-time basis with the aid of the world's best research and analysis? Or is it some guy who trades one JPY contract out of his basement during the daytime before reporting to work for the night shift at a convenience store? (Not making fun here—I could have easily been that guy.) Which one is right, and which one is wrong?

SURPRISE!

The answer may surprise you. Although the small speculators are far from perfect, they are superior to the noncommercial traders when it comes to predicting big moves. Small speculators are not the contrarian indicator of the COT report; in fact, they are not really a useful predictor of market direction one way or the other.

The noncommercial traders are the contrarian indicators of the COT report. They tend to be wrong more often than the small speculators, especially when they all line up together on the same side of the trade.

The report of June 23, 2009, showed that noncommercials were short the yen and small specs were long. We can see from the chart that the small speculators made the right call; the JPY actually gained strength vs. the USD, as indicated by the falling weekly chart of the USD/JPY currency pair (see Figure 6.2).

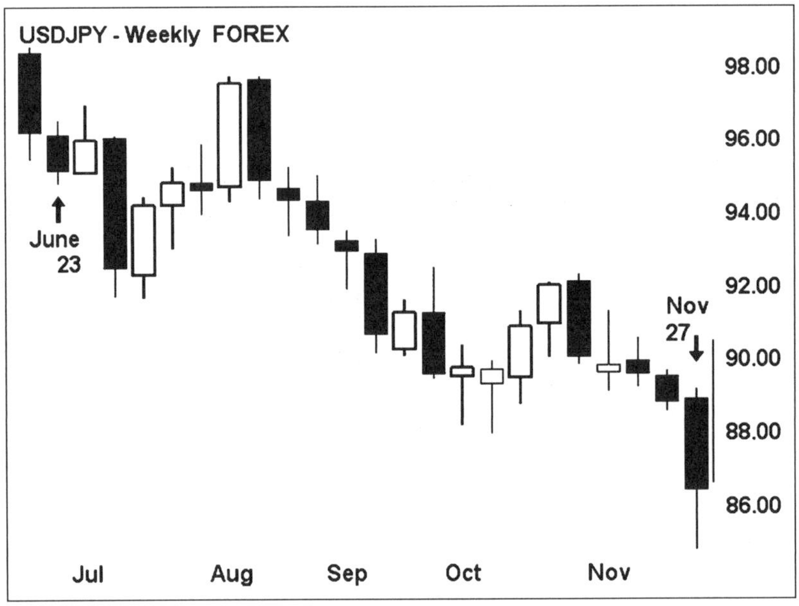

FIGURE 6.2 Small specs correctly predicted fall of USD/JPY.
Source: Created with TradeStation.

At the time the June 23 COT report was compiled, the yen was trading at about 95.00 to the USD. Not long after the release of this report, the JPY went on a rampage against the USD, and by early October the USD/JPY pair had fallen by nearly 1,000 pips. In this case, it seems that the big traders got it wrong, and the little guys got it right.

AGAINST THE DOLLAR

As mentioned earlier, all of the currencies that are listed in the Commitment of Traders report are traded vs. the U.S. dollar, so when you analyze the report, it is understood to refer to the JPY's positioning vs. the USD. Also, in the U.S. currency futures markets (and unlike the spot currency markets), USD is always the base currency (the second member of the currency pair).

Therefore, while USD/JPY is the order of the currency pair in the spot market, the futures market quote is the equivalent of JPY/USD. Because of this difference, a futures chart of the Japanese yen will appear to move higher when the JPY is rising (see Figure 6.3).

While the Japanese yen futures chart appears to be headed in the opposite direction of the USD/JPY spot chart, in reality, the yen is moving in the same direction (higher) vs. the USD on both charts (see Figure 6.4).

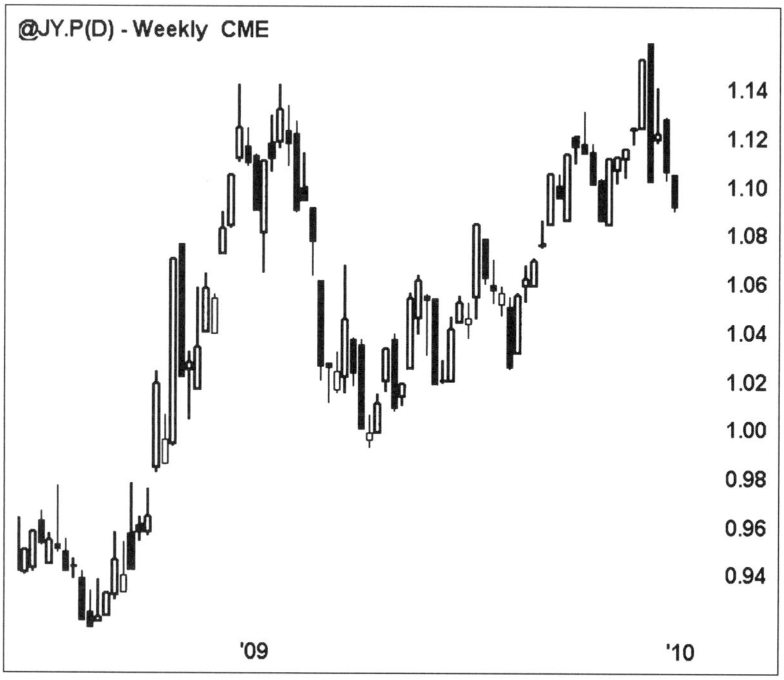

FIGURE 6.3 Japanese yen is strengthening on this futures chart.
Source: Created with TradeStation.

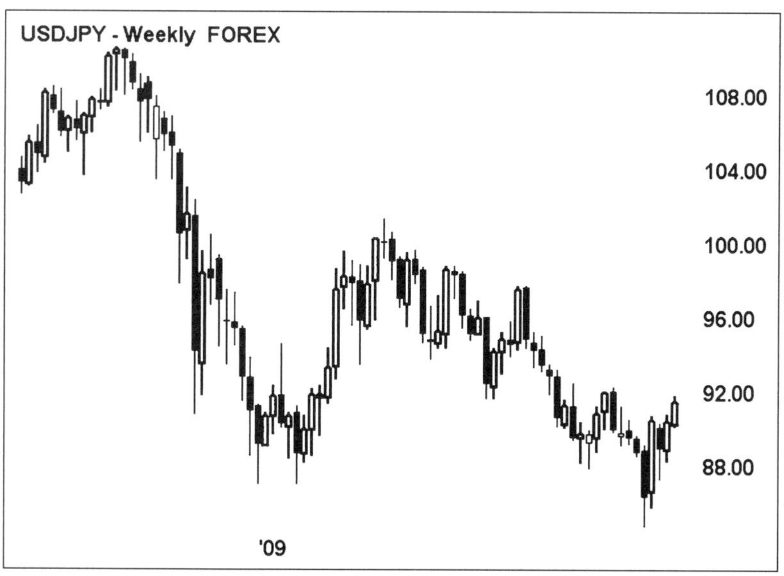

FIGURE 6.4 USD/JPY spot chart is an inverted image of the futures chart in Figure 6.3.
Source: Created with TradeStation.

A RELENTLESS POUNDING

As it turns out, the noncommercials have lousy timing when it comes to turning points in the Forex market. This is even more evident when they position themselves in an extreme manner. For a case in point, let's take a look at a sequence of major reversals in the British pound that occurred at various points in 2007, 2008, and 2009.

Early November 2007: After a massive, multiyear rally, the GBP/USD currency pair traded at its highest point in decades, rising above 2.1100. The pound was in for a steep fall, but how could we have known this ahead of time? How were the noncommercials positioned just prior to this event?

They weren't just long; they were *massively* long just prior to the big selloff. As it turns out, they were also massively wrong (see Figure 6.5).

According to the COT report of November 6, 2007, noncommercial traders were long more than *four times* as many contracts as they were short (79,840 long vs. 19,514 short). Small specs were also net long, though to a much lesser degree. On November 9, 2007, the GBP/USD pair peaked just above 2.1150; it then began a relentless downward move, losing over 1,500 pips by January 22, 2008. The pair fell below 1.9400 before bouncing back up toward the psychologically important level of 2.0000 (see Figure 6.6).

Ouch! It sure looks as if the noncommercial longs were on the wrong side of this trade. If you think about it, the extreme positioning represented by a ratio of over 4 to 1 is giving us some very important information: that the overwhelming majority of the noncommercial traders are on the same side of the trade. Think about it: If everyone is already long the British pound, who is left to buy it? To drive the point home, let's see what happens next in mid-July 2008.

Mid-July 2008: After sliding down from the prior year's highs, GBP/USD has settled down and is trading around 2.0000. Which way will it go next? For clues, Figure 6.7 shows the positioning in the futures market at that time, according to the COT report of July 15, 2008.

While this does not represent extreme positioning, we can see that noncommercials are net long the GBP (50,345 long contracts vs. 43,922 short). Interestingly, the small specs are net short (23,321 short contracts vs. 20,870 long).

In this case, most of the small specs got it right while the majority of the noncommercials got crushed. Right after this report was issued, GBP/USD began a steep slide.

British Pound Sterling - Chicago Mercantile Exchange

Futures Only Positions as of 11/06/07

Code-096742

Reportable Positions							Nonreportable Positions	
Noncommercial			Commercial		Total			
Long	Short	Spreading	Long	Short	Long	Short	Long	Short
79,840	19,514	624	40,375	107,261	120,839	127,399	26,467	19,907

(Contracts of GBP 62,500) Open Interest 147,306

FIGURE 6.5 Noncommercials are massively long the British pound in November 2007.
Source: Chicago Mercantile Exchange.

FIGURE 6.6 GBP/USD plunges shortly after the COT report of Nov. 6, 2007.
Source: Created with TradeStation. © TradeStation Technologies, Inc. All rights reserved.

By September, GBP/USD had fallen by about 2,500 pips from its July 15 high above 2.0100 (see Figure 6.8).

But the devastation didn't end there; by the end of 2008, GBP/USD lost another 2,500 pips and traded below 1.5000—a loss of over 5,000 pips (see Figure 6.9).

Mid-January 2009: After the breathtaking selloff described above, the GBP/USD pair continued to grind its way lower. By January 23, 2009, the pair was trading near 1.3500, more than 7,500 pips below its highs from just over a year earlier. A massive short-covering rally in the British pound was about to occur. So how were the noncommercial traders positioned just prior to this sharp rally? Is there any way we could have seen this rally coming? (See Figure 6.10.)

As you can see from the COT report of January 20, 2009, noncommercial traders were caught massively short at a major turning point—this time by a margin of more than *6 to 1* (7,489 long contracts vs. 46,526 short). This is a dramatic example of extreme positioning. The noncommercials are overwhelmingly lined up on the short side—in this

British Pound Sterling - Chicago Mercantile Exchange

Futures Only Positions as of 07/15/08 — Code-096742

Reportable Positions							Nonreportable Positions	
Noncommercial			Commercial		Total			
Long	Short	Spreading	Long	Short	Long	Short	Long	Short
50,345	43,922	453	37,035	41,007	87,833	85,382	20,870	23,321

(Contracts of GBP 62,500) Open Interest 108,703

FIGURE 6.7 Big specs and small specs are positioned on opposite sides of GBP/USD.
Source: Chicago Mercantile Exchange.

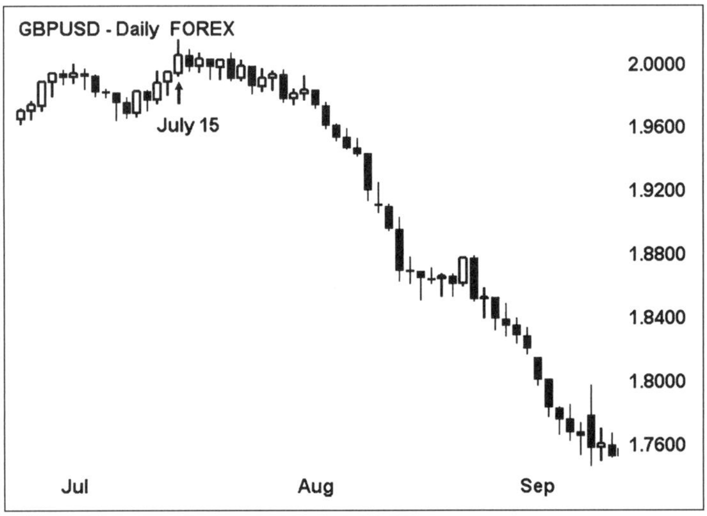

FIGURE 6.8 GBP/USD loses 2,500 pips in 3 months following the July 15, 2008, COT report.
Source: Created with TradeStation. © TradeStation Technologies, Inc. All rights reserved.

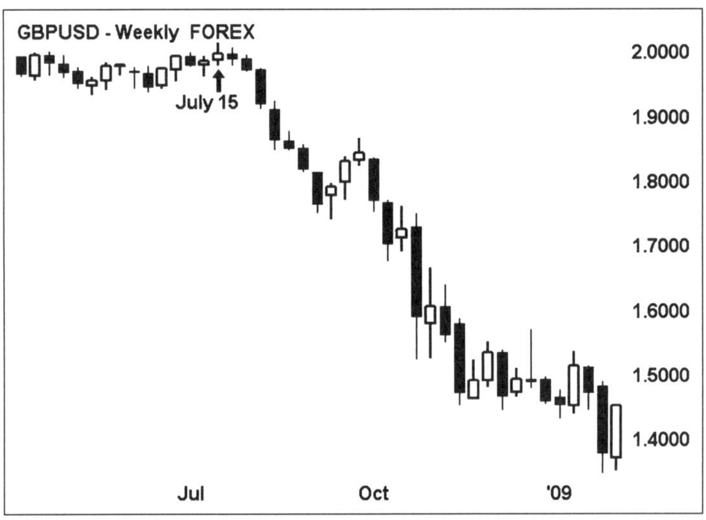

FIGURE 6.9 GBP/USD loses 5,000 pips in 6 months following the July 15, 2008, COT report.
Source: Created with TradeStation. © TradeStation Technologies, Inc. All rights reserved.

British Pound Sterling - Chicago Mercantile Exchange
Code-096742
Futures Only Positions as of 01/20/09

Reportable Positions							Nonreportable Positions	
Noncommercial			Commercial		Total			
Long	Short	Spreading	Long	Short	Long	Short	Long	Short
7,489	46,526	68	49,259	18,613	56,816	65,207	30,882	22,491

(Contracts of GBP 62,500) Open Interest 87,698

FIGURE 6.10 Big specs are massively short GBP/USD just prior to a rally; small specs are long.
Source: Chicago Mercantile Exchange.

FIGURE 6.11 GBP/USD rallies 1,200 pips shortly after the COT report of January 20, 2009.
Source: Created with TradeStation. © TradeStation Technologies, Inc. All rights reserved.

case, the wrong side—of the GBP trade. Once again, it turns out that the small specs were on the right side of the trade (30,882 long contracts vs. 22,491 short).

On this occasion, the previously beleaguered GBP/USD currency pair shot higher by over 1,200 pips in about two weeks' time. By now, the noncommercials must have been wondering if they would ever get it right (see Figure 6.11).

I used a 240-minute chart to illustrate the dramatic nature of this move higher. You can see that from late January through early February 2009, a vicious rally occurred in the British pound.

But that rally paled in comparison to the one that was just about to occur. After a pullback from the February high, GBP/USD settled back, drifting below 1.3700. Then, beginning in early March 2009, a new, even bigger rally began. Surely, after the events chronicled above, the noncommercials would finally get one right. Let's check their positioning according to the COT report of March 3, 2009 (see Figure 6.12).

Once again, the noncom traders are caught on the wrong side of the trade, this time by a margin of about 2.7 to 1 (14,845 long contracts vs. 40,294 short). And once more,

British Pound Sterling - Chicago Mercantile Exchange
Futures Only Positions as of 03/03/09 Code-096742

Reportable Positions							Nonreportable Positions	
Noncommercial			Commercial		Total			
Long	Short	Spreading	Long	Short	Long	Short	Long	Short
14,845	40,294	64	51,539	29,093	66,448	69,451	27,727	24,724

(Contracts of GBP 62,500) Open Interest 94,175

FIGURE 6.12 COT report of March 3, 2009, shows big specs are short GBP/USD.
Source: Chicago Mercantile Exchange.

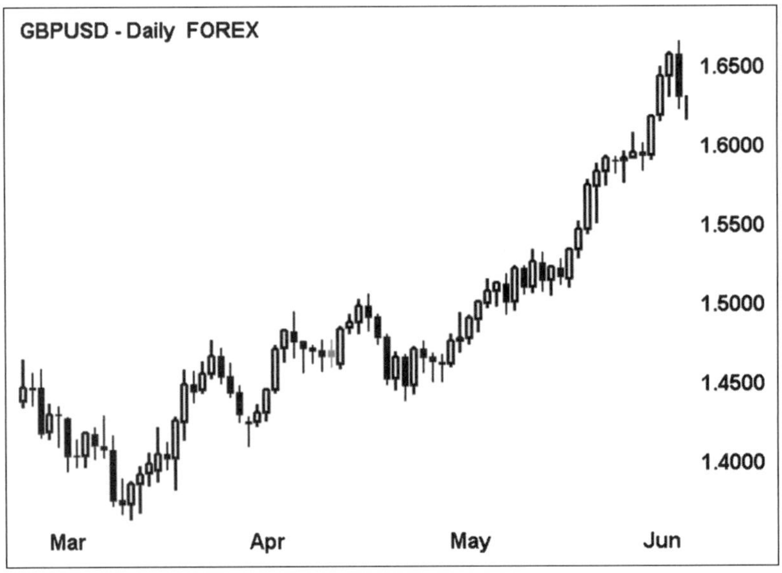

FIGURE 6.13 GBP/USD rallies sharply after the March 3, 2009, COT report.
Source: Created with TradeStation. © TradeStation Technologies, Inc. All rights reserved.

the small specs made the right call, although by a slight margin (27,727 long contracts vs. 24,724 short).

So what did the noncommercial traders miss out on this time? How about a three-month, 3,000-pip rally in GBP/USD? (See Figure 6.13.)

I'd like to point out that these examples do not represent minor fluctuations, but significant turning points in the GBP/USD currency pair. In every case that we examined, the noncommercials were caught on the wrong side of the trade. They have proven to be a valuable contrarian indicator, especially at major turning points.

When using the COT report, it's important to be cognizant not only of current long vs. short ratios, but the direction in which the numbers are moving. Is the positioning becoming more extreme, or are the net long and short positions evening out? The more extreme the difference in positioning by long and short noncommercial traders, the more likely it is that a major move in that currency is about to occur.

"Whether he likes it or not, a man's character is stripped at the poker table; if the other players read him better than he does, he has only himself to blame. Unless he is both able and prepared to see himself as others do, flaws and all, he will be a loser in cards, as in life."

—Anthony Holden, Poker Player and Author

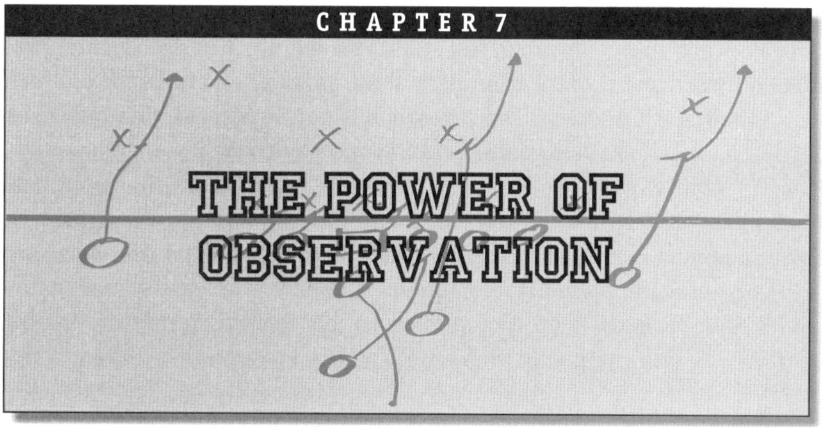

CHAPTER 7

THE POWER OF OBSERVATION

"You can observe a lot just by watching."
—Yogi Berra, 3-time Most Valuable Player, Baseball Hall of Fame

If you've ever traded stocks for a living, or even spent time as a casual observer of the equity markets, you may have witnessed the following scenario: A company releases a negative earnings report. When the earnings shortfall is announced and the stock opens for trading, it falls hard. A few hours later, you take another look at the stock and you see that it has bounced all the way back up and is now "green"—the stock has recouped its losses and is now trading higher than it was before the bad news was announced.

Or perhaps you've witnessed this scenario: You hear news that a company has been upgraded by a major analyst. The stock trades higher in the morning but by the end of the day, it is down sharply, despite the good news.

What is going on here? Are these market reactions illogical, or is there something else at work?

That "something else" is one of the most powerful and useful things in all of trading, and it appears in the Forex market, the commodities markets, the stock markets, and in every trading market. The "something else" to which I refer is market sentiment.

EXPLAINING TRIG TO A 6-YEAR-OLD

Consider this: One day long ago, early in my career, I was trading stocks as an employee for a boutique trading firm. On that day, the market was down hard, and many of the people in my trading room were shorting tech stocks, particularly shares of semiconductor stocks. "C'mon, Ed," I said to myself. "The semis are getting crushed! Time to get short!"

I searched until I found a chip stock that hadn't fallen yet, and then I shorted the daylights out of it. Much to my surprise, the stock just wouldn't budge. The market continued to sail southward and traders around me began to hoot and holler; they were scoring big bucks on their short positions, and meanwhile my stock wouldn't fall. I cursed and banged my fist on the desk. "This damn stock won't go down!" I yelled.

One of the more experienced traders heard me from across the room. "Oh really? And what stock is that?" he asked, and I gave him the four-letter symbol. Then the trader eyed me with a pained expression, as if he were deciding how to best explain trigonometry to a 6-year old. He patiently explained: "Look, you've just struck gold—you've found a stock that, at least for today, refuses to fall in a down market. Instead of trying to short it, why don't you wait and see if the market turns? If it does, then go long that stock."

Later in the day, the market did change direction and the stock went higher, just as he suggested. I was too proud to take his advice, and at the time I didn't really understand what he meant, but I learned a lesson that day. He went long the stock that afternoon—the same stock I had tried to sell short—and it rocketed higher.

Here's the point: The market's sentiment toward that stock on that day was very positive, so much so that the shares wouldn't fall even when everything around it was getting destroyed. Forget about the reasons why, because we can't always know the reason behind every move. Nobody possesses all of the relevant information about any stock, commodity, or currency at any given time.

The only thing that really mattered in this situation was that there were buyers—maybe big ones—who wanted to buy that stock. Perhaps they knew something—they possessed some good research, or maybe even inside information. Or maybe the news that was hurting the other semiconductor stocks was already factored into the price of that stock. The reason doesn't matter; the only thing that matters is that someone was buying, and they were driving the price higher. The good news is this: We don't have to know what that buyer knew in order to capitalize on the move.

BAD NEWS, GOOD REACTION

The same situation occurs in the currency markets all the time. For example, let's look at the GBP/USD chart from May 21, 2009. On that day came an announcement that seemed to catch traders by surprise and sent a shock wave through the currency markets. Standard and Poor's, an influential agency that provides credit quality ratings on a variety of investments, had reduced its outlook on the creditworthiness of the United Kingdom.

Specifically, S&P downgraded its outlook on the United Kingdom's AAA credit rating from "stable" to "negative." S&P was reacting to the mountain of debt that the United Kingdom had piled up in an effort to bail itself out of a credit crisis and extricate itself from a global economic meltdown.

We have all heard of companies that have had their debt downgraded, even to the point where a company's bonds are given a "junk" rating. And we all know someone who has been charged exorbitant fees by lenders because of misuse of credit cards.

But this was different. The government debt of the entire United Kingdom was being sullied, and the ability of the U.K. government to pay off its debts was being called into question. Just as a person who has difficulty paying his or her credit card debt is forced to pay a higher interest rate, the United Kingdom might be forced to pay higher yields to attract investors to its bonds. In response, the British pound fell hard against the U.S. dollar, at one point losing more than 250 pips in less than one hour.

And then a funny thing happened. Slowly at first, then with increasing speed, the British currency began to rebound. Eight hours after the S&P credit warning, the GBP/USD currency pair was actually higher than it had been prior to the announcement (see Figure 7.1).

What was the first clue that big buyers were active in the British pound? If you look at the chart prior to the S&P announcement, you'll notice that the currency had been pretty strong *before* the bad news became public. In fact, GBP/USD had traded below 1.4500 on April 21, and then climbed more than 1,000 pips in one month's time prior to the negative S&P announcement (see Figure 7.2).

This tells us that there was already at least one big buyer in the GBP, probably more than one. We don't know who was buying or why, but that isn't important.

Maybe these buyers, probably an institution or institutions, know or believe something that is more important than today's news. You and I can't always know what these buyers know. We may not have access to their research, but we don't have to know what

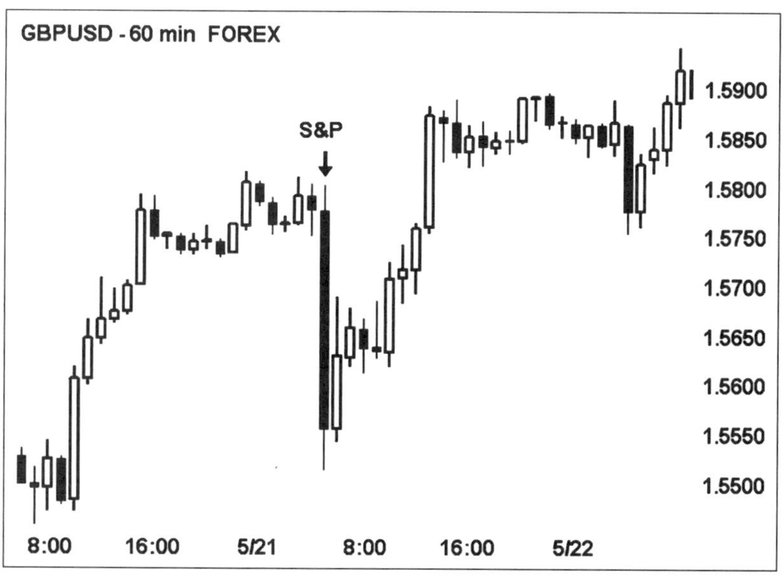

FIGURE 7.1 GBP/USD ignores S&P's downgrade of United Kingdom's credit outlook.
Source: Created with TradeStation. © TradeStation Technologies, Inc. All rights reserved.

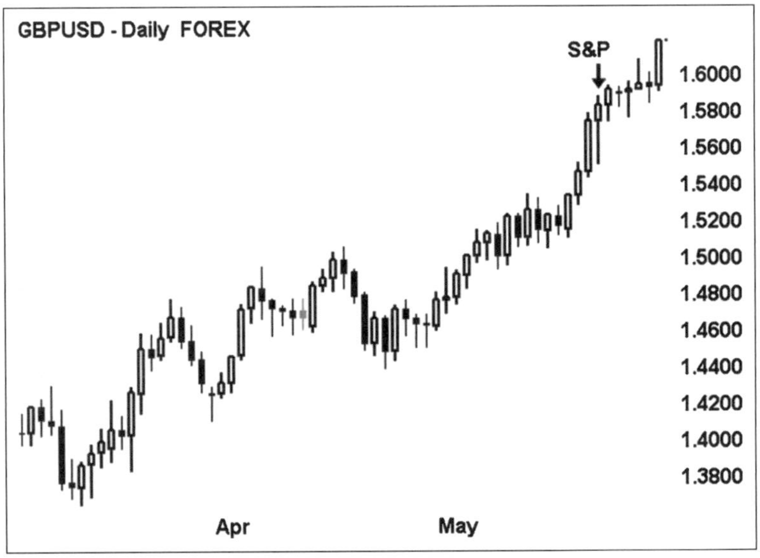

FIGURE 7.2 Big buyers were active in GBP/USD long before the S&P downgrade.
Source: Created with TradeStation.

they know. The only thing that matters to us is that there is a big buyer or buyers out there. If we see a currency react well to bad news on a consistent basis, that means that buyers are stepping in—and that means we are also going to buy.

I guess those big buyers made the right move, because by June 3, 2009—about two weeks after the S&P's downgrade of the U.K. economy—the GBP/USD pair climbed above 1.6600. In that short span of time, the pound was trading over 1,000 pips above the intraday low of the day of the downgrade. I don't know what information those buyers possessed, but it must have been correct (see Figure 7.3).

RUNNING FOR COVER

Consider this: In 2008, the U.S. dollar put on its best performance in years, crushing the euro, the British pound, and nearly every other major currency. GBP/USD fell more than 5,000 pips from the beginning of 2008 until the end of the year, and EUR/USD fell 2,500 pips in just a few months time. Even the U.S. Dollar Index had a great year, at one point climbing from 74 to 90. When it came to the U.S. dollar, especially during the third quarter of 2008, if you weren't long, you were wrong (see Figure 7.4).

Why was the USD rocking so hard in the third quarter of 2008? It's important to understand the reasons behind the move, so that we'll know how to react to similar situations if we encounter them in the future. Fear was running high as the financial world seemed to be collapsing all around us, and when traders are frightened, they move their capital to the safest place possible.

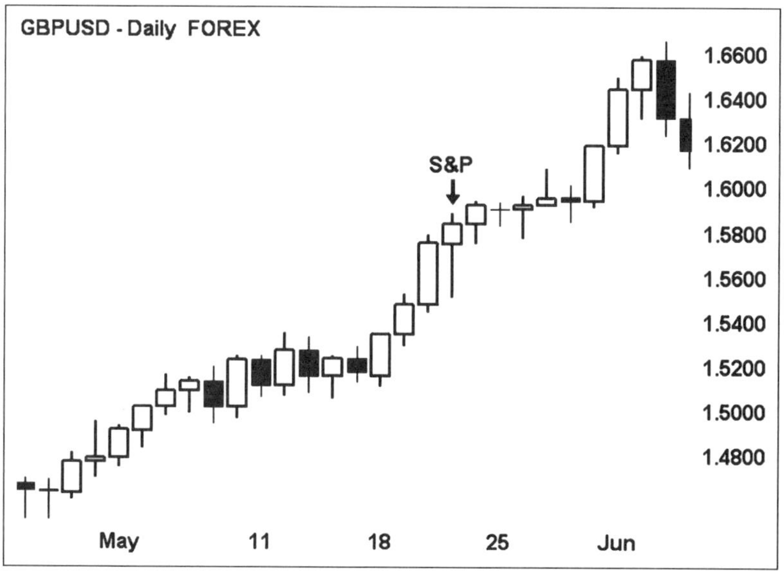

FIGURE 7.3 GBP/USD continued its climb after the S&P news was quickly absorbed.
Source: Created with TradeStation. © TradeStation Technologies, Inc. All rights reserved.

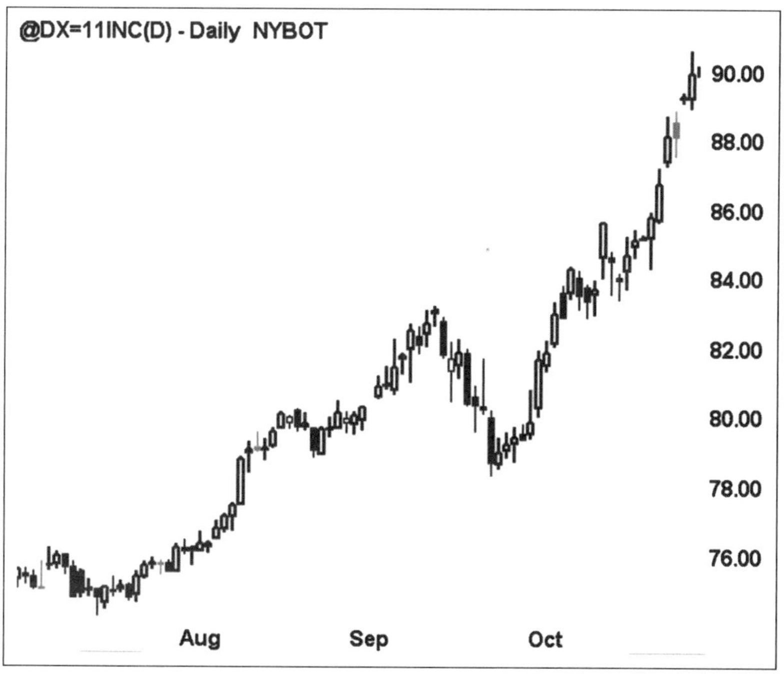

FIGURE 7.4 USDX rockets higher as the world's financial system teeters on the verge of collapse.
Source: Created with TradeStation. © TradeStation Technologies, Inc. All rights reserved.

As the world's reserve currency, the USD stood to gain the most as investors moved their wealth out of unstable currencies and financial markets around the world. U.S. Treasuries are especially attractive in times of turmoil, as they are considered among the safest investments in the world, and so money poured into them from around the globe. This influx of capital is one of the main reasons why the USD gained so much strength in 2008.

Another reason for the strength of the greenback was the sudden loss of confidence in many of the currencies of developing nations. These currencies tend to outperform during good economic times and underperform during bad times. Capital was evaporating by the hour for individuals and companies who had their wealth concentrated in emerging currencies like the Brazilian real, the Russian ruble, and the Mexican peso. In order to protect wealth, the logical move was to get out of those volatile currencies. The next move was to convert those funds to a relatively stable currency like the U.S. dollar.

BIGGER THAN THE NEWS

All of these factors led to strength in the USD, but there was something even more critical at work here. What really matters to a trader's bottom line is the ability to identify a market's positive or negative sentiment toward a currency—and even more important, not to fight against it. The sentiment toward the USD was very positive at that time, and that was all that mattered.

There was an incredible amount of bad news in the United States that year—the U.S. stock markets crashed, energy prices hit record highs, the housing market imploded, and major financial institutions collapsed as if they were made of tissue paper. A reasonable person might suspect that under those circumstances, the greenback would perform poorly.

Yet through it all, the USD reigned supreme, and those who identified this positive sentiment earliest—and resisted the urge to fight it—benefited the most. The day-to-day economic news was awful, but that didn't matter to the USD bulls. The flight to U.S. Treasuries and the greenback was bigger and more important than the news of the day.

CAPITALIZING ON SENTIMENT

Since the sentiment toward the USD was so strong and positive, I focussed on key economic reports. What was I hoping for? I was waiting for news that might weaken the USD, so that I could buy dollars cheaply. The bull trend in the USD was very strong, and astute observers noticed that although the greenback might weaken temporarily on bad news, it would quickly bounce back because traders were buying the greenback regardless of the news.

The strong positive sentiment for the dollar trumped any economic report. If everyone is fleeing toward the USD, would a weak U.S. manufacturing report or a negative consumer confidence report really make any difference? Essentially, I started using bad news as an opportunity to buy dips in the U.S. dollar.

THE FIRST CLUE

For an early sign of this change of sentiment, let's take a look at an event that occurred on July 31, 2008. EUR/USD had enjoyed a spectacular run, reaching new highs around the 1.6000 level. Then the pair began to consolidate and began trading in a range between 1.5300 and 1.6000. The pair had been consolidating for about three months, when it suddenly began to sell off during the last two weeks of July. The U.S. dollar was beginning to gain strength, and the euro was losing favor (see Figure 7.5).

On the morning of July 31, two economic reports were released simultaneously; the advance Gross Domestic Product (GDP) report for the second quarter, and the Unemployment Claims number. The first report would tell the pace at which the U.S. economy grew during Q2, and the second would reveal the number of individuals who filed for unemployment insurance for the first time during the prior week.

The currency market's reactions to these numbers are usually based on the expectations of economists; analysts are surveyed by news services such as Bloomberg, Dow Jones, or Thomson Reuters, and the market's expectations are based on the results of the surveys. According to those surveys, analysts anticipated that the U.S. economy grew at 2.4 percent, and 395,000 new unemployment claims would be filed.

When the numbers were released at 8:30 a.m. New York time, it became clear that the analysts had overestimated the strength of the U.S. economy, which only grew at

FIGURE 7.5 EUR/USD slides lower within a consolidation during late July 2008.
Source: Created with TradeStation.

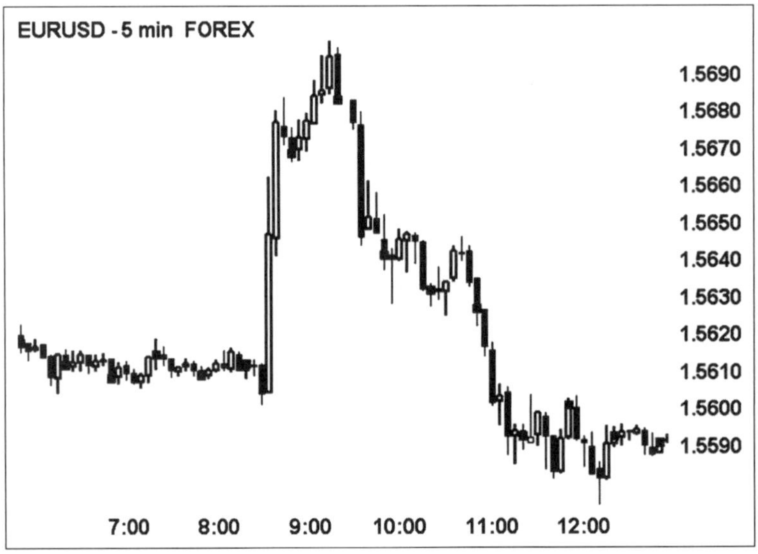

FIGURE 7.6 EUR/USD pops higher but quickly reverses.
Source: Created with TradeStation.

1.9 percent in the second quarter. Economists were looking for 2.4 percent growth in GDP and had missed the mark by a wide margin of 0.5 percent.

The news on unemployment was even worse, with 448,000 workers filing claims for the first time. This was much higher than the anticipated result of 395,000, a huge miss of 53,000 for the analysts. Clearly, the U.S. economy was in much worse shape than anticipated, and in response, the euro shot higher against the U.S. dollar. EUR/USD popped up by about 75 pips in just 10 minutes, and gained close to 100 pips in 45 minutes (see Figure 7.6).

And then a funny thing happened: EUR/USD came crashing back to earth as the U.S. dollar came roaring back with a vengeance. Just three hours after two truly awful economic reports had smashed the greenback, all of the USD's losses had been regained.

This powerful move caught many traders by surprise: What the heck had just happened? Although it seemed odd at the time, in the following weeks we began to see frequent and decisive positive movement in the greenback whenever negative economic news would strike. In fact, it seemed that the worse the news, the greater the rally in the dollar! The game plan became clear, and buying the USD on negative economic news became standard operating procedure for many currency traders.

DOUBLE SHOT

Two months later, the events that played out on September 25 of that year drove the point home. By that time, EUR/USD was no longer in a consolidation phase, having fallen out

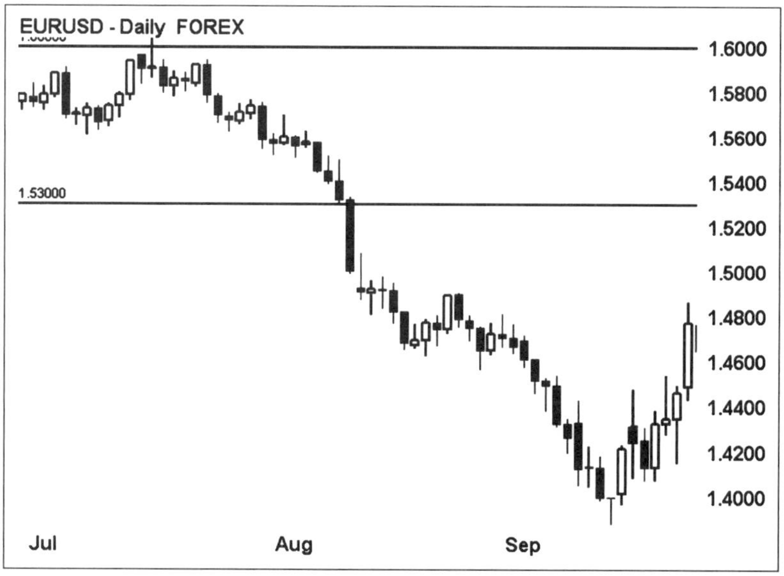

FIGURE 7.7 EUR/USD breaks major support, plunges, and bounces.
Source: Created with TradeStation.

of its prior trading range. After breaking support at 1.5300, the pair went into a free-fall, dropping all the way to 1.4000 as the greenback gained the upper hand against the single currency. Then in mid-September, EUR/USD caught a nice bounce up to 1.4800, but the countertrend rally appeared to be losing steam (see Figure 7.7).

On September 25, currency traders anxiously awaited the release of a series of economic reports. At 8:30 a.m. New York time, one report showed that orders for durable goods contracted by a disappointing –4.5 percent during the month of August. This was much worse than the expected result of –1.6 percent.

At the same time, the weekly unemployment claims number was released, and it was also much worse than expected: 493,000 new claims had been filed, much higher than the anticipated number of 450,000. Once again, it was a double shot of bad news for the U.S. economy. EUR/USD popped up by about 40 pips on the news, but within an hour, those gains had evaporated.

BETTING THE HOUSE

Now traders awaited a big housing report due at 10:00 a.m., which would reveal the annualized rate at which new homes were being sold—an important indication of the strength of the U.S. economy. The expected result was that new homes in the U.S. were selling at an annual rate of 510,000, according to the estimates of analysts.

Just imagine the reaction as the report revealed that new homes were selling at a shockingly low annual rate of just 460,000; the analysts had missed the mark by 50,000

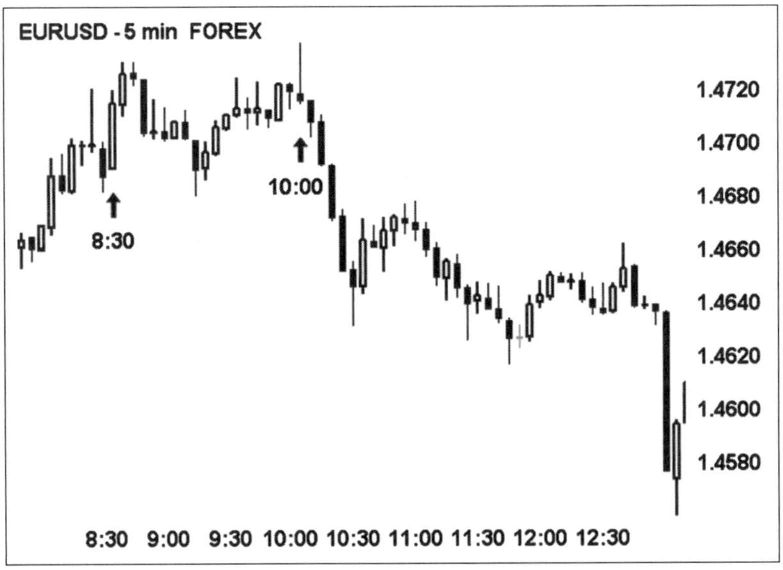

FIGURE 7.8 USD strengthens vs. EUR despite weak economic news.
Source: Created with TradeStation.

houses! The EUR/USD pair popped up by about 20 pips, but within 5 minutes, it was right back where it started. Clearly, traders had caught on and were now buying the USD on bad economic news. The five-minute candle showed a shooting star pattern, another indication that the price was about to reverse.

And reverse it did—the EUR/USD currency pair had been trading at 1.4720 just prior to the release of the housing report, but just 30 minutes later it traded at 1.4630, a move of 90 pips. Then the pair managed a feeble bounce, but it was short-lived. Just three hours after the housing report was released, EUR/USD had fallen all the way to 1.4560, a loss of 160 pips from its starting point (see Figure 7.8).

THE PREPARED MIND

Sentiment is best identified through observation. When you are involved in markets on a daily basis, you begin to notice certain things. For example, you might observe that the price of a commodity keeps going higher every day, regardless of whether the news is positive or negative. Or you might notice that a currency falls persistently, even when the news is good.

If you observe a currency (or a stock, or commodity) that moves consistently higher (or lower) whether the economic news is good or bad, you may have found something very valuable. You just may have identified strong market sentiment, one of the most valuable discoveries that you can make.

In these scenarios, very often there will be a clear trend on the chart, which in itself indicates strong sentiment or a high level of commitment. Put your powers of observation to work, take careful note of what you are seeing, and the rewards will follow.

> "In the fields of observation, chance favors only the prepared mind."
>
> —*Louis Pasteur, Famous Chemist and Microbiologist*

CHAPTER 8

OTHER PEOPLE'S MONEY

"Yes, it's that simple: use OPM—other people's money. That's the way to acquire great wealth."

—From the book *Success through a Positive Mental Attitude*, by Napoleon Hill and W. Clement Stone

People often ask me how to turn a small amount of money into a giant pile of cash. The sad truth is, it's not easy to trade your way from, say, $5,000 into millions of dollars on your own. A trader who undertakes such a task fights an uphill battle, because big profits often walk hand in hand with big risks. The problem with big risks is they tend to catch up with us, eventually resulting in a big loss.

But all hope is not lost, because traders who can produce a track record that proves their ability to trade real money (sorry, this does not include demo accounts) might be qualified to manage funds in addition to their own, or Other People's Money (OPM). In order to do this, you will have to be able to prove that you can trade profitably over a significant period of time (a minimum of six months, preferably two years or more).

Ladies and gentlemen, this is where the real work—and the real money—is. But where does one find this money? It is all around us; there are always investors willing to place money with a legitimate trader, and good traders are always in demand. You may decide to "run money" for individuals, or perhaps you can help fill the needs of an institution.

The latter is not as far-fetched as it may sound: Institutions need traders too! For example, suppose that a hedge fund is already trading in stocks and commodities and decides that it needs exposure to the currency markets. That institution might seek out a trader who specializes in currencies and allocate a relatively small portion of its capital to that trader. If the trader performs well, the institution might increase the capital allocated to that trader.

ACCOUNT MANAGEMENT

Customer account management is a very different ball game from running a hedge fund. The rules for hedge funds are complex and varied depending upon your location, and those rules are becoming more complicated all the time. A hedge fund manager runs a very opaque operation, and the investors rarely know what the fund manager is doing with their money.

Conversely, when it comes to account management, the investors often see *every* trade that the account manager is placing. In many cases, no money actually changes hands; the investor opens his or her own account and then grants the trader the authority to place trades in the account. This permission is granted through the signing of a limited power of attorney (LPOA).

We are not going to go into various legalities here, for example, which licenses are required, and so forth, for two reasons: First, Forex traders are a wide and diverse audience. If this book is half as successful as its widely read predecessor, *Forex Patterns and Probabilities*, then it is being read in dozens of countries right now. Each of those countries has its own laws regarding money management, and this book is not intended to be a legal treatise.

The second reason is because those myriad laws are constantly changing and becoming more complex, especially after the scandals of the early part of the 21st century. Rather than bemoaning this fact, we should encourage greater scrutiny of managed accounts, as the "bad apples" need to be sorted out from the rest. Increased scrutiny will inspire greater confidence in the many good account managers who are out there—the ones you never hear about on the evening news.

LIMITED POWER

The LPOA limits the trader's authority to the actual placement of trades; at no point is the trader allowed to withdraw funds from the account. If you are ever asked to sign such a document, whether you are the investor or the trader, be certain that this is clearly stated.

In most cases, the investor can see all of the transactions being placed in the account—after all, it is the *investor's* account. If at any point the investor becomes uncomfortable with what is happening in the account, he or she can cancel the LPOA, immediately revoking the trading authority of the account manager.

Similarly, the account manager can also sever the LPOA if the client becomes too bothersome. You might be surprised at how often this happens. Some clients require constant hand-holding, and this can interfere with the account manager's ability to operate freely. This occurs frequently when trading for individuals, especially if they are not well capitalized. This type of investor is often referred to as "scared money."

Institutions, on the other hand, tend to write big checks and then leave the account manager alone. As experienced professionals, they understand that constant nagging does not aid the account manager in his or her decision-making process; in fact, it is more likely to harm the results.

If you are managing money and you ever feel yourself hesitate before entering a trade because you are concerned about the potential negative reaction of a client, then it is time for you to fire that client. Never fear, there are plenty of good clients out there—provided that you can continue to provide consistent, profitable results without taking inordinate risks.

"ONE AND TWENTY"

Just how is the account manager compensated for providing this service? Allow me to introduce you to the usual method of payment, often referred to as "one and twenty." In this scenario, the account manager keeps 1 percent of the assets under management (AUM) and 20 percent of the profit (assuming that there *are* any profits).

The actual level of compensation is negotiable, and account managers who are in demand may charge more. For example, 2 percent of AUM and 25 percent of any anticipated profit might be the price an investor is charged to place money with a "hot" account manager. On the other hand, managers who are keen to raise capital may forego any charge on the AUM, thus resulting in a possible compensation of "zero and twenty."

Finally, there are money managers who do not accept any portion of profits and are only paid a fee based on a percentage of the assets under management. As you can imagine, there are many potential compensation scenarios for money managers.

SMALL POTATOES

Let's assume that an investor gives you an opportunity to trade his $1,000,000 USD account. Does that sound like a lot of money? In the world of finance, it is small potatoes. We'll also assume that your goal as the trader is to generate a profit of 2 percent per month, while guarding tightly against risk. Remember, if there is no profit at the end of the year, you will receive 20 percent of nothing, but you get to keep the 1 percent of the AUM regardless of whether there is any profit.

A consistent monthly gain of 2 percent should result in an annual profit of about 27 percent (the result is higher than 24 percent because the projected gains are being compounded on a monthly basis). Although this goal might seem easy, keep in mind that this is a game of consistency.

Any joker can earn a 2 percent profit in a month, and some of us may gain it in an hour. The problem is, most traders give it back about an hour later! Meanwhile, the trader who can end every month with a profit of at least 2 percent can be a star in the world of money management.

(For a greater understanding of monthly goals and how to set them, please refer to Chapter 17 of my first book, *Forex Patterns and Probabilities*).

Let's assume that despite your best efforts, you come up short of this goal, finishing the year with a respectable total profit of 20 percent. Here is how the trader's compensation would be calculated according to "one and twenty":

AUM = $1,000,000
1% of AUM = $10,000

The 1 percent annual AUM fee is not usually delivered in one lump sum. Instead, it is normally calculated as 1/12 of 1 percent every month, and the funds are automatically transferred from the investor's account to the trader's account at the beginning of every month. In order for this automatic transfer to occur, both the investor and the trader must have accounts with the same broker and must file the proper paperwork with that broker.

Forex brokers tend to be very helpful when facilitating this type of arrangement, because a good money manager with the ability to raise capital could potentially bring dozens of accounts (and millions of dollars) to the broker. They will "roll out the red carpet" for a good account manager, because of the amount of business the broker stands to gain.

Okay, that takes care of the 1 percent AUM. Now let's focus on the profit portion of the money manager's compensation:

Annual Profit = 20%
20% of $1,000,000 = $200,000

Let's assume that at the end of the year the profit on the $1,000,000 account is 20 percent, which equals $200,000. You worked hard all year, and although you fell short of your goal of a 27 percent profit, the end result of your labor is that you've turned 1 million dollars into 1.2 million dollars. You didn't set the world on fire, but you did a respectable job.

In addition to 1 percent of assets under management, the trader is entitled to 20 percent of the profit. In this case, the account manager's portion equals 20 percent of $200,000. Therefore, your slice of the profit pie comes to $40,000:

20% of $200,000 = $40,000

Now we can calculate the money manager's gains for the year, just based on this one account:

1% of AUM = $10,000
Plus 20% of profit = $40,000
Total Profit $10,000 + $40,000 = $50,000

Congratulations, you are now $50,000 richer! In addition to that, you now have one year's experience as a successful account manager. You may be able to leverage this experience into a high-paying position at a hedge fund. Or you may decide to continue to grow your own money management business.

At this point, some traders are undoubtedly saying, "Why should I do all that work and go through all that hassle for a mere $50,000? I already make more money than that trading my own account, so why would I want to get involved with Other People's Money?"

SOMEWHAT LARGER POTATOES

Well, that decision is up to you, but keep in mind that you were going to place these trades in your own account anyway. You are essentially getting $50,000 for allowing someone else to "piggyback" on your trades—not an insignificant sum. You leverage your own account, so if you're a consistently profitable trader, why not leverage your trading results as well?

LAMM AND PAMM

How is this "piggyback" effect achieved? Most commonly, the Forex broker has several allocation systems from which to choose. Two such allocation systems are the percentage allocation management module (PAMM) and the lot allocation management module (LAMM).

When using LAMM, trades of a similar lot size are placed in both accounts (the trader's account and the investor's account) regardless of account size. If a trader using LAMM purchases one standard lot for his or her own account, a one standard lot trade is automatically and simultaneously placed in the customer's account. You don't have to place separate trades in each account, because the two accounts are linked together—the trade is placed automatically. In fact, many accounts can be linked together in this manner.

However, what if you have a $50,000 account and your client has a $5,000,000 account? Although one standard lot may be appropriate for a $50,000 account, it doesn't make much sense to place a one lot trade in the customer's account, because the size of that account would make such a trade inconsequential. In this case, a percentage allocation module would be much more appropriate.

When using PAMM, trades are allocated on a percentage basis instead of a fixed number of lots. For example, suppose you have a $100,000 account, and in addition you are managing an account worth $500,000. Since the account you are managing is five times the size of your own account, any trade you place in your account will be replicated on a percentage basis in the investor's account.

In other words, when using PAMM, if you place a trade for one standard lot in your own account, the same trade will be placed simultaneously for five standard lots in the investor's account (assuming that the investor's account is five times bigger than your own account). PAMM-style lot allocation makes sense when the accounts in question differ greatly in size, or if the trader is managing many accounts of various sizes.

ROOM TO GROW

Also, consider this—as we mentioned, in the world of money management, one million dollars is not a lot of money to have under management. There are hedge funds out there that manage $10, $20, $30 billion. Under our current scenario, there is plenty of room to grow, and we can scale our profits right along with our growth. Consider the following scenario.

Let's say that after the first year, our investor is pleased with the trader's performance. He decides to allocate more capital to our account manager—after all, he is now $150,000 richer thanks to our trader's efforts (total profit of $200,000 minus the account manager's compensation of $50,000 leaves the investor with a profit of $150,000).

Pleased with the first year's results, the investor ups the ante, giving our trader a total of $5,000,000 to manage. In addition, he tells a few close friends about this "hot new trader" and they decide that they want in on the action, allocating another $5,000,000 to our account manager for a total of $10,000,000 AUM.

Let's also assume that the account manager replicates his feat from the previous year, ending with a 20 percent annual gain. What will his money management income look like now?

AUM = $10,000,000
1% of AUM = $100,000
Total Annual Profit = 20%
20% of $10,000,000 = $2,000,000 (total annual profit)
20% of $2,000,000 = $400,000 (trader's portion of profit)
Total Profit $100,000 + $400,000 = $500,000

Ah, so now I have your attention! In the second year, the account manager was paid in the same manner (one and twenty) and achieved the same results (20 percent profit) as he did in the first year. But since he had 10 times the amount of money under management during the second year, he walked away with ten times more profit than he did the first year.

As you can see, the more money that is held under management, the greater the potential income for the money manager. Also, I am using realistic annual returns of 20 percent; this is not some ridiculous pie-in-the-sky projection, but a realistically achievable figure. Please note that I did NOT say that it would be easy, but it is certainly achievable! But even with consistent returns of 1 percent per month or less, a trader can do quite well managing other people's money.

Of course we can keep adding zeros to the AUM to create truly astronomical profit figures, and when you do this, it becomes easy to understand how hedge fund managers and other traders can earn such tremendous sums of money. Good money managers are some of the most highly compensated people in the world—similar to pro athletes and rock stars—so the potential to make big money is out there.

But if you do find yourself managing huge piles of cash someday, there is a problem that you will eventually encounter, known to traders as the "Law of Large Numbers."

MORE MONEY, MORE PROBLEMS

In its more common usage, the Law of Large Numbers refers to probability. For example, if you flip a coin once and it comes up heads, then the results of your coin flipping are the following: 100 percent = heads and 0 percent = tails. If you continue to flip the coin, it becomes more likely that the result of heads—and the result of tails—will be closer to 50 percent of the total flips. The larger the sample of flips, the more likely this is to occur.

In trading, this phrase is used in a different manner. To money managers, the Law of Large Numbers refers to the concept that the more money a trader has under management, the more difficult it becomes to continuously replicate the gains. For many traders, it's easier to earn a 20 percent profit on $1,000,000 than it is on $10,000,000 or $100,000,000.

The more money you have under management, the harder it becomes to maintain your performance. For example, it might become difficult for an account manager to nimbly enter and exit positions when he or she is throwing around 100-lot trades at the drop of a hat, so be forewarned. This problem is exacerbated when dealing with instruments like stocks, which are less liquid than currencies. In this scenario, it becomes harder to enter and exit a meaningful position size.

Most traders have a comfort zone regarding the amount of assets under management they are willing to handle, and many refuse to accept additional funds at some point because they are no longer comfortable with the amount of money they are managing. They may also believe that having too much money under management will dilute their results.

GOOD HELP IS HARD TO FIND

Also, the more money you have under management, the more difficult it will become to manage it on your own. Eventually, you will have to bring in some hired help, which also means that at some point you're going to have to start hiring (and firing) people.

Running a company and managing employees is an entirely different skill set from trading, and there is a danger that it could distract you from your real job of finding and placing good trades. Again, it is not impossible to do both or to allocate some of that responsibility to others, but you can see how we are drifting farther and farther away from actual trading. You might find yourself with more nontrading responsibility than you desired. People management and money management are not the same at all!

Finally, please remember that the "one and twenty" compensation plan is not written in stone, it is just a guideline. As we mentioned earlier, if a money manager finds that his services are in high demand, he may raise his rate, for example, he may require 2 percent or even 3 percent of AUM and 25 percent of any profits. On the other hand, a new money manager who is looking to build clientele might trade for only a percentage of profits and temporarily forego any payment for AUM. Another tactic is to charge only a small percentage of AUM and forego any slice of the profit pie.

Just like everything else in trading, in the end the fees charged will be determined by supply and demand—in this case both the demand for your services, and the supply of other money managers providing a similar level of service.

THE DARK SIDE OF MONEY MANAGEMENT

Now for the other side of the coin: Maybe someday you'll consider allowing someone to handle your account for you. There is nothing wrong with hiring a reputable account manager to make decisions and place trades on your behalf, and there are plenty of good traders out there who might be up to the task.

The problem is that there are plenty of snakes out there too, looking to take advantage of unsuspecting clients. One thing that I have noticed over the years is that the same slimy scammers seem to keep crawling out from under the rocks, over and over again. Many of these shady dealers operate from countries that have lax standards and minimal enforcement of financial regulations.

The collapse of the financial markets in 2008/2009 shone a bright light on some of the seedier aspects of the money management business, most notoriously personified by Mr. Bernard Madoff. Madoff may have scammed more than $60 billion from his unsuspecting clientele, all of whom believed that this former chair of the National Association of Securities Dealers (NASD) was a reputable money manager.

Madoff appeared to earn steady, unspectacular returns for years—in fact, his results were too consistent. He was supposedly achieving returns of about 10 percent per year, but his returns seemed to be unaffected by market conditions; in the real world, returns vary from month to month and year to year because market conditions are always changing. The scam, and dozens of others like it, unraveled when the markets collapsed and clients tried to pull their money out—only to learn that their money was gone.

MADOFF SCHEME?

There isn't much to smile about when it comes to losing money as a result of fraud, and later in this book we will discuss ways to avoid being scammed. But there is one slightly humorous side effect of all of these scandals—at least as far as yours truly is concerned. In the wake of these scams, the term "Ponzi scheme" has once again achieved common usage in the public vernacular. This phrase refers to Charles Ponzi, the notorious Boston con man who rose to prominence during the early 20th century.

Thanks to Mr. Madoff and his ilk, rarely does a day go by when I don't hear some good-natured ribbing about my last name. If you were a doctor, and your last name just happened to be "Frankenstein" or "Kevorkian," or maybe even "Zhivago," then you'd understand.

Hey, Charles Ponzi was a piker compared to Madoff: He only stole millions, as opposed to Madoff's billions. Maybe we should change the name of this scam from a "Ponzi scheme" to a "Madoff scheme"? Nah, I guess that's asking too much.

FINAL THOUGHTS ON OPM

Here is the main reason why it is so important to understand financial markets and trading—in the end, nobody is going to take better care of your money than you are. Be very careful about whom you entrust with your funds. Watch your money like a hawk, and always be on guard for anything that seems strange or unrealistic. Always know the procedure to withdraw your funds, just in case problems arise.

Finally, if you should someday decide to manage Other People's Money, always keep the following in mind:

> "The basic unwritten premise in 'Use OPM' is: that you will operate on the highest ethical standards of integrity, honor, honesty, loyalty, consent, and the Golden Rule and apply these in your business relationships."
>
> —*From the book* Success through a Positive Mental Attitude,
> *by Napoleon Hill and W. Clement Stone*

PART III

WINNING THE CHAMPIONSHIP

CHAPTER 9

THE EASIEST POINTS YOU'LL EVER SCORE

"I've missed more than 9,000 shots in my career. I've lost almost 300 games. 26 times, I've been trusted to take the game-winning shot and missed. I've failed over and over and over again in my life. And that is why I succeed."

—Michael Jordan, 5-Time NBA Most Valuable Player,
6-Time NBA Champion

In basketball, it is called the layup; in American football, it is the "extra point." Every sport has a play that is considered to be nearly automatic, almost a "sure thing." In Forex trading, just as in sports, there is no such thing as a "sure thing." However, there is one thing that does come pretty close.

CENTRAL BANK INTERVENTION

When faced with an unfavorable exchange rate scenario, a central bank will sometimes try to "push" the exchange rate in a desired direction. The central bank accomplishes this by buying or selling its own currency in the open market in order to achieve a more favorable exchange rate—an event known as "intervention."

When intervention occurs, it creates some of the best opportunities you'll ever see in any trading market. There are numerous examples of intervention during recent history, and we're going to take a look at a few of them—first to understand the meaning of intervention and the various reasons behind it, and then to learn how to profit from it.

A classic example of intervention occurred in early 2004, when the Bank of Japan intervened in the currency markets in an effort to weaken the Japanese yen.

THE BANK OF JAPAN, 2004

Over the three-year period from 2001 through 2003, the USD/JPY currency pair formed a massive head and shoulders pattern, with the head of the pattern near 135.00 and the neckline located in the vicinity of 115.00 (see Figure 9.1).

When that neckline was finally broken in September 2003, the U.S. dollar collapsed vs. the Japanese yen, leading to rapid appreciation in the Japanese currency.

This strength in the yen was considered undesirable to Japan's leaders, because of the negative impact it would have on Japanese exports. Japan is a net exporter and its economy depends on the country's ability to export products to the rest of the world. USD/JPY quickly fell and finally found support in the area just above 105.00 (see Figure 9.2).

Major Japanese companies like Toyota, Canon, and Sony were faced with huge potential losses due to the effect the strong yen was likely to have on their sales. Big Japanese exporters usually hedge to protect themselves from a strengthening currency, because a strong yen is their Achilles heel. But this move in the yen was greater than most of them had anticipated: The USD/JPY pair had moved too far, too fast, and now many of these exporters were faced with rapidly escalating losses.

Out of concern for the potential damage that would be done to Japan's export-based businesses, equity markets, and economy in general, officials from Japan's Ministry of

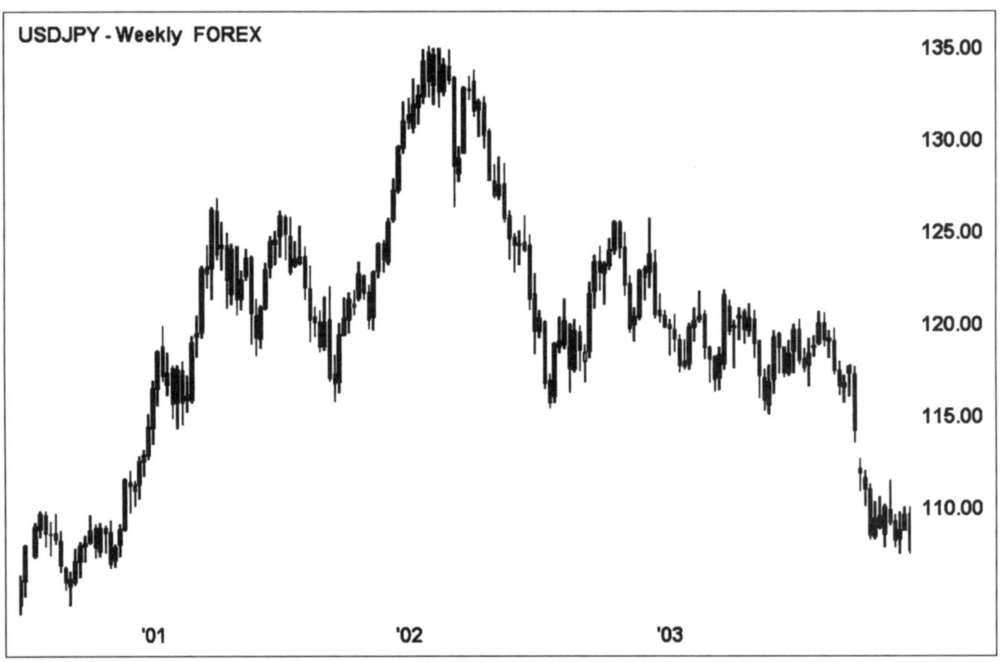

FIGURE 9.1 Massive head and shoulder pattern on USD/JPY.
Source: Created with TradeStation. © TradeStation Technologies, Inc. All rights reserved.

FIGURE 9.2 USD/JPY falls, then finds support above 105.00.
Source: Created with TradeStation.

Finance (MoF) made a series of statements in late 2003 and early 2004 indicating that they would intervene directly in the currency markets in order to weaken the yen, and thus improve the outlook for exporters.

A Coded Message

By indicating that they might drive USD/JPY higher, MoF officials were trying to entice traders to join in and take long positions in the pair. The wording of the MoF's statements sounded innocent enough, as Japanese officials would often comment that they were "watching exchange rates closely." When those words crossed the newswire, the reaction of one of the traders in the room was priceless.

"The MoF is watching exchange rates closely? So what? So am I! We are all watching exchange rates closely! Thank you, Captain Obvious!" We all laughed, but the mirth turned to gasps as we watched the USD/JPY pair blast higher.

The words "watching exchange rates closely" may not have sounded meaningful, but to the experienced trader, they held significance. Whenever these seemingly innocuous comments hit the newswire, the USD/JPY pair would spike higher in response (see Figure 9.3).

At other times, officials from the Bank of Japan (BoJ) or the Ministry of Finance would chime in with comments like, "Exchange rates should reflect fundamentals." Again, this sounds like an extremely benign remark, and yet the market's response was dramatic. It was as if Japanese officials had said, "We are joining to jam this thing higher,

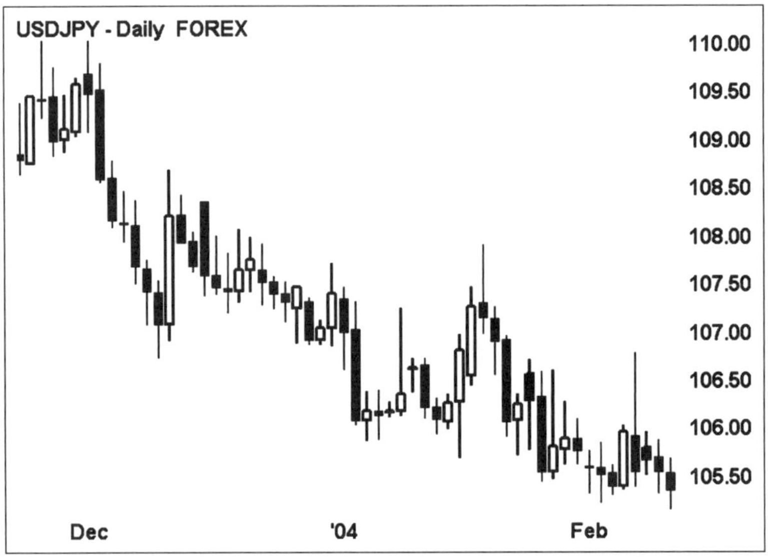

FIGURE 9.3 Comments from BoJ and MoF officials often create spikes in USD/JPY.
Source: Created with TradeStation.

and if you're smart you won't get in our way. In fact, we invite you to join us as we push USD/JPY to the moon."

The spikes in USD/JPY occurred because experienced Forex traders understood that the comments from Japan's Minister of Finance were not meant to be taken literally. The MoF was sending a coded message to the markets, telling shorts to get out of the way.

Finally, after weeks of hints and warnings, the Bank of Japan began to push USD/JPY higher in February of 2004. In a relentless move that lasted for three weeks, the BoJ bought U.S. dollars and sold Japanese yen, driving the USD/JPY exchange rate from just above 105.00 to about 112.00, a move of 700 pips. This was a bonanza for individual traders, who had already been tipped by the BoJ and the MoF that the move was coming (see Figure 9.4).

The Bank Tips Its Hand

Take a minute to think about this, and I'll explain to you the beauty of this situation. A huge, huge buyer has revealed itself, in the hope of turning you, the trader, into a buyer as well. But why would a central bank "show their hand" and announce their intentions?

After all, in the world of equities, institutional traders, like mutual funds and hedge funds, go out of their way to disguise their intentions. These institutions fear that if the trading public knew they were attempting to buy a large quantity of shares, traders would start acquiring the stock and push the shares higher. As traders drive the price higher, it becomes more expensive for the institution to acquire the shares. That's why institutions have to hide their intentions in the stock market.

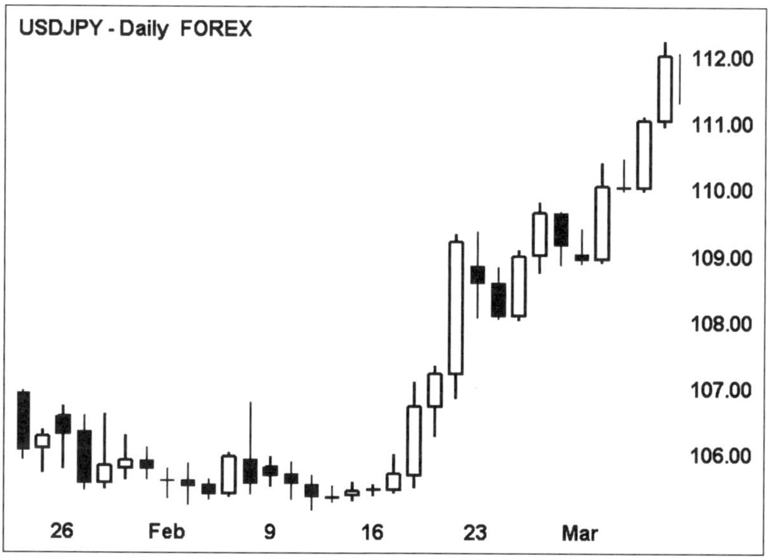

FIGURE 9.4 BoJ intervention moved USD/JPY higher by 700 pips.
Source: Created with TradeStation.

Here is the big difference: In the case of intervention, the central bank is not really trying to "acquire" the currency, and they are not competing with traders to obtain shares. Their end game is to push the exchange rate in the desired direction, period.

Because the Forex market is so liquid, this can be an expensive proposition. Imagine that the USD/JPY currency pair is a massive weight, and the Bank of Japan, through the Ministry of Finance, wants to see this weight lifted higher. The central bank is really trying to get others to do the "heavy lifting" for them and move the exchange rate so they don't have to.

The Best Part

Here comes the best part: The central bank doesn't care if you or I make money on this event. Unlike the mutual fund in the example above, currency traders are not competing with central banks. In fact, when it comes to intervention, central bankers and individual traders are often working together.

Less than a month after the intervention commenced, the USD/JPY pair was allowed to resume its downward movement. But the three-week-long counter-trend move that was created by the intervention gave Japanese exporters sufficient time to reestablish their hedges and protect their businesses against further yen strength.

Later that year, USD/JPY began an uptrend—unrelated to central bank intervention—that would last for several years, as the U.S. Federal Reserve began a series of rate hikes. The Fed eventually raised the U.S. Fed Funds rate from 1 percent to 5.25 percent, creating a "carry trade" for those who were long USD and short JPY.

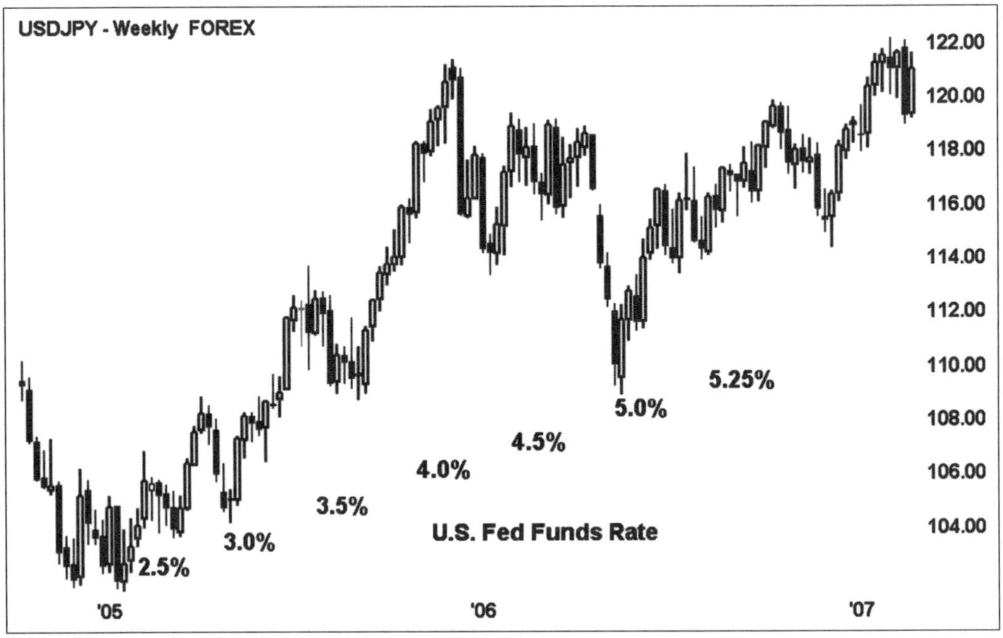

FIGURE 9.5 USD/JPY rises for years as Fed Funds rate climbs.
Source: Created with TradeStation. © TradeStation Technologies, Inc. All rights reserved.

Because of this, the Bank of Japan did not need to continue major interventions vs. the USD beyond the spring of 2004 (see Figure 9.5).

Keep a close eye out for these situations, as a central bank will give traders a "freebie" every once in a while as a means to their own ends. If you read the financial press, publications like the *Wall Street Journal* and the *Financial Times* are good sources for information about potential central bank interventions. Often, when intervention occurs, central bankers speak openly about their intentions to the financial press; that's how they enlist traders to join them in their efforts.

Now that we understand a little about the topic, let's take a look at what was probably the most infamous intervention in recent history, the United Kingdom's intervention of 1992.

THE GREAT BRITAIN POUND, 1992

Ultimately, Japan's intervention of 2004 was a success, but it's important to note that despite the tremendous amounts of capital that governments and central banks have at their disposal, intervention does not always succeed.

Just as it is more difficult to manipulate the price of a big, widely held stock than that of a thinly traded one, it is much more difficult to directly influence exchange rates in the currency market than it is to influence the price of an individual stock.

Remember, currencies are vastly more liquid than stocks, and therefore it can be difficult and very expensive for anyone—even major governments and central banks—to manipulate exchange rates.

The potential failure of an intervention is another reason why governments and central banks seek the help of traders by signaling their intentions in advance. Again, think of Forex intervention as a government or central bank lifting a heavy weight; often, the intervening agent will enlist the help of traders—you and me—to assist with the heavy lifting.

One of the most notorious examples of a failed intervention occurred in 1992, when the government of the United Kingdom unsuccessfully attempted to prop up the British pound. This failure illustrates that the vast size of the currency market makes it a difficult market to manipulate, even for the government of a country the size of the United Kingdom.

Notice that this decision was made by the U.K. government and not the Bank of England. At the time, the Bank of England was not independent of the U.K. government, and benchmark interest rates for the United Kingdom were determined by the Chancellor of the Exchequer.

The Bank of England remains the world's second oldest central bank; it was founded in 1694 (the world's oldest central bank is the Swedish Riksbank, which was founded in 1668). It wasn't until 1997 that then-Chancellor of the Exchequer Gordon Brown handed responsibility for setting interest rates to the Bank of England.

Setting the Stage

In 1992, Great Britain entered into an agreement called the European Exchange Rate Mechanism, or ERM. The ERM had been set up to keep exchange rates in Europe within tight ranges, in order to help facilitate international trade among European countries. Many believe that this was also done in preparation for the upcoming introduction of the euro in 1999.

Essentially, Britain agreed to keep its currency within a specified range vs. the German currency, the deutsche mark (symbol DEM). This meant that the United Kingdom had made a commitment to support the pound and keep it within a tight range vs. the DEM, and to accomplish this, the U.K. government agreed to intervene to support the GBP if it fell below 2.778 deutsche marks. At the time the United Kingdom first entered the ERM, one British pound was worth about 2.95 deutsche marks.

The timing of the United Kingdom's entry into the ERM couldn't have been worse: In 1992, the economy of the United Kingdom was suffering from a recession that began in 1990. This economic slowdown was exacerbated by a decision to keep U.K. interest rates high.

Normally, when a country goes into a recession, interest rates are lowered to stimulate growth. The British economy really needed a reduction in rates; however, if the United Kingdom were to cut rates severely, it would likely cause the pound to fall against the German currency, thus violating the terms of the ERM.

Germany's rates were high at the time, due in part to the reunification of East Germany and West Germany. A wide interest rate differential between the GBP and the DEM certainly would have put additional pressure on the pound, creating a carry trade (long DEM, short GBP). This would complicate efforts to keep the British currency within its designated range, and so the United Kingdom kept its benchmark rate high.

Enter Soros

Due to these and other fundamental factors working in favor of the DEM and against the GBP, many speculators considered it unlikely that the government of the U.K. would succeed in propping up the pound. Some of these speculators placed huge bets that the pound would fall vs. the deutsche mark and against other currencies. Among these speculators was George Soros, a trader who headed the Quantum Fund, who came to be known as "the man who broke the Bank of England" due to the events that were about to transpire.

Soros and other speculators had done the math: They estimated how much money it would cost to keep the pound in its desired range and determined that at some point, the U.K. government would simply have to give up. As Soros and other speculators shorted the pound mercilessly, the U.K. government tried to fight back through intervention in the open markets and by raising interest rates—a ploy to entice yield-seeking investors to buy the pound (and thereby help the U.K. government to "lift the weight"). Market forces kept pushing the pound lower, and in response the U.K. government would fight back and push the currency higher.

Desperate Measures

Then on September 16, 1992, in a desperate attempt to strengthen the pound, U.K. Prime Minister John Major and Chancellor Norman Lamont raised interest rates during the day from 10 percent to 12 percent, and promised to raise the rate to 15 percent.

Major and Lamont also authorized the spending of billions in a doomed effort to keep the GBP within the range allowed by ERM. But it was too late; as they struggled frantically to lift the pound, Soros and other investors were pushing hard in the opposite direction. Something had to give.

Finally, that evening, the British government gave up and announced its exit from ERM—a day that is known in the United Kingdom as Black Wednesday. Over the next two months, the pound fell sharply, with much of the loss coming in the first few days. The Great Britain pound lost heavily vs. the deutsche mark, and it tumbled hard against other currencies as well, such as the U.S. dollar (see Figure 9.6).

This chart of GBP/USD shows a nearly 5,000 pip plunge during September and October of 1992, as Cable (a popular nickname for the GBP/USD pair, due to an undersea cable that links the two countries) fell from 2.0000 and finally found support below 1.5000. GBP/USD didn't reach that lofty level again until 15 years later, in 2007 (see Figure 9.7).

FIGURE 9.6 GBP/USD falls 5,000 pips after intervention fails.
Source: Created with TradeStation.

FIGURE 9.7 It took 15 years for GBP/USD to regain the 2.0000 handle.
Source: Created with TradeStation.

According to official files released by the Treasury under the U.K. Freedom of Information Act, the entire fiasco ended up costing the country more than 3.2 billion pounds. Trading losses equaled 800 million pounds, and the United Kingdom would have made an additional 2.4 billion on sterling's devaluation if they had simply held on to their currency reserves instead of exchanging them for pounds.

As for Soros, he is alleged to have made over one billion dollars in profit on the trade, and many other speculators profited as well. The lessons of Black Wednesday are clear. Intervention—whether initiated by a central bank or by a government—is not always a "sure thing."

THE RESERVE BANK OF AUSTRALIA, 2008

Beginning in 2002, the Australian dollar began a massive, multiyear rally against the U.S. dollar. When the Australian dollar collapsed along with commodities prices in late 2008, the AUD/USD pair lost nearly 4,000 pips over the course of a few months, falling from near parity (it had traded just below 1.0000 vs. the USD) to almost 0.6000 (see Figure 9.8).

This massive rally in the U.S. dollar created a problem for many countries, including Australia. For example, suppose you are a businessperson in Australia who has taken a loan in U.S. dollars. The loan must be repaid with U.S. dollars, and your wealth is held in

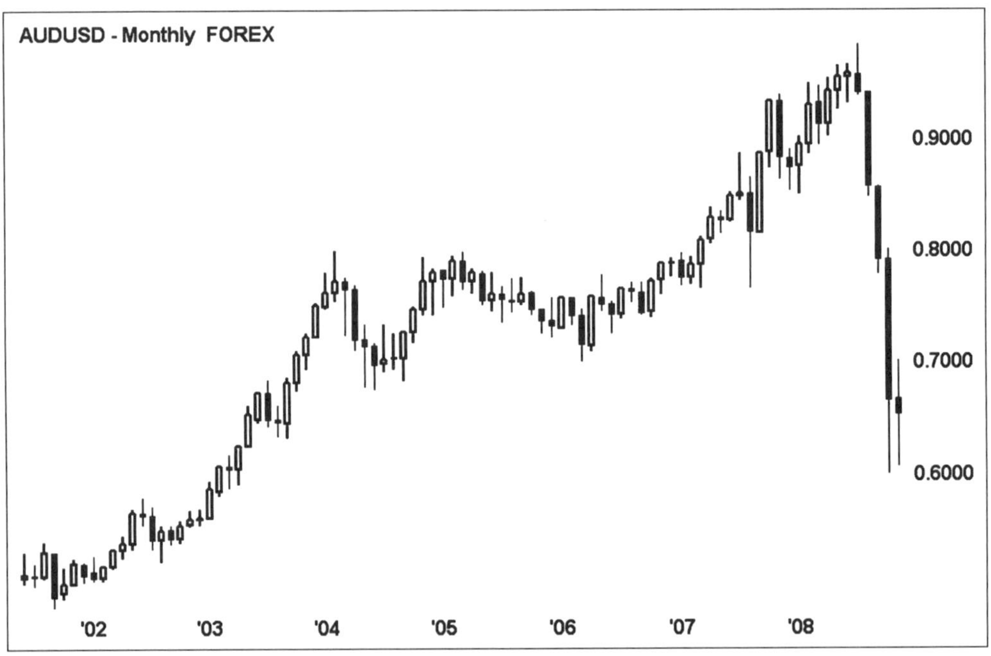

FIGURE 9.8 AUD/USD plunges after a multiyear rally.
Source: Created with TradeStation. © TradeStation Technologies, Inc. All rights reserved.

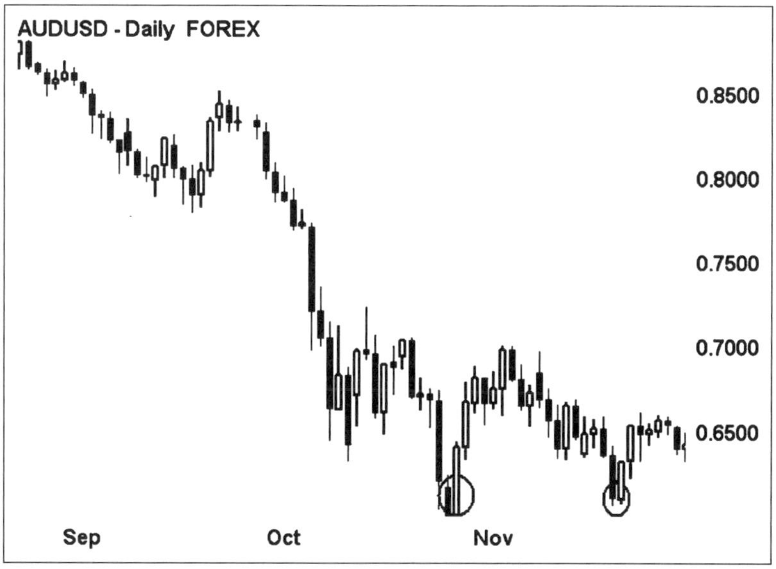

FIGURE 9.9 RBA intervenes in October and November 2008.
Source: Created with TradeStation.

Australian dollars. If the aussie loses 40 percent of its value vs. the greenback, then the loan becomes 40 percent more expensive—and 40 percent more painful to repay—from your perspective.

If this situation were allowed to continue, many Australian businesses could fail. To stem the tide and break the currency's fall, the Reserve Bank of Australia (RBA) took action and began to intervene in an effort to strengthen the Australian dollar.

Although they never named a particular price level, it seems pretty clear that the RBA drew a line at 0.6000, as the pair vaulted after coming within 10 pips of that key psychological level on October 28, 2008. Later, the RBA admitted to spending $3.15 billion Australian in October 2008 to push the exchange rate higher. Additional interventions would come in November, as the pair again took a dive toward 0.6000 (see Figure 9.9).

Putting in the Bottom

It's clear that despite having limited currency reserves of just $44 billion USD, the RBA helped to put in the bottom in the AUD/USD pair. Generally speaking, central banks are not concerned with profit and loss statements, but in this case the RBA was clearly a winner, with the AUD/USD pair trading above 0.8000 by June 2009.

It was around that time that the RBA announced that it had begun to replenish the USD reserves that had been spent to lift the aussie in late 2008. You might say the RBA went long AUD/USD around 0.6000, and closed the trade 2,000 pips higher, around 0.8000. Nice trade!

In September 2009, the RBA announced that it would pay the Australian government a record dividend of 5.98 billion aussie dollars. In a September 17 article on Bloomberg.com, the governor of the RBA stated:

> *"This is the highest dividend ever paid by the bank, but it reflects unusual circumstances," Governor Glenn Stevens said in the report. "It can be expected with a high degree of confidence that future dividends will generally be much smaller."*

The Australian government had reaped a huge gain through the intervention. Conversely, the earlier failed intervention of the British pound cost the U.K. government a pretty penny, as they had purchased pounds at a high price. Clearly, central banks have a great deal at stake when they intervene in the currency markets, so they do not undertake such actions lightly.

THE RUSSIAN RUBLE, 2009

You'll note that in the previous section, we mentioned that the Reserve Bank of Australia never actually *stated* that they would intervene to support the aussie at 0.6000, though it was clear to traders that the RBA put in the bottom at that level. In most cases, a central bank will not name a specific price level for an intervention. To understand why, let's take a look at an intervention that occurred in early 2009 in the Russian ruble.

When the U.S. dollar made remarkable gains in late 2008, it did so at the expense of currencies such as the Australian dollar and the Russian ruble. For Russia, the world's largest energy exporter, the global economic meltdown created a unique challenge. With the price of a barrel of oil sliding back below $40 in early 2009 (after rallying above $140 in 2008), there was a sharp decline in capital flows to the country. The Russian ruble was under tremendous pressure: One U.S. dollar had been worth 23 rubles in July 2008, but by January 2009, one USD was worth more than 30 rubles.

Faced with a rapidly depreciating currency, Russia decided to take action. With the USD/RUB exchange rate rapidly approaching 31 after trading at 23 just six months earlier, Russia's central bank announced that it would not let the exchange rate rise beyond 36. Note that in our case studies of the Bank of Japan and the Reserve Bank of Australia, those central banks did not name specific price levels when discussing their respective intentions.

A Crucial Mistake

The Central Bank of the Russian Federation had made the crucial mistake of naming the approximate level at which they planned to intervene to strengthen the ruble. Basically, they had signaled to traders that there was no threat of intervention unless and until the

USD/RUB exchange rate rallied all the way from 31 to 36! Traders took this as a green light to short rubles until the level was reached.

You can guess what happened next—now that traders had been given the "all clear" signal, the USD/RUB currency pair gapped up and shot higher. By February 2, 2009, the exchange rate traded above 36—and the Russian central bank then intervened, as they had promised earlier.

The important lesson is this: Although central banks will often reveal their intentions, it is not in their best interests to reveal precise intervention levels. Ultimately, the Russian central bank's intervention was a success, as the USD/RUB stayed below 37. The crisis ended as the world's economies improved, sending oil back above the $80 level and buttressing the ruble. But the Russian central bank could have avoided that shock rally to 36 if they had been less revealing of their intentions.

CHAPTER 10

HITTING IT FOR SIX

"Down in the mine I dreamed of cricket; I bowled imaginary balls in the dark; I sent the stumps spinning and heard them rattling in the tunnels. No mishap was going to stop me from bowling in the real game, especially this one."

—Harold Larwood, ICC Cricket Hall of Fame

In the game of cricket, when a batsman hits the ball over the boundary without the ball bouncing, he scores six points. Similar to a home run in baseball, it is the most impressive shot a player can make. Well, now that you understand a few things about intervention, we're going to put together everything that we've learned on this topic. Now we have the tools at our disposal to hit it for six!

THE SWISS NATIONAL BANK, 2009

Now that we have an understanding of intervention and the reasons behind it, we'll take an in-depth look at a dramatic example—the Swiss National Bank's intervention in the EUR/CHF currency pair. This intervention occurred sporadically at uneven intervals during the year 2009, and it created some fantastic money-making opportunities for currency traders. It can serve as a template for making money during future interventions if and when a similar situation occurs.

Many of our intervention examples focus on events that began with the financial crisis that erupted in 2008 (the roots of the problem go back further, but I digress). We mentioned in the previous chapter that the U.S. dollar became very strong during this crisis as traders fled riskier assets for the safety of U.S. Treasuries. One of the currencies that took a hard tumble vs. the greenback was the Swiss franc.

But while the swissy was falling vs. the USD, it was actually gaining on other currencies, most notably the euro. The Swiss franc has long been noted as a safe haven currency, and the financial crisis pushed traders toward safe havens like the U.S. dollar, and to a lesser extent, the swissy. As a result of this and other factors, the euro depreciated sharply vs. the Swiss franc during the latter part of 2008 and during the first few months of 2009.

In March 2009, the Swiss National Bank (SNB) decided that they had had enough of the Swiss franc's appreciation vs. the euro. At a scheduled policy meeting, the central bank announced at 13:00 GMT that they would cut a key interest rate by 25 basis points. That action did not come as a surprise; most major central banks were cutting rates to the bone at that time. But the SNB also released an interesting comment regarding intervention in the Swiss franc, which was reported on the Dow Jones Newswire service just one minute later:

13:01 GMT SNB to FX Purchase to Stall Franc Rise Vs Euro

The March 12, 2009, announcement created a huge spike on the daily chart of EUR/CHF, as traders rushed to get on the same side of the trade as the SNB (see Figure 10.1).

In a game-changing move, the Swiss central bank had revealed their intentions to the market, essentially stating that they would sell Swiss francs and buy euros. Traders were caught off guard and the market's reaction was swift and immediate, with the EUR/CHF pair blasting higher by over 400 pips in about half an hour (see Figure 10.2).

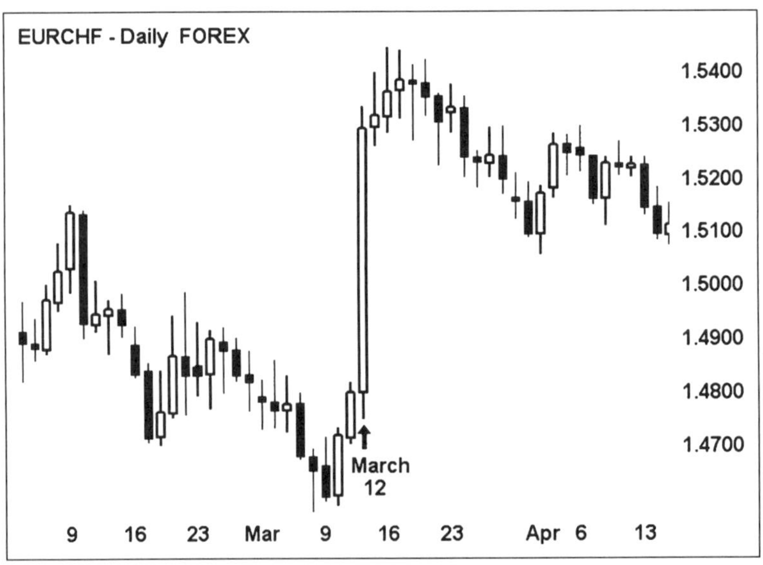

FIGURE 10.1 The Swiss National Bank announces EUR/CHF intervention, resulting in a spike in the EUR/CHF pair.
Source: Created with TradeStation. © TradeStation Technologies, Inc. All rights reserved.

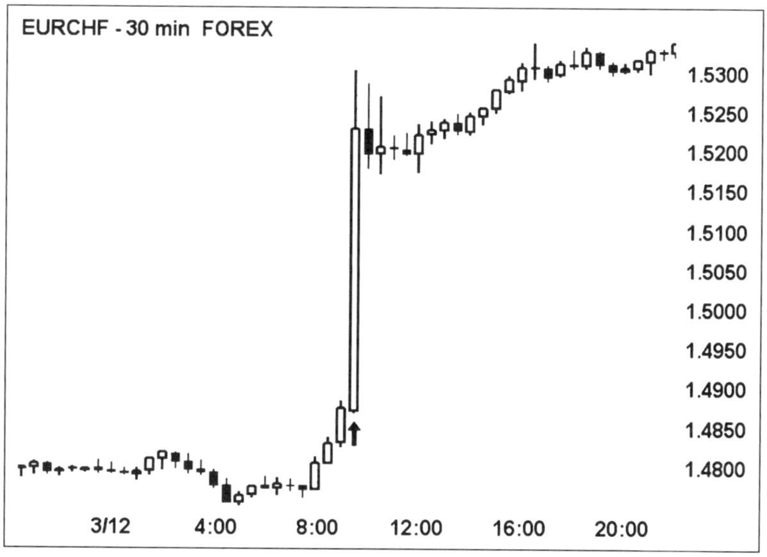

FIGURE 10.2 30-minute chart reveals the ferocity of the EUR/CHF move.
Source: Created with TradeStation.

In addition to the intervention, the SNB also announced that they would begin quantitative easing by purchasing Swiss bonds. Here are some excerpts from the news headlines of that day:

13:47 GMT UPDATE: SNB To Start Buying Foreign Currency, Swiss Bonds

ZURICH (Dow Jones)—The Swiss National Bank said Thursday that it will start purchasing foreign currency on foreign exchange markets and buying Swiss franc bonds issued by private-sector borrowers. These steps, along with an interest rate cut, are aimed to prevent any further appreciation of the Swiss franc against the euro, the SNB said in a statement.

14:20 GMT UPDATE: Swiss Central Bk Cuts Rates, Turns To Intervention

ZURICH (Dow Jones)—Switzerland's central bank Thursday cut interest rates to a historic low and announced foreign exchange and bond market operations, departing from a non-interventionist policy in the past few years. After Thursday's quarterly monetary-policy meeting, the Swiss National Bank cut the target for the three-month Swiss franc London interbank offered rate, its benchmark rate, by 25 basis points to 0.25%, revisiting a historic low from 2003.

While the rate cut had been widely expected, the SNB's other actions—the purchase of foreign currency to curtail the Swiss franc's rise, and the purchase of Swiss franc bonds issued by private sector borrowers—came as a surprise to many traders and led to an immediate weakening of the Swiss currency.

PUMPING THE PESO

Interestingly, on the very same day, Mexico's central bank was intervening on behalf of the beleaguered peso, which had recently reached new all-time lows against the U.S. dollar. Unlike the situation in Switzerland, the Banco de Mexico's objective was to strengthen their currency:

15:07 GMT Bank of Mexico Sells $100M in Auction at Avg MXN14.9524/Dlr

The Dow Jones Newswire headline indicates that the Bank of Mexico sold U.S. dollars and purchased Mexican pesos, helping to push the USD/MXN exchange rate above 15 for the first time in days. Eighty percent of Mexico's exports are sent to the United States, which had entered a steep recession. In addition, a sharp drop in the price of oil had damaged the Mexican economy, since the country is a net exporter of crude oil.

That was certainly an exciting day for traders who focus on central bank interventions, but the fun wasn't over yet. If you missed the initial thrust in EUR/CHF, you were about to get another chance to sell the Swiss franc vs. the euro.

A SECOND CHANCE

Although the SNB did not announce that they would defend a particular exchange rate level, it soon became apparent that they were still active in the currency market. On May 15, 2009, after the effects of the initial intervention announcement had worn off, the EUR/CHF pair began to float gently back toward 1.5000. It traded within a few pips of that huge round number, and then it suddenly took off as if it had been shot out of a cannon (see Figure 10.3).

What had happened? Although it was never officially confirmed or denied, there were reports that the Bank of International Settlements (BIS) had intervened on behalf of the Swiss National Bank. It might be helpful to think of the BIS as a bank for central banks.

It's interesting to note that the intervention occurred on a Friday, around lunchtime in New York. At that time, it was around midnight on Friday night in Japan, it was 6 p.m. in Basel, home of the BIS, and it was 5 p.m. on Friday in London, the Forex trading capital of the world. The SNB/BIS had chosen to intervene at a time of the day (and week) when the currency market was likely to be "thin." Perhaps they chose this time because markets are easier to move when there are fewer buyers and sellers, and when there is less participation overall.

A THIRD CHANCE

By now the trade had become pretty obvious: In March, the SNB had publicly stated that they would not allow the Swiss franc to weaken vs. the euro. Even though they hadn't

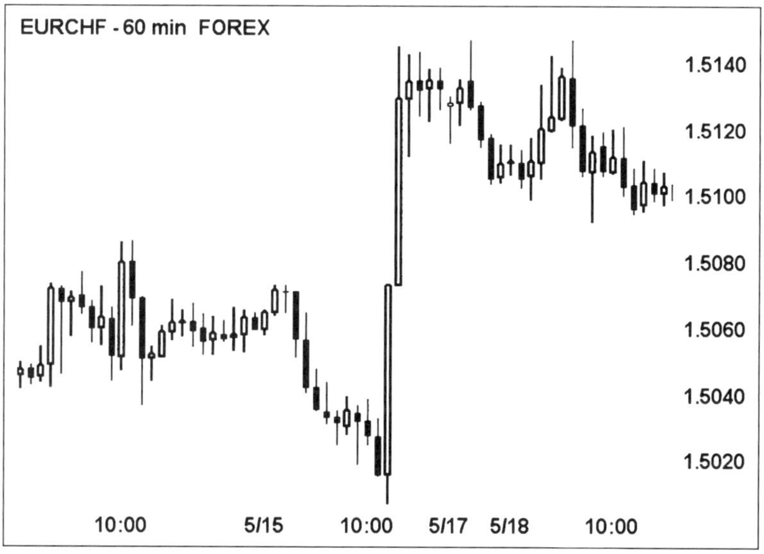

FIGURE 10.3 EUR/CHF gains 140 pips in two hours; traders believed the BIS intervened on behalf of the SNB.
Source: Created with TradeStation.

declared that they would defend a particular level, it was fairly evident after the May 15 intervention that the "line in the sand" on EUR/CHF was 1.5000. Subsequently, SNB officials made numerous comments to the financial press, indicating that they would continue this interventionist policy for the foreseeable future.

Now the real fun was about to begin; how much easier could it be? Traders began to simply load up on EUR/CHF every time it approached 1.5000, placing their stops just beneath that key level. On June 18, 2009, their patience was rewarded: When the currency pair drifted close to 1.5000, a big buyer stepped in and jammed it up above 1.5130. Not a bad payday for one hour's work (see Figure 10.4).

A FOURTH CHANCE

That trade was basically free money for traders who understood what was happening and took action. It had to be one of the easiest trades ever—well, at least until the following week, because six days later, the pair was testing 1.5000 once again. Just in case there was still anyone left who didn't know what was going on, the following headline crossed the Dow Jones Newswire:

> ***10:40 GMT EUR/CHF Edges Toward Post-Intervention Low***
>
> *EUR/CHF is edging toward the March 12, post-intervention low of 1.5006 seen on June 18. On that occasion traders reported the BIS stepped in and the cross spiked to a one-week high of 1.5150. EUR/CHF now trades at 1.5013. (GST)*

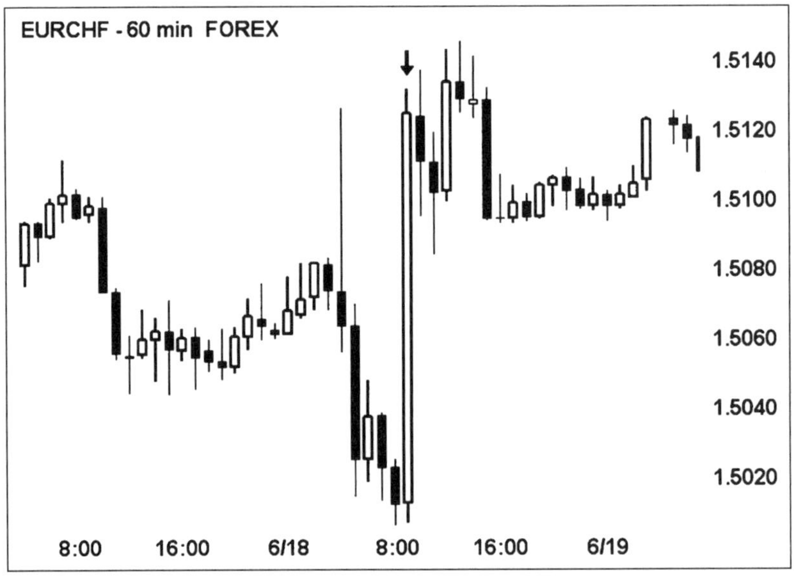

FIGURE 10.4 EUR/CHF jumps about 130 pips in one hour after drifting close to 1.5000.
Source: Created with TradeStation.

Okay, based on that headline and on the previous actions taken by the SNB, how could anyone not know what was about to happen next? The nice folks at Dow Jones were warning us that EUR/CHF was just a few pips away from 1.5000. Better hurry up and get that order in . . . and load the boat! Here is the headline that crossed the newswire six minutes later:

10:46 GMT EUR/CHF Spikes From Suspected 1.50 Intervention Threshold

The SNB had done it again! Less than an hour later, this Dow Jones headline told the tale:

11:33 GMT EUR/CHF Intervention "Aggressive"—Trader

EUR/CHF soars to a fresh 2 month high of 1.5270, with a UK-based trader saying the BIS is "aggressively" bidding the cross via the electronic broking system. He estimates the BIS has bought in excess of EUR3B so far Wednesday. (GST)

And from there, the trade just kept on running—this time, the SNB/BIS put an exclamation point on the intervention, allowing EUR/CHF to float to within 15 pips of 1.5000 before ripping it higher by nearly 300 pips! When added together, the three most recent interventions combined were worth nearly 600 pips. Serious money!

NO EXCUSES

By this point, I have to say that if you are a Forex trader, there was no excuse to have missed that last trade. Prior to June 18, most of us suspected that 1.5000 held the key, but I could still forgive someone for missing that particular intervention. But by June 24, it was common knowledge that the SNB/BIS had already intervened at that key psychological level twice in just over a month, and that the Swiss National Bank would not tolerate a strong CHF. Anyone who missed the trade on June 24 simply wasn't paying attention.

The SNB was basically offering free rides on EUR/CHF—this time giving traders a gain that represents a good month for many of us. Money was lying there on the table, and all you had to do was reach down and pick it up. Everyone was talking about it, and the financial press was all over it. The newswires even sent an alert, so any trader who bothered to do the least bit of research should have nailed it (see Figure 10.5).

TEACHING THE SHORTS A LESSON

The SNB had succeeded in pushing EUR/CHF higher, but there was a problem—every time they pushed it up, the pair kept floating back down toward 1.5000. Could it be that some traders were playing both sides of the intervention—riding EUR/CHF up from 1.5000, and then, when it appeared that the intervention had ended, shorting the pair in an attempt to ride it back down?

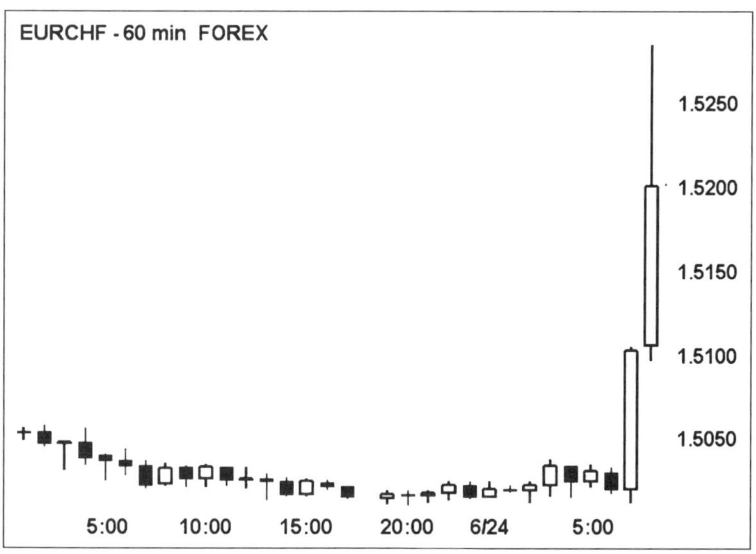

FIGURE 10.5 EUR/CHF blasts off for a gain of nearly 300 pips after another intervention.
Source: Created with TradeStation. © TradeStation Technologies, Inc. All rights reserved.

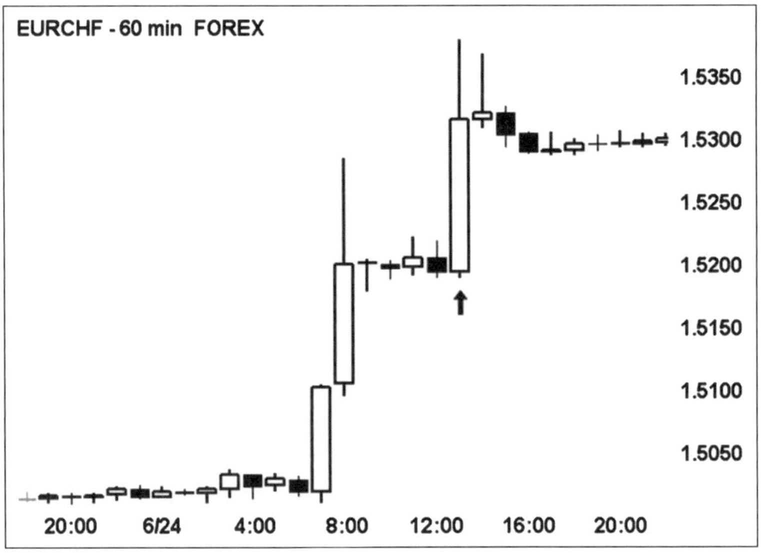

FIGURE 10.6 SNB pauses, then resumes intervention to trap shorts.
Source: Created with TradeStation.

Try to see it from the SNB's point of view: What if you were going to all this trouble to lift this giant weight, and every time you lifted it, someone pushed it back down. How would you feel about that? While the SNB had no comment on this, it's not hard to imagine that they were displeased with traders who were shorting EUR/CHF. Perhaps the SNB had become too predictable and needed to shake things up a bit.

That's exactly what happened next. On June 24, after intervening at the usual area just above 1.5000 and pushing EUR/CHF higher by nearly 300 pips, the pair floated back down and came to rest near 1.5200. The SNB waited; one, two, three, four hours passed—plenty of time for traders to get short for the ride back down to 1.50, right?

Wrong. The SNB had other plans. After giving shorts sufficient time to "load the boat," the SNB resumed its intervention—this time from a higher level. Shorts were trapped as the pair ripped higher, this time rising all the way to 1.5350! The shorts learned a hard lesson that day—don't mess with the Swiss National Bank! (See Figure 10.6.)

NO FIXED THRESHOLD

Here's a thought—prior to that June 24 intervention, SNB governing board member Thomas Jordan confirmed that the central bank was active in the markets, and that the SNB had performed its first unilateral interventions since 1992. Also, on June 18, an SNB statement indicated the central bank would take "firm action to prevent an appreciation of the Swiss franc against the euro." The continuing interventions came as no surprise to traders who paid close attention to the financial press. Once again, the SNB had clearly displayed its intentions for all to see.

Interestingly, Jordan claimed that there was no "fixed threshold," meaning that interventions might occur at levels other than 1.5000. "Markets should not become used to a certain level of intervention," he said. Why would he make such a statement when it was perfectly obvious that the intervention level was 1.5000?

One reason could be to prevent CHF speculative bulls from pushing EUR/CHF down to that 1.5000 level. Central banks will rarely indicate a specific level because it is an invitation to those on the other side of the trade to test the bank's resolve. Most traders interpreted Jordan's comment to mean that the SNB would likely intervene from a higher level in the future, somewhere above 1.50, in order to once again confound the shorts. But while it was becoming less clear *where* the next intervention would occur, the question of *when* it would take place was coming into focus.

THE EUROPEAN CENTRAL BANK'S ROLE

An interesting point about the intervention of June 24, 2009—on that day, the European Central Bank (ECB) performed a special operation. In an effort to inject liquidity into the banking system, the ECB offered unlimited funds to banks at a fixed rate of 1 percent, for a term of one year. Banks responded by scooping up 442 billion euros worth of loans, courtesy of the ECB.

But what sort of impact was created by this massive ECB operation? Banks were borrowing euros, not buying them, and now they had euros coming out of their ears. What if some of those banks then exchanged some of those euros for other currencies, such as the Swiss franc? If a substantial amount of those borrowed euros were sold for Swiss francs, it would cause the EUR/CHF exchange rate to move lower—possibly leading to an intervention by the SNB.

Many traders concluded that the two events of June 24 were related; perhaps banks had borrowed large sums of euros from the European Central Bank, and then sold some of those euros to purchase other currencies, such as the Swiss franc. In this scenario, those banks were actually selling euros and buying Swiss francs—an action that would have the effect of depressing the EUR/CHF currency pair. When it fell to near 1.5000, the SNB stepped in and intervened.

If this was the case, then many traders concluded that the next ECB credit facility, scheduled for September 30, 2009, might create a similar reaction. And so on that day, the European Central Bank once again offered to lend euros to banks, and this time 75 billion euros were borrowed. The banking crisis had subsided, cutting the demand for the ECB's loans. Currency traders waited to see if the SNB would step in once again in the aftermath of the tender offer. The EUR/CHF pair floated lower, slipping below 1.51 but never really approaching the vaunted area of 1.5000.

But remember, Jordan had announced earlier that there was no set level of intervention, at 1.5000 or elsewhere. We also saw the actions of the SNB on June 24, when they intervened first from 1.50, then waited, and then intervened again from a higher level.

Would it be that much of a surprise if the SNB were to intervene from a level above 1.50? Would an intervention and a tender offer again occur simultaneously, as had happened on June 24?

A FIFTH CHANCE

Yes, they would. On September 30, 2009, the same day that the European Central Bank loaned 75 billion euros to banks at 1 percent interest for a term of one year, the Swiss franc once again skyrocketed. The intervention began from a higher level, as Mr. Jordan's comments indicated that they would. Starting this time from about 1.5075, the EUR/CHF currency pair blasted higher by about 165 pips to 1.5240. The entire move lasted about one hour (see Figure 10.7).

THE END OF THE PARTY

On December 16, 2009, the ECB offered what it said would be its final credit facility. The liquidity issues faced by the banks seemed to have been resolved, for the most part, so the ECB was winding down its special operations.

The terms of this facility were different from the previous ones: Instead of offering 12-month loans at a rate of 1 percent, this time the rate was indexed to the ECB's benchmark rate. So, if the ECB raised rates during the following 12 months, the rate paid by

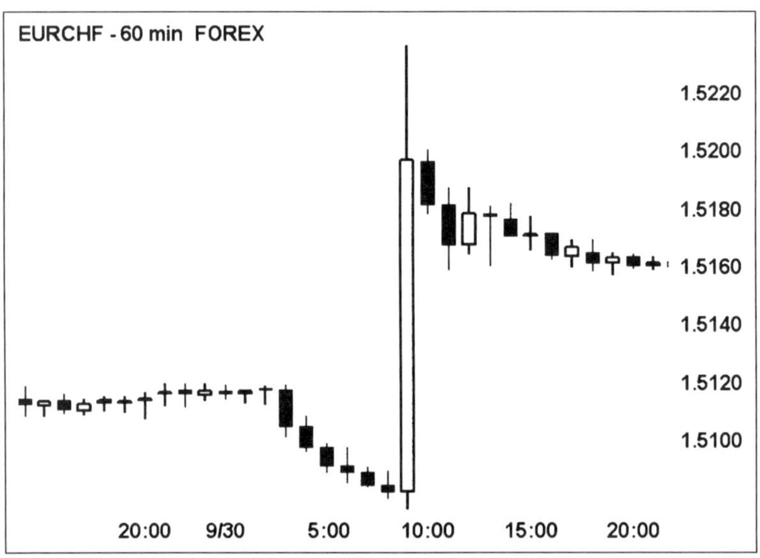

FIGURE 10.7 SNB varies tactics and intervenes from a higher level.
Source: Created with TradeStation. © TradeStation Technologies, Inc. All rights reserved.

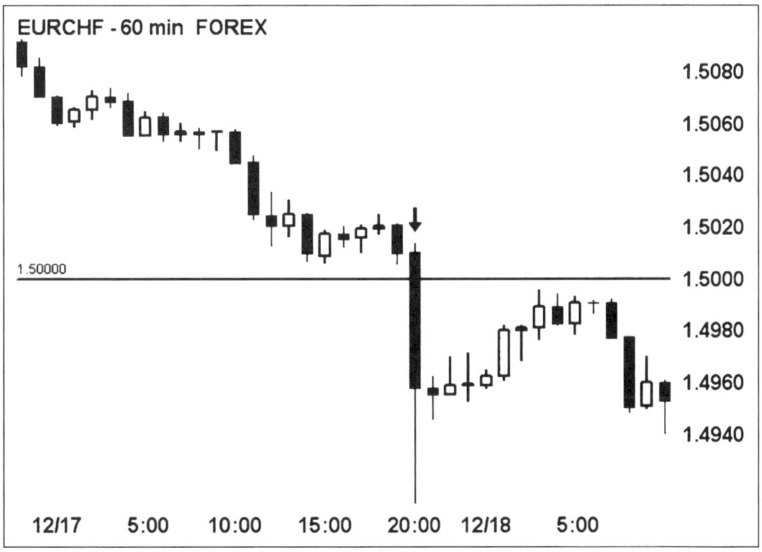

FIGURE 10.8 SNB finally allows EUR/CHF to break 1.50.
Source: Created with TradeStation. © TradeStation Technologies, Inc. All rights reserved.

the banks for borrowing euros would rise commensurately. The banks responded by borrowing 97 billion euros from the ECB. Would this action create volatility—and perhaps another intervention—in the EUR/CHF pair?

On the 16th, EUR/CHF slowly crept lower; this continued on the 17th, and the pair paused for several hours just above 1.5000. It was time to get long some EUR/CHF and wait for the SNB to push it up.

Only the push never came. This time, EUR/CHF was allowed to break 1.5000, and my stop was hit. The pair spiked lower, taking out numerous stops along the way (see Figure 10.8).

This occurred just as I was putting the finishing touches on this book, and I'm glad it did. As good as this trade was to me in 2009, I wouldn't want to create the impression that such a trade never leads to a loss. Everything ends eventually, and the EUR/CHF trade was no exception. Now the task would turn toward identifying the next similar trading opportunity.

NOT EXACTLY BREAKING THE BANK

As we learned from the case of Mr. Soros and his billion-dollar payday, breaking the bank can be a very profitable trade. But there is a key difference between the Swiss National Bank interventions of 2009 and the failed 1992 British pound intervention that made Soros so wealthy and famous. Please pay very close attention to the difference between these two events.

You see, when the U.K. government decided to intervene in 1992, it was done in an attempt to *strengthen* their currency, the British pound. But during its interventions of 2009, the Swiss National Bank was working to actively *weaken* the Swiss franc.

The main difference is this—if a central bank is trying to strengthen its own currency, it must be buying its own currency. So what was the Bank of England selling to buy British pounds? Remember, buying pressure is necessary to push the GBP/USD exchange rate higher. If the United Kingdom had been selling GBP to buy GBP, this would not have created the desired effect, as they would have been both buying and selling the same currency. Such an action would likely have had no impact on the pound.

If a central bank buys its own currency, it normally uses a reserve currency, such as the U.S. dollar, to do so. But central banks other than the Federal Reserve have a limited supply of U.S. dollars; they can't simply print more if they start running low. So, when intervening to strengthen its own currency, a central bank may have a limited supply of firepower with which to operate. That is one reason why the 1992 intervention failed.

Ah, but when intervening to *weaken* its own currency, a central bank sells that currency—as happened in the case of the SNB intervention in EUR/CHF. When selling its own currency, a central bank does not have a limited supply of currency to sell—they can always print more, and then sell it.

In theory, the SNB could simply print and sell Swiss francs for an indefinite period of time. Clearly, traders who had shorted the EUR/CHF pair in the hope of becoming the next George Soros hadn't considered that fact. Because of the ability to print more money, it is considerably easier for a central bank to weaken its own currency than it is to strengthen it.

WRAPPING UP

Many traders made big money on the EUR/CHF pair in 2009, thanks to the interventions described in this chapter. Someone once asked me why anyone would trade any other way, and I really had to think about my answer for a minute. Given the opportunity, there really is no better way to trade than to join forces with a central bank. I can't think of an easier money-making scenario in any trading market than the one described in this chapter.

I guess the main problem with intervention is that the opportunity doesn't always present itself; major central banks don't always have a need to perform these types of operations, at least when dealing with the more liquid and popularly traded currencies. But when they do, it really does create some of the best trading opportunities available in any market, anywhere.

While it is still possible to lose money on an intervention trade, the odds are on the side of the trader who pays close attention and takes the side of the central bank—especially if that central bank is actively weakening its currency. But there are other ways to make money in the Forex market.

CHAPTER 11

HOW TO TRADE LIKE A HEDGE FUND

"I always turn to the sports section first. The sports page records people's accomplishments; the front page has nothing but man's failures."
—Earl Warren, 14th Chief Justice of the United States

Do you want to trade like a hedge fund? If not, why not? Ask yourself this question: Who makes money in the Forex market, individual traders or institutional traders? The sad fact is, most individual traders will lose money, whether they are trading stocks, commodities, options, or Forex. This is because most of them simply don't have good strategies and are too focused on short-term gains. They are missing out on the big moves while trying to squeeze out a few pips.

Many people who enter the markets really don't have enough knowledge to succeed, although it is impossible for them to know this at the time. There is an old saying, "You don't know what you don't know." Usually, individual traders don't know that they don't know enough about what they're doing, and they possess just enough knowledge to injure themselves. It brings to mind another old saying, "A little knowledge is a dangerous thing."

THE BLIND LEADING THE BLIND

This is exacerbated by the fact that many of those who purport to teach Forex are not trading experts, but marketing experts. Most of them don't really know enough about Forex to teach someone how to trade successfully.

So, we wind up with people who don't know what they're doing, teaching people who don't know that the people who are teaching them don't know what they're doing. Is it any wonder that most individual traders lose money?

Meanwhile, institutional traders tend to be more successful. They have an organization behind them that acts as a support group. They use strategies that at least give them a fighting chance to win, whereas many individuals trade in a manner that is almost *guaranteed* to result in a loss (for more on this, see Chapter 18 of *Forex Patterns and Probabilities*).

Institutional traders also have the benefit of oversight; most institutions have an in-house risk management department, just to be certain that none of their traders takes a big loss or places foolish trades. The disadvantage to the individual is that he has no one looking over his shoulder, keeping him out of trouble.

Consider this: Why do institutional traders exist? If institutional traders didn't make money for their employers, wouldn't those employers simply close their doors, or at least shut down their proprietary trading operations? The very existence of these prop trading desks, some of which have been around for decades, tells us something about the value an institutional trader represents to his or her employer.

It's been said that if you want to succeed at something, all you need to do is model your behavior after someone else who is already successful. But if it makes sense to "do what the winners do," then why is it that so many individual traders emulate the losers of this game instead of the winners?

THE GUNSLINGER MENTALITY

I think many of us have an idea in our heads of what we expect trading to be, and often it is very different from what trading is like in the real world. We want to be short-term, quick-hit day traders—almost every one of us—and we all have some sort of reason or excuse for clinging to this gunslinger mentality, this vision of how we believe trading "should be." We have a fixed idea in our mind of how we want to play the game, but unfortunately this vision might not be based on reality.

But for some of us, our desire to succeed at this game is great enough that we are willing to abandon our preconceived ideas and trade in ways that we might not have previously considered. Maybe we should base our trading decisions on something that actually works, instead of basing them on something we wish would work.

Try to keep an open mind about institutional trading methods, and always remember that you can use more than one trading technique—in fact, you should use different techniques in different situations. Your personal trading style doesn't have to exist in a narrow category; it can be a combination of various techniques and time frames. There is a right time and a wrong time for almost any trading strategy.

ONE WAY TO EMULATE THE WINNERS

One of the great advantages of the currency market is that an individual can trade just like a hedge fund. Sadly, most individuals who attempt to trade Forex either do not realize this, or do not realize what a huge edge this creates. Many traders, especially institutional traders, use a tactic called the carry trade to take advantage of interest rate differentials, which could be described as the difference in interest rates between two countries.

Here's how it works: A trader establishes a position, and of course in every Forex trade, the trader is long one currency in the pair and short the other. Each currency also has an interest rate associated with it, usually represented by the benchmark rate established by the central bank responsible for that currency.

The trader collects interest when he is long the higher yielding of the two currencies. Conversely, a trader pays interest when he is long the lower yielding of the two currencies. Sounds simple, right? Okay, it's not *that* easy, but that is the carry trade in a nutshell. Let's look at an example.

First, the simple version—let's say that we are placing a trade in hypothetical currency pair ABC/XYZ. Within that pair, currency ABC has a yield of 6 percent, and currency XYZ has a yield of 2 percent. We could say that the *differential* between ABC and XYZ is 4 percent.

If you take a long position in currency pair ABC/XYZ, that means you are long currency ABC and short currency XYZ. Since you are long the higher yielding of the two currencies, you collect the differential, which in this case is 4 percent. However, if you sell short ABC/XYZ, you will be short currency ABC and long currency XYZ. In other words, you will be short the higher yielding currency and long the lower yielding currency; in this case, the trader must pay the 4 percent differential in interest.

Again, this is a simplified version of the carry trade, to give you a general grasp of how it works. We'll get deeper into the specific mechanics of this trade as we go along.

REWARD AND PUNISHMENT

You could say that traders who go long ABC/XYZ are rewarded with interest, and traders who short ABC/XYZ are penalized for doing so, to the tune of about 4 percent. Some traders open long positions just to collect the interest, while others might avoid shorting the pair in order to circumvent the 4 percent "penalty."

Under normal circumstances, if ABC offers a significantly higher yield than XYZ, the currency pair ABC/XYZ would tend to rise, as traders enter the position that offers a reward (long ABC/XYZ) and avoid the position that creates a penalty (short ABC/XYZ). In other words, the "interest reward" creates buyers for ABC/XYZ, and the "interest penalty" discourages sellers from shorting the pair. This often creates a bias toward buying in the pair, which in turn drives the pair higher—but only under normal circumstances.

What do I mean by "normal circumstances"? Usually, the fact that one currency sports a higher interest rate than the other is not a random occurrence. A higher rate is often, but not always, an indication of a strong economy. But if you're buying a higher yielding currency *and* at the same time investing in a strong economy, and simultaneously shorting a lower yielding currency *and* a weak economy, the chances of your success grow exponentially. In cases like this, the differential in rates is likely to expand—something that makes this trade even more attractive, as we'll see.

PERCEPTION OF CHANGES IN THE DIFFERENTIAL

If traders believe that the interest rate differential between ABC and XYZ is likely to increase, they become more likely to go long the ABC/XYZ currency pair. Notice that I didn't say traders would wait for the differential to increase; by the time changes occur to the interest rate, it's already too late. They enter the trade due to the *perception* that the differential will increase in the future; by the time any anticipated changes in interest rates become reality, the smart money is already in the trade.

Conversely, if there is a perception that the interest rate differential will narrow, traders tend to exit the carry trade. This is important to understand, even if you don't particularly care about collecting interest (which is the "icing on the cake"). This gives the trader insight as to why and when currency pairs with wide differentials are likely to change direction. For example, if the market perceives that the interest rate differential of ABC/XYZ will become narrower in the future, a short position might be appropriate.

So where do traders acquire the perception that interest rate differentials might increase or decrease? One way is by paying close attention to central bank statements. For example, let's say that the chairman of the central bank responsible for currency ABC has indicated that he's very concerned about inflation.

How do central banks fight inflation? The most common method would be for the central bank to raise its key interest rate. By voicing its concerns, the central bank is tipping its hand, letting traders know that rates might be going higher in the future, so that the market won't be surprised when a rate hike actually occurs. Conversely, a central bank might indicate in a statement that it is concerned about slow economic growth. This is a clue that the central bank might seek lower interest rates in the future to stimulate growth.

Central banks give these clues frequently, and these clues often appear in the statements that accompany interest rate decisions. Often, the volatility that surrounds a decision by the Fed, the BoE, and other central banks is not due to the interest rate decision itself, but to the statement that accompanies it.

In these cases, central banks are signaling their intentions to avoid "shocking the markets". When markets are caught off guard, it can create unwanted excess volatility—something most central banks seek to avoid.

TWO SIDES TO THE COIN

Okay, so if ABC's central bank is likely to raise rates, what about the central bank for currency XYZ? Remember, there are two currencies in every Forex transaction, so for every trade we place, we have to keep our eye on two central banks. Let's suppose that the central bank responsible for currency XYZ has not changed interest rates for quite some time and has made no indication that it plans to do so in the future.

Why would ABC's central bank raise rates, but not the central bank for XYZ? Perhaps XYZ's economy is underperforming the economy of ABC; if growth is slow and inflation is benign, XYZ's central bank has no real need to raise interest rates, and may even be tempted to cut rates in the future. Or, perhaps XYZ's central bank is dealing with lower inflation relative to ABC's central bank.

By observing the comments of central bank officials and by keeping a close eye on economic reports (such as the GDP and inflation rates for both ABC and XYZ), and by understanding the underlying policies of the central banks involved, the trader and the market in general can build an informed opinion as to the future interest rate differential between ABC and XYZ.

Does that sound complicated? Don't be intimidated; because the universe of tradable currencies is small, it's not that difficult to keep up-to-date on the major currencies and their respective central banks. Think about it: If the NYSE consisted of only eight stocks, equity traders would know every last detail about those eight stocks. There wouldn't be much else for them to talk about!

Well, most currency traders deal with only about eight currencies: EUR, USD, GBP, JPY, CHF, CAD, AUD, and NZD. Since we only have to follow comments from eight central banks, it isn't that difficult for traders to get a feel for what they are saying. This makes it easy to form an opinion as to what the central banks' next move will be. The trader can confirm this opinion by observing the interest rate futures of those countries.

ANOTHER POSSIBLE SCENARIO

Here's another scenario: Perhaps the central bank for XYZ simply has a policy of always keeping interest rates low compared to other central banks. Why would they want to keep interest rates low? Perhaps the country has an export-based economy, like Japan. By keeping interest rates down, the Bank of Japan is enticing traders to short the Japanese yen vs. higher yielding currencies, such as the Australian dollar or the New Zealand dollar.

The constant selling pressure created by this policy acts to weaken the yen, thereby making Japanese exports cheaper to buyers around the world. In the early part of this century, the highest benchmark interest rate reached by the Bank of Japan was a mere 0.5 percent—far lower than the rates of other major central banks. This policy has also made the Japanese yen a popular *funding currency*—in other words, the low-yielding currency that traders wish to sell short—for the carry trade.

ALL GOOD THINGS MUST END

So when will the carry trade finally fail? The trade may run successfully for a long time, possibly years, allowing the traders who are long ABC/XYZ to collect substantial interest while holding a position that is appreciating at the same time. In other words, they are having their cake and eating it too!

But nothing lasts forever: The carry trade tends to fall apart when traders begin to perceive that the interest rate differential is going to contract. Notice that they do not wait for the interest rate differential to actually contract. Instead, they exit the trade, often en masse, when they *perceive* that the interest rate differential is about to narrow. By the time the differential actually narrows, the party is over, the keg is kicked, and Elvis has left the building.

What would create the perception that the rate differential is about to narrow? Perhaps XYZ's economy finally kicks in and starts growing at a faster rate; maybe XYZ now needs to raise interest rates to keep growth and inflation at manageable levels. Or maybe it becomes apparent that ABC's growth is slowing, or the chairman of ABC's central bank states that he is no longer concerned about inflation—an indication that interest rates are likely to move lower, thus narrowing the differential. If ABC's economy falls into a recession, the interest rate differential may disappear completely.

Of course, by monitoring the interest rate futures for both ABC and XYZ, and by monitoring comments from their respective central banks, you can guard against any surprises.

> "To give yourself the best possible chance of playing to your potential, you must prepare for every eventuality."
>
> —*Seve Ballesteros, Pro Golf Champion*

CHAPTER 12

HOW TO TRADE LIKE A ROCK STAR

"How do you go from where you are to where you want to be? I think you have to have an enthusiasm for life. You have to have a dream, a goal, and you have to be willing to work for it."

—Jim Valvano, NCAA Champion Basketball Coach

Now that you understand the basic mechanics of this trading style, some questions remain—where to place the entry and the protective stop? When and how should we add to our positions? And of course, how should we exit the trade? For the answers to these questions, read on!

CASE STUDY: GBP/JPY CARRY TRADE

To solidify our knowledge of the carry trade, let's consider the case of the Great Britain pound vs. the Japanese yen. In November 2003, the Bank of England began a series of rate hikes to increase its benchmark bank rate, which had bottomed out at 3.5 percent. The hikes would eventually culminate in July 2007, with the BoE's bank rate peaking at 5.75 percent (see Table 12.1).

Meanwhile, during that same decade, the Bank of Japan's benchmark overnight call rate never rose above 0.5 percent (see Table 12.2).

As we mentioned earlier, the Bank of Japan has a tendency to keep interest rates low in order to boost exports. This makes JPY an excellent currency to sell short in order to collect interest under the right conditions, such as when the interest rate differential between GBP and JPY is perceived to be expanding. When it became clear that the differential was about to increase, the currency pair began to move higher (see Figure 12.1).

Note that GBP/JPY reached its low point for the year 2003 on October 13, when it fell to 179.43, and didn't trade below 180.00 again until October 2008, five years later.

TABLE 12.1 Changes in the BoE's Bank Rate

Date	Bank Rate
Jul 2007	5.75
May 2007	5.50
Jan 2007	5.25
Nov 2006	5.00
Aug 2006	4.75
Aug 2005	4.50
Aug 2004	4.75
Jun 2004	4.50
May 2004	4.25
Feb 2004	4.00
Nov 2003	3.75
Jul 2003	3.50
Feb 2003	3.75

Source: Bank of England

The low was reached in October even though the Bank of England didn't raise rates until November 6, 2003, to 3.75 percent. Traders felt confident that the rate hike was coming because it had been signaled by BoE officials prior to its occurrence. You could say that the market perceived that U.K. rates were going to rise, and at that point, the GBP/JPY pair began its move off its 2003 lows (see Figure 12.2).

The BoE's Monetary Policy Committee (MPC) kept raising rates steadily, and as the differential widened, the GBP/JPY pair climbed steadily higher, rising 7,000 pips from 180.00 to 250.00. The rate hikes helped to create an uptrend in GBP/JPY that lasted for years, as traders entered long positions to collect interest and avoided shorting the pair so they wouldn't have to pay interest.

TABLE 12.2 Changes in the BoJ's Overnight Call Rate

Date	Overnight Call Rate
Dec 2008	0.10
Oct 2008	0.30
Feb 2007	0.50
Jul 2006	0.25
Mar 2001	0.00
Feb 2001	0.15
Aug 2000	0.25

Source: Bank of Japan

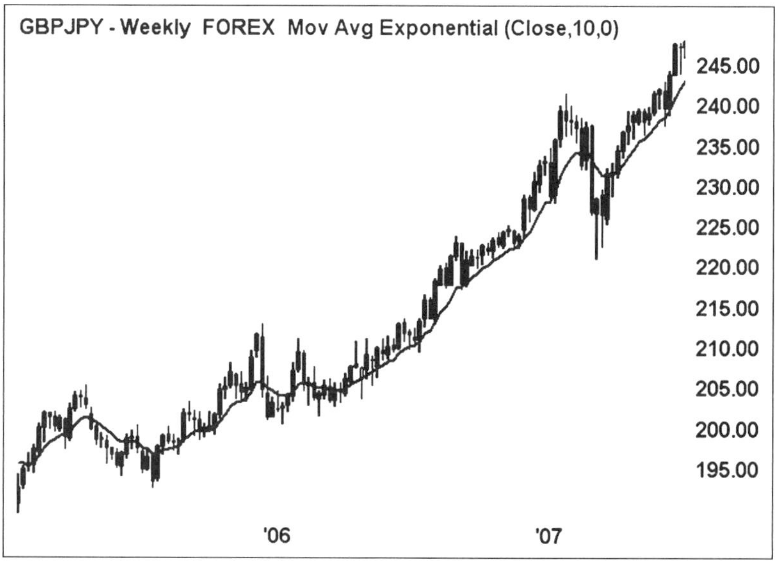

FIGURE 12.1 GBP rises vs. JPY as the interest rate differential between Great Britain and Japan increases.
Source: Created with TradeStation.

FXEd AND THE CARRY TRADE

In a prior chart (Figure 12.1), you might have noticed that the GBP/JPY exchange rate found support on its 10-week exponential moving average (EMA) for long stretches during 2006 and 2007, making it a potential long setup for the FXEd Trend Trade (for more on this technique, see Chapter 9 of *Forex Patterns and Probabilities*).

Initially, I used this trade setup on daily charts only, but I've found that it is an excellent tool for entering carry trades when used on the weekly chart. I've also expanded the technique to include the 20-period EMA in addition to the 10-period EMA, as described in *Forex Patterns and Probabilities.* Additionally, I've relaxed the rules regarding the proper order of moving averages, since it would be extremely difficult to achieve the proper order of moving averages on a weekly chart.

We now have a technical method (the FXEd technique) that we can use to enter a fundamental trade (the carry trade). By combining the two, we are blending the technical and fundamental aspects of trading. I always try to think of technicals and fundamentals as two different sides of the same coin. When you blend technicals and fundamentals and consider them in tandem, it is a sign that you're maturing as a trader.

When did the GBP/JPY trade finally fall apart? Note that the peak occurred in August 2007, months before the Bank of England started a campaign of rate reductions that eventually reduced the GBP yield to just 0.5 percent. Once again, traders didn't wait for BoE rate cuts to start selling the British pound; the selling commenced when the market perceived that the interest rate differential between GBP and JPY was about to narrow.

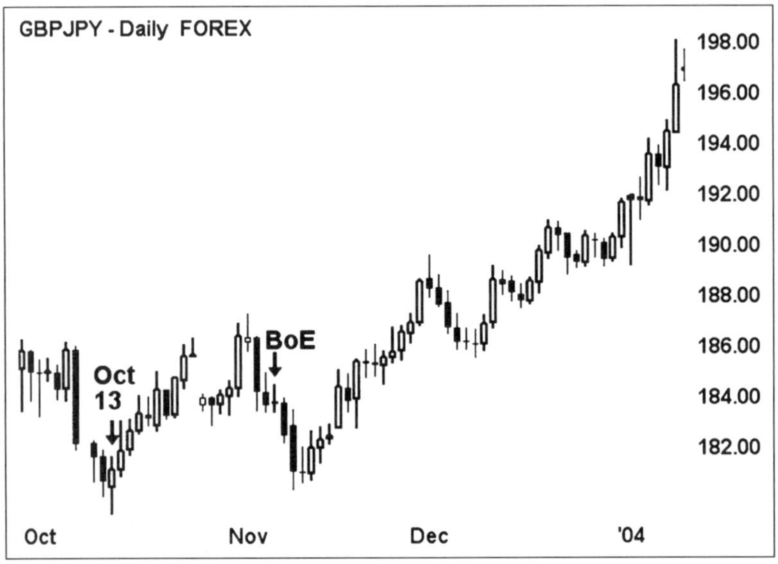

FIGURE 12.2 GBP/JPY bottoms out prior to a BoE rate hike.
Source: Created with TradeStation.

What followed was a crash of epic proportions in the GBP/JPY pair, as the differential narrowed to almost zero (see Figure 12.3).

Here's an interesting note—after the pair finally bottomed in early 2009, it began to recover prior to any rate hikes from the BoE. Once again, the market was anticipating and acting upon perceived changes in the interest rate differential before they actually occurred (see Figure 12.4).

YOU'RE TALKING A LOT, BUT YOU'RE NOT SAYING ANYTHING!

Tune your television to most financial networks, and you'll see guests falling all over themselves in an attempt to speak without actually saying anything. Most of the commentary could be summarized as follows: "The market might move up, or it could move down, unless it decides to move sideways." That pretty much covers all the bases!

Worse still, it takes many of these analysts a good three or four minutes of jargon-laced rhetoric to reach this nonconclusion. The result is a useless and boring waste of airtime.

One of the reasons why I've made dozens of appearances on financial television networks since the release of *Forex Patterns and Probabilities* is because I'm not afraid to tell viewers exactly what I'm trading, and why. Because of this, I've been a frequent guest on networks such as CNBC, CNN, the BBC, Bloomberg Television, Fox Business News, and ForexTV. As a trader, I'm used to making decisions and I'm not afraid to share that decision-making process, whether in books, on television, or in a magazine.

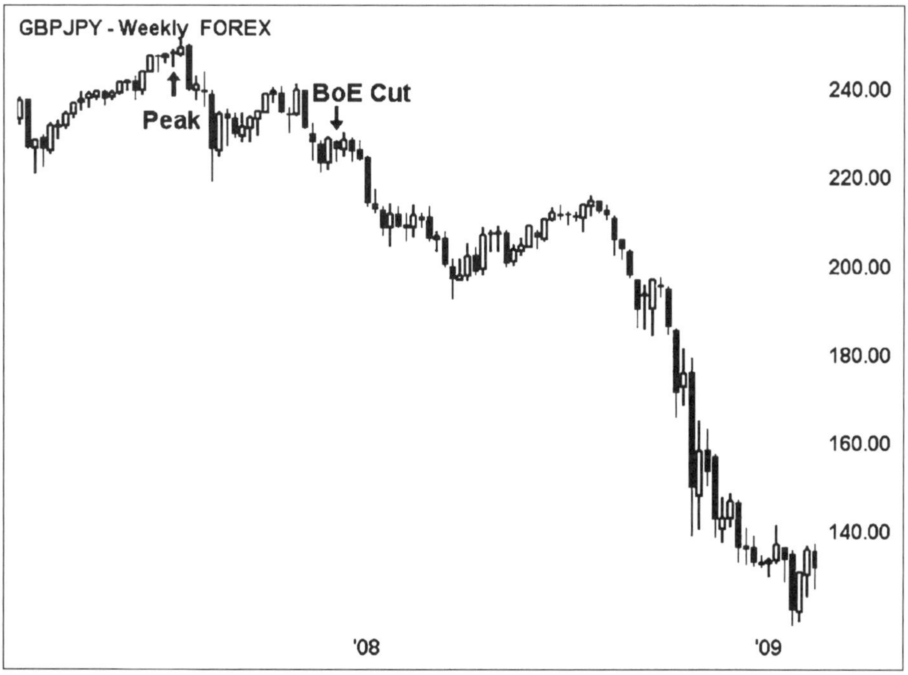

FIGURE 12.3 GBP/JPY loses over 10,000 pips; the selloff began before the differential began to narrow.
Source: Created with TradeStation.

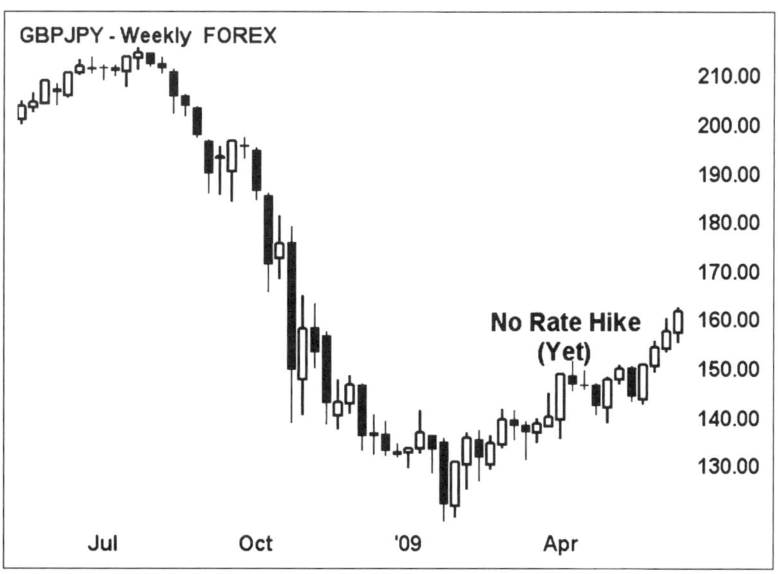

FIGURE 12.4 GBP/JPY rises from its lows as traders perceived that the differential would widen.
Source: Created with TradeStation.

The popular trading magazine *Technical Analysis of Stocks & Commodities* featured an interview with me in their August 2009 issue. The interview itself was conducted on June 8, 2009. Toward the very end of the interview, in response to a final question, I was very forthcoming about one of my then-current positions, and here is my unedited, word-for-word answer to that question:

> *Q: Any last words for our readers?*
>
> *A: Always look at the big picture. I have been holding an aussie position for about two months now, and I hope I'm still in it two months from now. I hope it goes on and on, because if I am still in it that means it's still going strong. That one trade could do more for me than day after day of 125 round trips a day and it is a lot less labor-intensive. Plus, there is positive carry on that aussie dollar trade. There is interest collected on it every day, whether it goes up or down. That, to me, is the way to go.*

Now, that is a pretty bold, very public call in the normally noncommittal world of the financial press. I told the magazine and the rest of the world that I was long aussie, and that I hoped to stay that way for a very long time. I took the risk of looking very foolish in print if I had been wrong and aussie had tanked.

(By the way, the phrase "125 round trips a day" refers to my old style of trading NASDAQ stocks on Level II. This refers to an earlier time in my career, when day trading tech stocks was the most profitable game in town.)

TECHNICALS AND FUNDAMENTALS LINE UP TOGETHER

What was it about aussie that I found so attractive? For one thing, the Reserve Bank of Australia had conducted interventions in late 2008, just a few months earlier. It was clear that the RBA had put in the bottom on AUD/USD at 0.6000. As we learned earlier, it's nice to be on the same side of the trade as a central bank.

Another factor mentioned in the article was "positive carry," meaning that I could collect interest on the trade. At a time when many major central banks were cutting their benchmark rates to virtually zero, Australia's cash rate never fell below 3 percent (see Table 12.3).

On the technical side, one supporting factor was the double bottom formation that is clearly visible on the weekly chart. This bullish technical pattern, when it appears after a sharp selloff, often indicates that a rally is about to occur.

Add to this the bounce that occurred just above the 10-week EMA, which happened in early April. While this bounce did not create an entry, it caused me to take notice, because it was an indication that the 10 EMA might become a support level. Now that we had both technical factors and fundamental factors working in harmony, the aussie began to look extremely attractive (see Figure 12.5).

TABLE 12.3 RBA Cash Rate Bottomed at 3% in 2009

Date	Cash Rate Target
Dec 2009	3.75
Nov 2009	3.50
Oct 2009	3.25
Apr 2009	3.00
Feb 2009	3.25
Dec 2008	4.25
Nov 2008	5.25
Oct 2008	6.00
Sep 2008	7.00
Mar 2008	7.25
Feb 2008	7.00

Source: Reserve Bank of Australia

ENTRY AND STOP

On the next bounce off the 10-week EMA, it would be time to enter. That opportunity presented itself during the week of April 24, 2009—a little less than two months prior to the *Stocks & Commodities* interview. If you missed the initial entry, the setup occurred again the following week. Aussie was breaking out of the double bottom and bouncing off its 10-week EMA (see Figure 12.6).

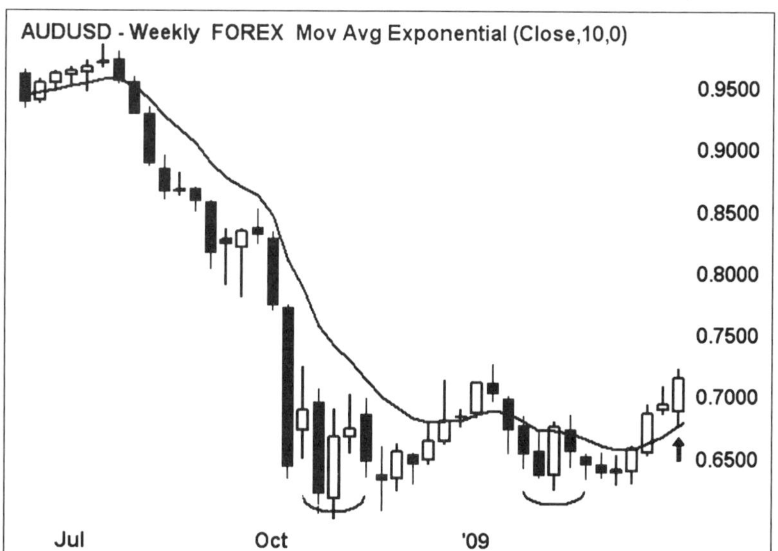

FIGURE 12.5 AUD/USD intervention, plus double bottom, plus possible 10-EMA support.
Source: Created with TradeStation. © TradeStation Technologies, Inc. All rights reserved.

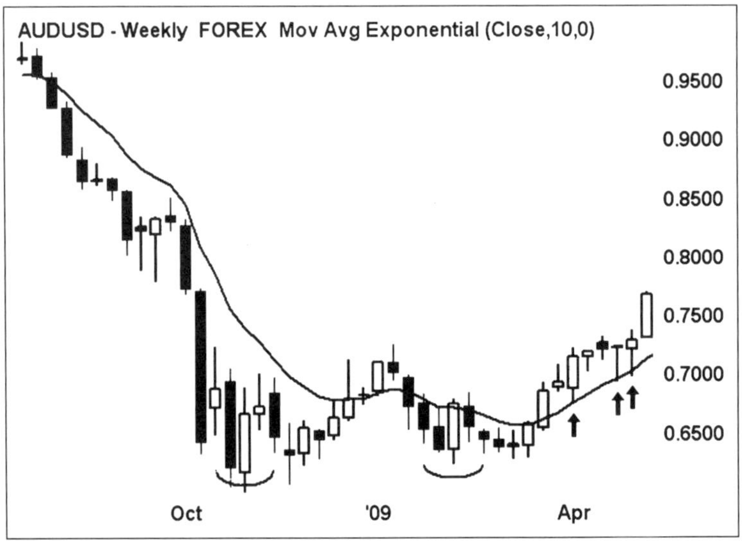

FIGURE 12.6 AUD/USD bounces repeatedly off its 10-week EMA.
Source: Created with TradeStation.

Let's examine the entry for the trade. In the FXEd Trend technique, the moving average is the entry point. The moving average is listed as 0.6971 in Figure 12.17, so we enter a long position at that point (see Figure 12.7).

In reality, when the price reaches a moving average it has a tendency to depress that moving average, so the actual entry point may have been a few pips lower. We will use 0.6971 as the entry point even though optimally, the entry could have occurred at a lower

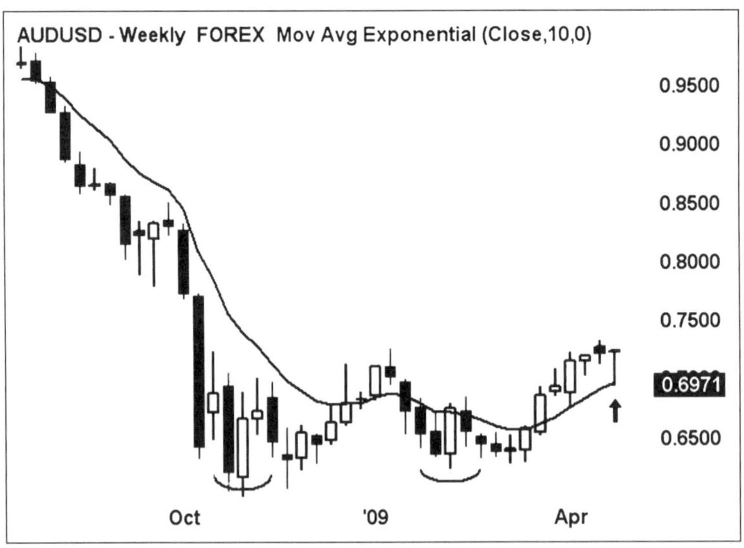

FIGURE 12.7 AUD/USD entry point is 0.6971, the weekly 10-EMA.
Source: Created with TradeStation.

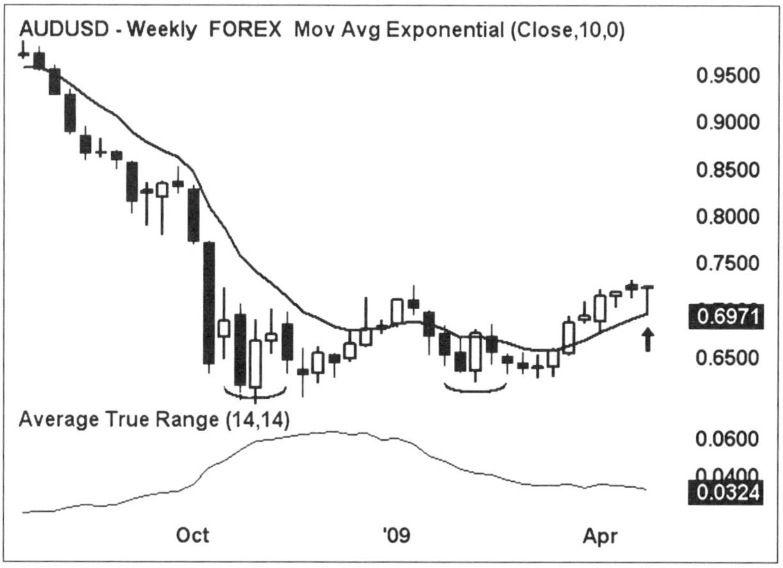

FIGURE 12.8 Stop created at 0.6809 using half of the weekly ATR (324), subtracted from the moving average.
Source: Created with TradeStation.

(better) price. The low price for the candle is 0.6952, indicating that a lower entry price could have been accommodated. Naturally, if the entry had occurred at a lower price, the stop would also have been lower, and therefore harder to hit.

Of course, whenever we enter a trade, our first concern is the placement of the stop. In the FXEd Trend Trade, we use half of the average true range, or ATR, to determine the location of the stop. ATR tells us how much volatility we can expect from a currency pair and is based on the average volatility for the 14 most recent candles—in this case, 14 weeks.

The chart indicates that at the time, AUD/USD boasted an ATR of 324 pips per week. Half of 324 = 162, so we will place the stop 162 pips beneath the entry point/moving average of 0.6971, resulting in a stop located at 0.6809 (see Figure 12.8).

TRADE LIKE A ROCK STAR

Now 162 pips might sound like a rather wide stop, but does that mean that we're risking a lot of money? Possibly: If you trade two standard lots, in which AUD/USD has a constant value of $10 per pip, the risk on this trade would total $3,240. That figure might be unacceptable for many traders, especially beginners. Our first job as traders is to protect the account; our second job is to make money. Always be on guard against a large loss.

But with the flexibility now available to retail Forex traders, there is no need to take great risks. Many accounts allow the trader to trade mini lots, in which AUD/USD has a

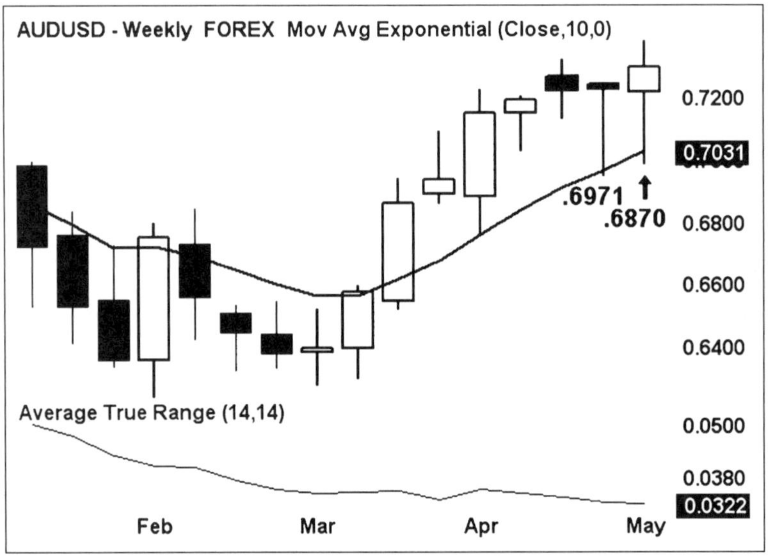

FIGURE 12.9 Stop is raised to 0.6870 as the next candle closes.
Source: Created with TradeStation.

value of $1 per pip. The previous trade, placed with two mini lots, would result in a total risk of just $324.

If that is still too much money to risk losing, the trade could be done in a micro account. With a pip value of just 10 cents, two lots in this trade placed in a micro account would result in a total risk of just $32.40. As you can see, almost anyone can "trade like a rock star" without taking inordinate risks, regardless of the amount of money in their account.

Okay, so we have dealt with the entry and the stop, but what about the target? If you're familiar with this trading technique, you already know that there is literally no target price; we will simply trail the stop until it is hit, and that is how we will exit the trade. When the next candle closes—which in this case will be over a week after the entry, since we are trading on a weekly chart—then we will calculate the new location for the stop, if it hasn't already been hit (see Figure 12.9).

TIGHTENING STOPS TO REDUCE RISK

After the candle representing the week of May 1, 2009, closes, the 10-week EMA rests at 0.7031, and the ATR reads 0.322. Half of the ATR is 161. Now subtract 161 pips from the moving average of 0.7031 (tip—if using a calculator, simply remove the decimal points in order to make this easier) and you'll get a result of 0.6870 (7031 – 161 = 6870). This is the new location of the stop, up from 0.6809.

We have just lowered the risk on the trade from 162 pips per lot to 101 pips (6971 – 6870 = 101). Using our earlier example, two standard lots now represent a risk of $2,020,

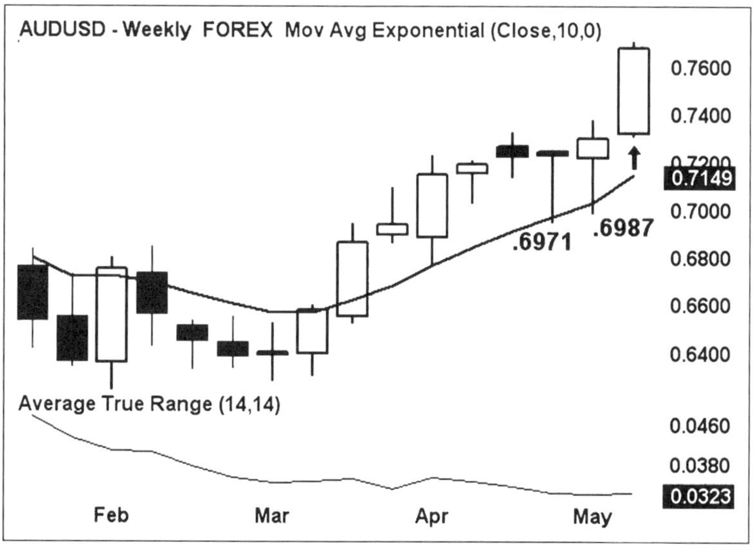

FIGURE 12.10 Stop is raised to 0.6987 as another candle closes.
Source: Created with TradeStation.

down from $3,240. On two mini lots, we are risking $202, and on two micro lots, the risk is just $20.20.

When the next candle closes, we'll move the stop again if we're still in the trade. How will we know if the stop has been hit? Simply check the low price of the candle; if the low of the candle is higher than the stop by more than a few pips, then you are still in the trade.

You might need to allow a few extra pips to account for the spread, depending on whether your charts are running off the bid or the ask (or an average of the two). If you're not sure whether your charts are indicating the bid price or the ask price of a currency pair, just ask your chart provider. Also, keep in mind that for every day we are long the AUD/USD currency pair, we will continue to receive interest in the account.

By the week of May 8, 2009, the moving average has climbed up to 0.7149. The ATR is now 323, and half of 323 = 161.5. Round up to 162, and subtract from 7149, and the result of 6987 will represent the new location of the stop (see Figure 12.10).

ELIMINATING RISK

Our initial entry point was 0.6971, so the stop of 0.6987 is above our break-even point by 16 pips. This means that the worst-case scenario will be a gain of 16 pips on two lots *if the stop is hit.*

While the potential for a loss has been eliminated, it's important to understand that there is no cap on the amount that might be gained. Instead of trying to predict how high Aussie might run, we are just going to sit tight and keep moving the stop in this manner until it is hit.

Also, consider this—you have been in this trade for several weeks now, and you have done very little work. All you are doing is recalculating the stop every week, which takes less than a minute of your time. What are you going to do with all of that free time? You could certainly use that time to place shorter term trades, or you could simply do whatever you please. That type of freedom is the reason why people pursue a career in trading in the first place.

When is the best time to adjust the stop? The best time to recalculate your stop is when the market reopens for business, after the weekend. This equates to Sunday evening around 5 p.m. U.S. East Coast time. Because a new weekly candle begins to form at this time, this is when you'll see a dramatic change in the moving average.

Since the Forex market tends to be fairly quiet at that time of the week, it is not necessary to move the stop immediately at that moment. Usually, you have a few hours before the Asian markets kick into full gear, so don't wait *too* long before moving the stop.

STAYING IN THE TRADE

Also, be honest with yourself—how many of you have already taken your profits? At one point during the most recent candle, the exchange rate for AUD/USD reached above 0.7700, so at that point your gain was about 800 pips in just over two weeks. For many of us, a profit this size is too much to bear—we can't stop thinking about it, and the temptation to close the trade early becomes too great to ignore.

There is something about human nature that makes us want to take profits too soon, so we'll add this rule—you can close half of the trade any time you wish, but with the other half of the trade you must trail the stop as prescribed above. I think you'll find that when you use your judgment to take profits, you'll almost always get out of the trade too early. Nothing hurts quite like taking a 30 pip profit and then learning that you could have earned 300 pips, or even 3,000. And that's not counting the interest you could have collected along the way.

That's why I created the FXEd technique—to force myself to stay in the trade, even when I felt it was time to get out. When I place these trades, I try not to think about them, because I know that what I believe is not important. Will it break resistance? Will it pull back to support? I know that I don't know the answer to these questions, so I just follow the plan.

In fact, once I've set this trade into motion, my own opinion about the currency pair doesn't matter—*not even to me*. I literally don't care what I think about what might happen next. I've committed to a plan, and I'm going to see it through—period.

JUMPING AHEAD

Let's jump ahead in our analysis to early July; by this time, quite a few weekly candles have passed, and the trade has been ongoing for months. We know that the stop hasn't

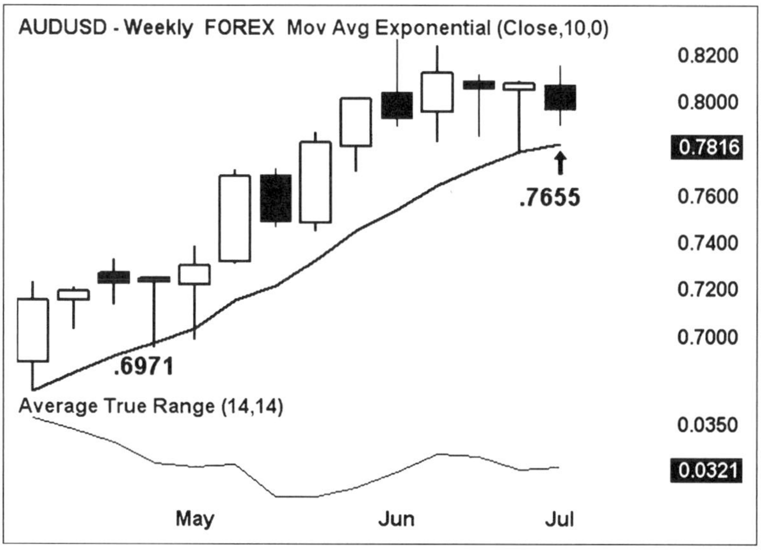

FIGURE 12.11 Stop is raised to 0.7655 after another candle closes.
Source: Created with TradeStation. © TradeStation Technologies, Inc. All rights reserved.

been hit, because the price hasn't crossed below the moving average for months. Where is our stop located now? (See Figure 12.11.)

By early July, the moving average has climbed all the way up to 0.7816. The ATR has been fairly stable, at 321. Half of 321 equals 160.5, so we'll place the stop 161 pips beneath the moving average (7816 – 161 = 7655).

When I'm trading, I always ask myself, "What is the worst thing that could happen right now?" Well, with the entry at 0.6971 and the stop at 0.7655, the worst thing that could happen is that you'll be stopped out for a gain of 684 pips per lot. If your trade consists of two standard lots, your profit has now reached $13,680; the profit on two mini lots would be $1,368, and two micro lots would show a profit of $136.80. This does not include interest, which you've been collecting every day. Not a bad reward for less than one minute's work per week!

On the next candle, AUD/USD pulls back sharply and drops below the moving average. Was the stop hit? No, because even though the price pierced the 10-week EMA, the low for the week was 0.7722 (please note that this chart includes a fractional pip, hence the reading of 0.77224). Since our stop was located at 0.7655, we are safe by 67 pips—in other words, the AUD/USD exchange rate never really came close to taking out our stop (see Figure 12.12).

ALWAYS TIGHTEN, NEVER LOOSEN

In Figure 12.12, the moving average is now located at 0.7810 and the ATR is 311. Half of 311 = 155.5, which we will round up to 156. This will result in a stop of 0.7654

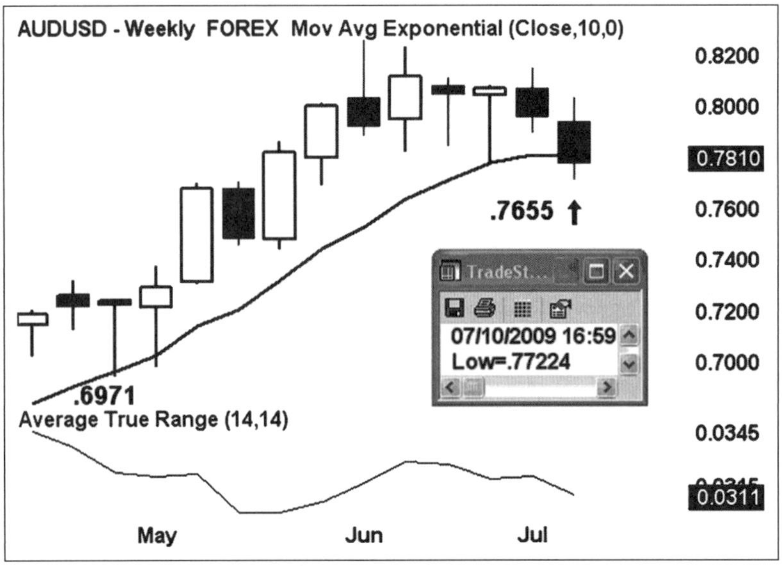

FIGURE 12.12 Price breaks EMA but misses stop by 67 pips.
Source: Created with TradeStation. © TradeStation Technologies, Inc. All rights reserved.

(7810 – 156 = 0.7654), which is lower than our previous stop of 0.7655. Does this mean we should lower our stop by one pip, from 0.7655 to 0.7654?

The answer is a resounding "No!" We never lower our stop when we're holding a long position, and we never raise a stop when we're in a short position. We can only tighten stops—move them closer to the price—and never loosen them. This is one of the cardinal rules of risk management. If you perform this calculation and the result indicates that you should loosen the stop, simply leave it where it is.

CLOSE CALL

The following candle had a low of 0.7702, missing our stop of 0.7655 by just 47 pips (see Figure 12.13).

That was the closest call so far, and it was to be the last close call for quite some time. Assuming that you didn't bail out of the trade too soon, you were about to enjoy four solid months during which the price stayed above the moving average.

ONWARD AND UPWARD

By late November, the moving average had risen all the way to 0.8999, with an ATR of 273. Half of 273 is 136.5 (round up to 137), so the stop was now located at 0.8862 (8999 – 137 = 8862).

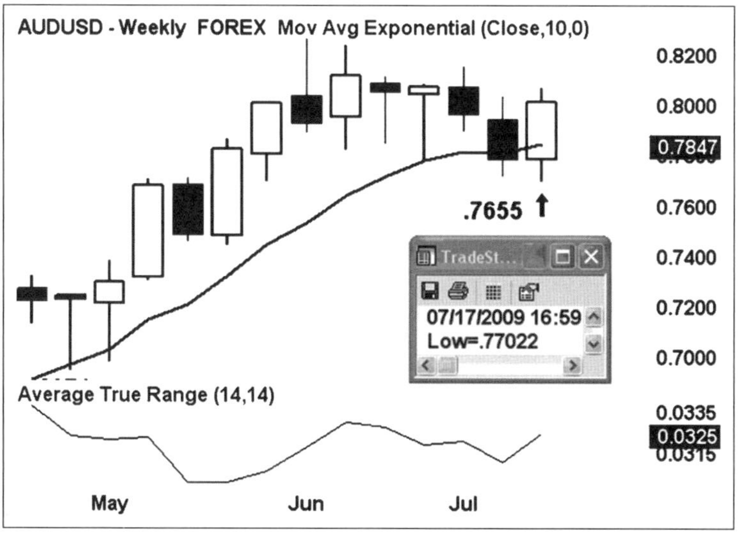

FIGURE 12.13 Price breaks EMA but misses stop by 47 pips.

Since our initial entry (many months earlier) was located at 0.6971, this means that our *worst-case* scenario is a gain of 1,891 pips per lot. You have now held the trade for over six months (see Figure 12.14).

Let's think about that for a minute: 1,891 pips on two standard lots would yield a profit of $37,820 if you closed it now—which you're not going to do, because the stop hasn't been hit yet. The risk on the trade was never greater than $3,240, and the potential gains are, well, incalculable. There is literally no telling how far this trade might run.

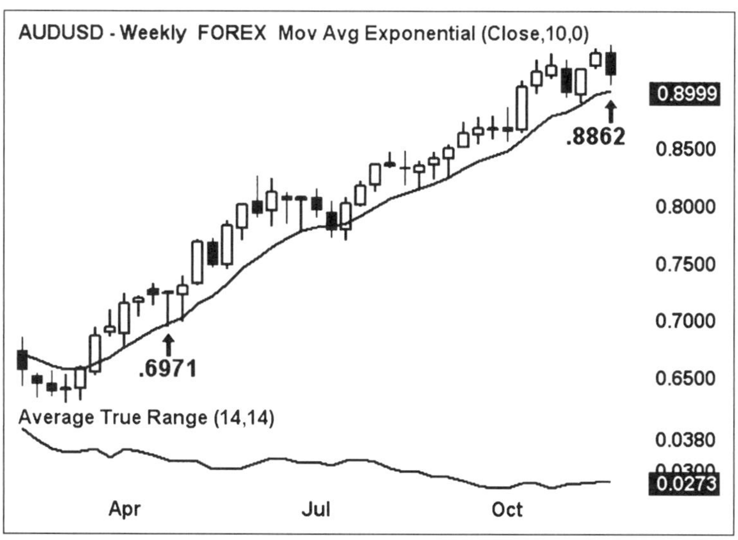

FIGURE 12.14 Worst-case scenario is a gain of 1,891 pips per lot.

CNBC APPEARANCES

In the months following the publication of the *Stocks & Commodities* article, I remained bullish on the Australian dollar. I communicated this very clearly and repeatedly on live television, particularly during a string of appearances on CNBC. Each video clip appears with the headings listed here, and these clips might still be available for your viewing pleasure on the CNBC web site or elsewhere online.

During this clip, I suggested that traders might want to diversify into commodity currencies, which turned out to be a pretty good call:

> *Airtime: Wednesday, September 23, 2009 | 6:20 p.m. ET*
>
> *Go long on a basket of commodity currencies, like the aussie, the kiwi and the Canadian dollar, says Ed Ponsi, president at FXEducator.com. He speaks to Stephen Halmarick, head of investment markets research at Colonial First State, CNBC's Karen Tso, and Sri Jegarajah.*

By October, aussie had soared hundreds of pips above its 10-week EMA. At that point, I urged caution, telling traders that if they weren't already long aussie, they should wait for a pullback to the 10-week EMA (see Figure 12.15).

> *Airtime: Tuesday, October 20, 2009 | 6:20 p.m. ET*
>
> *Don't buy into the aussie now, says Ed Ponsi, president at FXEducator.com. He tells CNBC's Karen Tso he is concerned about the aussie levels short-term.*

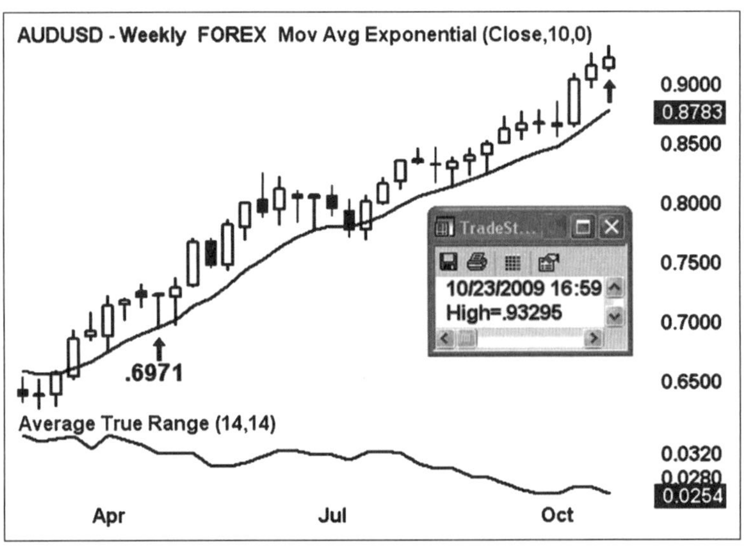

FIGURE 12.15 AUD/USD extends 546 pips above its10-week EMA.
Source: Created with TradeStation. © TradeStation Technologies, Inc. All rights reserved.

During the week of October 23, the price of AUD/USD reached a high of 0.9329—a number that was nearly 550 pips above the moving average, indicated at 0.8783. While still bullish on aussie, the price was simply too far extended beyond the moving average to justify an entry.

In the interview, I suggested that traders shouldn't buy at current levels, but should wait for a pullback instead. That pullback would occur in November, when aussie traded below 0.9000, dipping below the 10-week EMA by about 50 pips.

By mid-November, I predicted a short-term bounce in the USD. This was due in part to the COT report, which at that time indicated that the greenback was tremendously oversold. The market was *too short* the greenback, so it almost had to go up.

Airtime: Tuesday, November 10, 2009 | 5:20 p.m. ET

Expect a bounce in the dollar in the short term, says Ed Ponsi, president at FXeducator.com, speaking to Gavin Thomas, MD & CEO of Kingsgate Consolidated and CNBC's Karen Tso.

In addition to the bullish COT reports, the U.S. Dollar Index was having trouble getting through support at 75.00. Shortly after this appearance, the USD Index began a sharp rally; by late December, it traded above 79.00 (see Figure 12.16).

FIGURE 12.16 USDX bounces sharply from support.
Source: Created with TradeStation.

That short-term bounce in the USD helped to push aussie back to its 10-week EMA, creating a new entry point well below the October highs. After the November pullback in aussie, the currency once again began to rally. Finally, in December 2009, I predicted parity for the AUD/USD pair:

Airtime: Tuesday, December 1, 2009 | 5:20 p.m. ET

The aussie will reach parity at some point, says Ed Ponsi, president of FXEducator.com, speaking to Lewis South, chief economist at Macquarie Funds Management and CNBC's Karen Tso.

My specific prediction was that AUD/USD would reach 1.0000 by mid-to-late 2010. Aussie has not yet reached parity as of this writing, but I'm hoping it'll get there by the time you read this book. Once again, I'm going out on a limb in public.

And what if it never gets there? Well, even if the stop is hit, at this point it is still an awesome trade—the kind of trade that can turn a bad year into a good year, or a good year into a great year. And who knows, maybe I'm being too conservative in my prediction. After all, there is no telling how far this could go.

Speaking of stops being hit, it finally happened on AUD/USD during the week of December 18, 2009. Just like the EUR/CHF intervention trade, which also lasted for the better part of a year, the AUD/USD trade ended just prior to the completion of this book. It's almost as if the market wanted these trades to resolve themselves so that I could tell you how they ended. Eventually, all good things must end (see Figure 12.17).

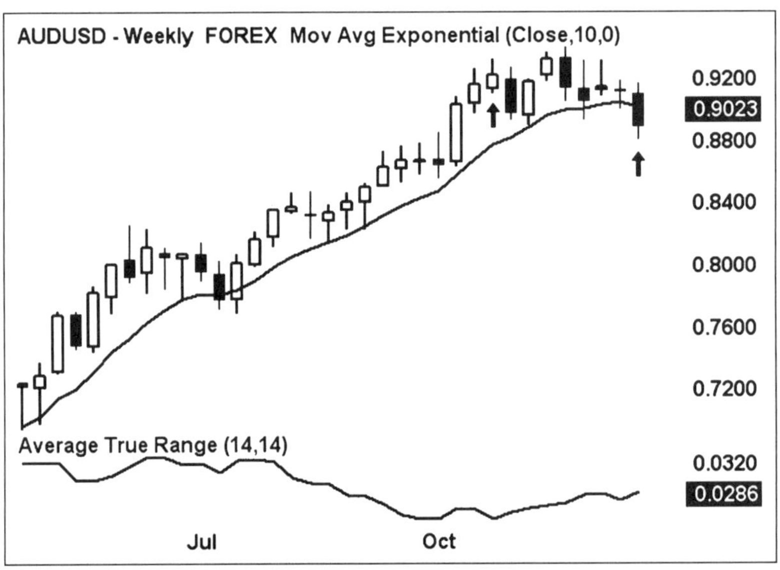

FIGURE 12.17 Stop is finally hit in December on AUD/USD trade.
Source: Created with TradeStation.

PYRAMID SCHEME

One question that comes up frequently in conjunction with the FXEd strategy is the question of adding to winners. Yes, you can add to a winning trade, but only if you have already moved your stop to break even or higher. At that point, you will have eliminated all risk from the trade, so there is no reason why you couldn't add to the position if the price returns to the moving average and the setup occurs again. This is often referred to as "pyramiding," and while this practice is not mandatory, it can turn a good trade into a great trade. Just make sure that you only add to winners, and never add to losers.

WHY WE DO IT THIS WAY

I'm sure that many traders bailed out long ago, due to any number of factors. Also, traders who used other techniques to go long aussie have already reached their targets and exited. Consider that any method you would have chosen to create a target probably would have taken you out of this trade long ago, resulting in a smaller profit and eliminating any chance for further gains. Did you cave in to fear or greed, and exit too soon? And if you did close the trade early, did you learn anything from the experience?

But as impressive as this trade may be, the gains are even larger than they appear, because for all the months that you've been holding this position, you've been collecting interest every day. But how much interest did we collect?

In an upcoming chapter, we'll learn how to "see into the future"; in other words, we'll learn how to estimate the amount of interest we are going to receive prior to placing the trade, and various ways to incorporate this information into our trading strategies.

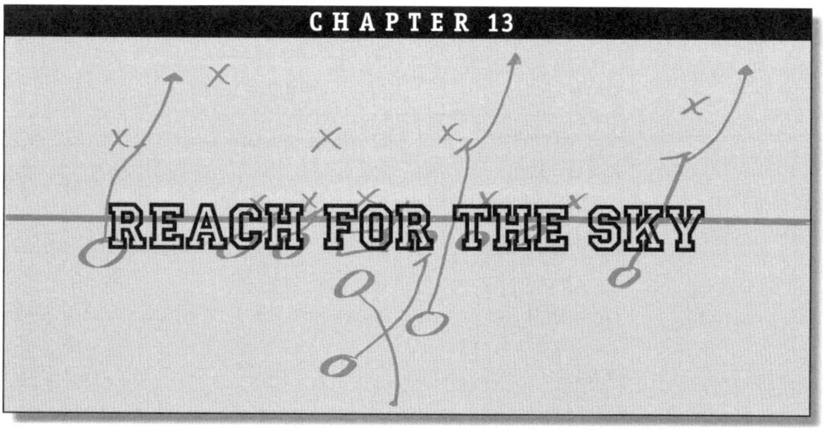

CHAPTER 13

REACH FOR THE SKY

"Most people give up just when they're about to achieve success. They quit on the one-yard line. They give up at the last minute of the game, one foot from a winning touchdown."

—H. Ross Perot, Self-made Billionaire

Finally, I just want to show a few quick examples of this hybrid between FXEd and the carry trade. While the prior example was pretty spectacular, I want to demonstrate that it is not unique. This trade setup occurred frequently while I was writing this book, and I'd like to present just a few examples of trades that occurred during that time.

When using this technique, the opportunities come in bunches; you won't see any entries for a while, then you'll be inundated with them. Be careful about highly correlated trades; for example, don't go long EUR/USD, GBP/USD, and AUD/USD at the same time, because that is really just one big "short the USD" trade. When a funding currency becomes weak, numerous currencies can set up against it, so be careful.

Just remember that nothing always works, so don't expect miracles. If there were such a thing as a trading style that always worked, this would be a very short book! On the other hand, good traders don't need miracles—they just need good strategies that result in wins that are large, relative to the size of the inevitable losses.

As you read this, please keep in mind that every FXEd trade is not necessarily a carry trade, and every carry trade is not necessarily an FXEd trade. There is no law that states that a carry trade must adhere to a moving average. Nor is there a law that states, "A currency pair that tracks a moving average must offer positive carry." But when the two strategies do intersect, the results can be phenomenal.

TABLE 13.1 Short-Term ECB Minimum Bid Rate History

Date	Min Bid Rate
May 2009	1.00
Apr 2009	1.25
Mar 2009	1.50
Jan 2009	2.00
Dec 2008	2.50
Nov 2008	3.25
Oct 2008	3.75
Jul 2008	4.25
Jun 2007	4.00
Mar 2007	3.75

Source: European Central Bank.

EUR/USD 2008

Earlier, I mentioned that I've expanded this technique to encompass not only daily and weekly charts, but 10 and 20 EMAs as well. Here's an example of a big move for the EUR/USD pair as it tracks its 20-week EMA. The move begins in 2007, as the ECB's benchmark minimum bid rate climbed from 3.75 percent to 4 percent (see Table 13.1).

While the Fed Funds rate was higher than the ECB's minimum bid rate for all of 2007, the differential was quickly narrowing, and by the end of 2007 it had nearly disappeared. As the ECB's rate rose from 3.75 percent to 4 percent, the Fed Funds rate fell from 5.25 percent to 4.25 percent. By the end of 2007, the differential had narrowed to a mere 0.25 percent (see Table 13.2).

TABLE 13.2 Short-Term U.S. Federal Funds Rate History

Date	Fed Funds Rate
Dec 2008	0.25
Oct 2008	1.00
Oct 2008	1.50
Apr 2008	2.00
Mar 2008	2.25
Jan 2008	3.00
Jan 2008	3.50
Dec 2007	4.25
Oct 2007	4.50
Sep 2007	4.75
Jun 2006	5.25

Source: Federal Reserve.

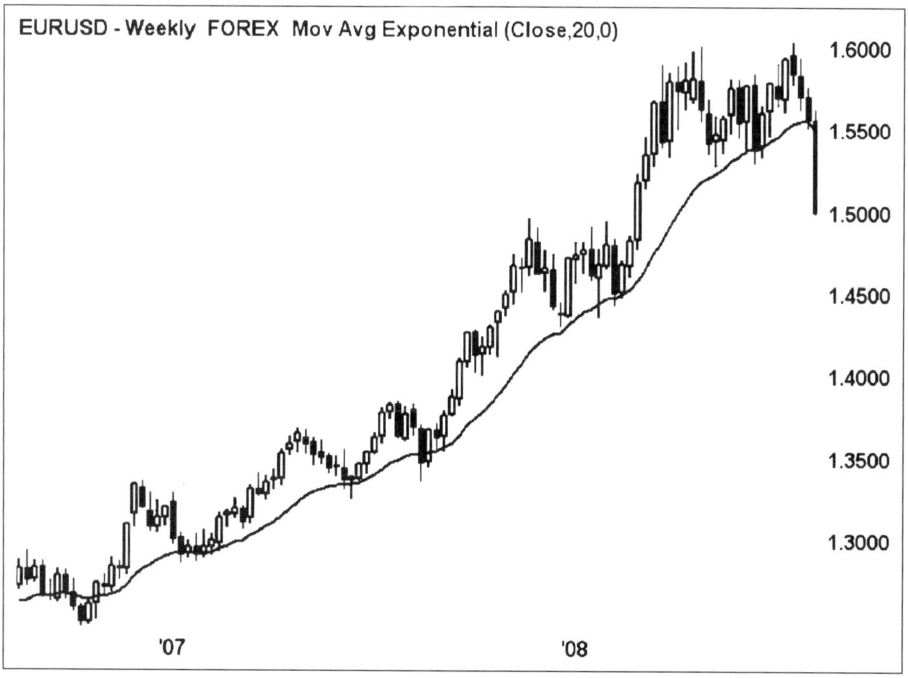

FIGURE 13.1 EUR/USD climbs its 20-week EMA.
Source: Created with TradeStation.

By early 2008, the long EUR/USD trade had positive carry, but traders had already begun buying in anticipation of this during 2007. It was a classic example of traders acting on perceived changes in interest rates, instead of waiting for the actual changes to occur.

The EUR/USD's climb accelerated in the spring of 2008, as the Fed started cutting interest rates in dramatic fashion. The cuts included a 75 basis point reduction on January 22, and another 75 basis point cut on March 18. Now EUR/USD had positive carry in its favor, helping to boost the exchange rate.

After rocketing all the way to 1.6000, the trade ended when the price finally broke through the 20-week EMA in August 2008. Crashing stock markets and a threatened collapse of the world's financial system sent traders running to the safety of U.S. Treasuries and the U.S. dollar (see Figure 13.1).

USD/CHF 2008

The USD/CHF currency pair has a high negative correlation to the EUR/USD pair; in other words, when one goes up, the other one usually goes down. So, it shouldn't come as a great surprise that while EUR/USD was finding support on its 20-week EMA in 2008, USD/CHF was finding resistance on its 20-week EMA at the same time (see Figure 13.2).

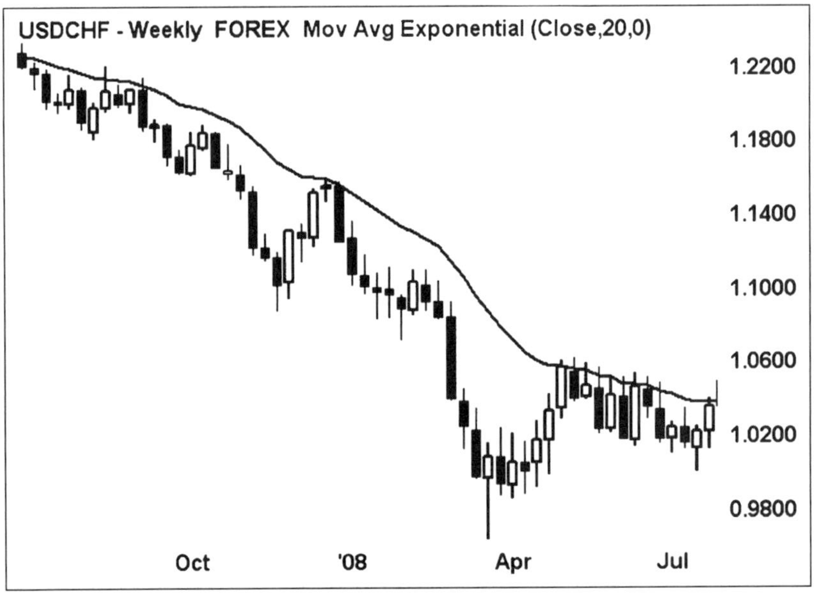

FIGURE 13.2 USD/CHF finds resistance on its 20-week EMA.
Source: Created with TradeStation. © TradeStation Technologies, Inc. All rights reserved.

When the moving average is acting as resistance, we sell short when the exchange rate makes contact with the moving average. In this case, the stop is placed above the moving average by half of the weekly ATR. As the price moves lower, the stop is tightened as it is lowered on each successive candle.

While this trade barely achieved positive carry (both the Fed and the SNB were cutting rates frantically), what did happen was that the interest rate differential between USD and CHF disappeared. Remember, every FXEd trade is not necessarily a carry trade, and every carry trade is not necessarily an FXEd trade. Table 13.3 gives a look at Swiss rates during the time of this trade.

TABLE 13.3 Short-Term SNB Interest Rate History

Date	SNB Target Rate
Mar 2009	0.25
Dec 2008	0.50
Nov 2008	1.00
Nov 2008	2.00
Oct 2008	2.50
Sep 2007	2.75
Jun 2007	2.50
Mar 2007	2.25

Source: Swiss National Bank.

Given a choice between trading EUR/USD or USD/CHF at that time, EUR/USD was the clear winner because of its positive carry. I wouldn't advise taking both trades because the pairs are too highly correlated. A trader who enters a long trade on EUR/USD and shorts USD/CHF at the same time has essentially placed the same trade twice. If the trader doesn't realize this, the two trades together may represent an unacceptable risk.

NZD/USD 2009

Here is a fascinating example of how multiple moving averages can act as support. On the daily chart of NZD/USD, we see the pair finding support on its 10-day EMA. When the 10-day breaks, the pair finds support on its 20-day EMA, and on the occasions when the 20-day EMA breaks, support is found on the 50-day EMA.

How can you tell which EMA is the 10-day, which is the 20-day, and so on? The EMAs are in "proper order," with the 10-day EMA above the 20-day EMA, and the 20-day EMA located above the 50-day EMA. As originally explained in *Forex Patterns and Probabilities*, the FXEd trade can set up on daily charts, too (see Figure 13.3).

At the same time that this was occurring on the daily chart, the pair was finding support on the weekly chart on its 10-period EMA. The 10-week EMA is similar in some ways to the 50-day EMA, as there are five full trading days in every week, and 5 days multiplied by 10 weeks equals 50 days (see Figure 13.4).

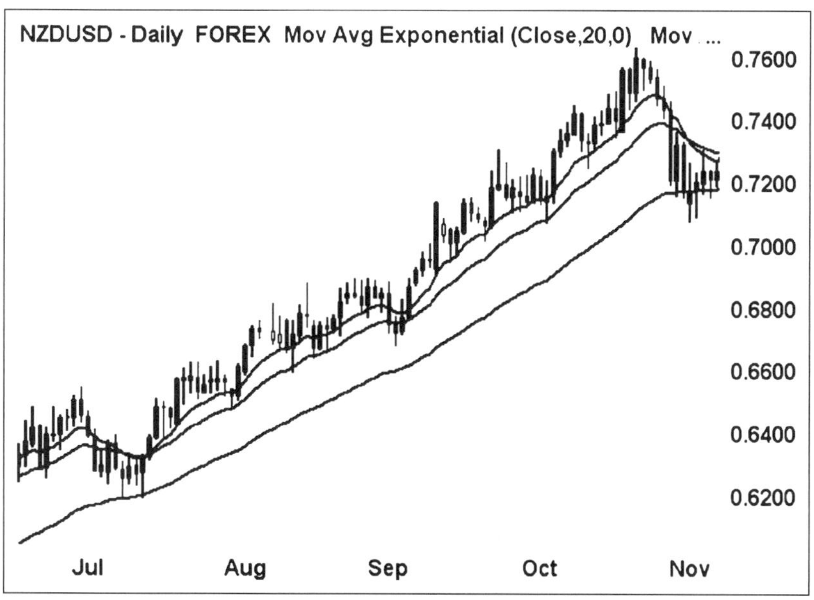

FIGURE 13.3 NZD/USD finds support on 10-, 20-, and 50-day EMAs.
Source: Created with TradeStation.

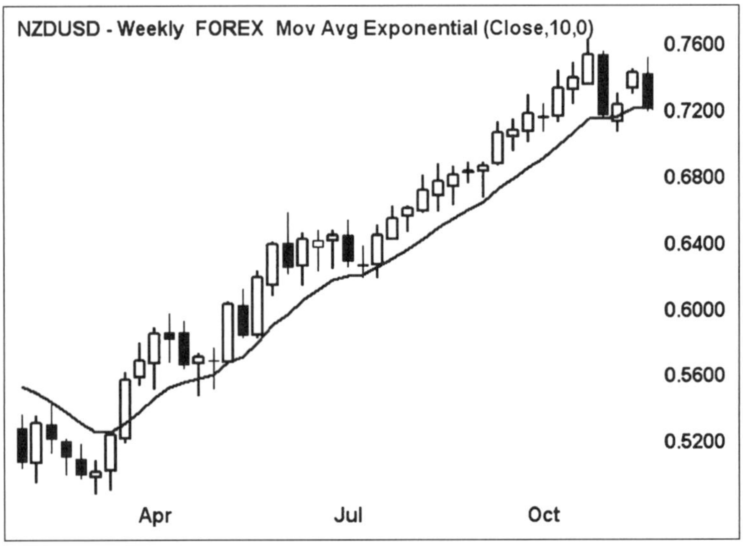

FIGURE 13.4 NZD/USD finds support on its 10-week EMA.
Source: Created with TradeStation.

New Zealand's benchmark interest rate was higher than the Fed Funds rate for the entire year of 2009, creating positive carry. Just like Australia, New Zealand maintained higher rates during the financial crisis than most developed countries, as the RBNZ's benchmark OCR rate bottomed out at 2.5 percent (see Table 13.4).

EUR/USD 2009

Just as the aussie and the kiwi were rocking in 2009, the euro was also cruising up its 10-week exponential moving average vs. the USD. The first bounce off of the 10-week EMA

TABLE 13.4 Short-Term RBNZ Overnight Cash Rate History

Date	RBNZ OCR Rate
Apr 2009	2.50
Mar 2009	3.00
Jan 2009	3.50
Dec 2008	5.00
Oct 2008	6.50
Sep 2008	7.50
Jul 2008	8.00
Jul 2007	8.25

Source: Reserve Bank of New Zealand.

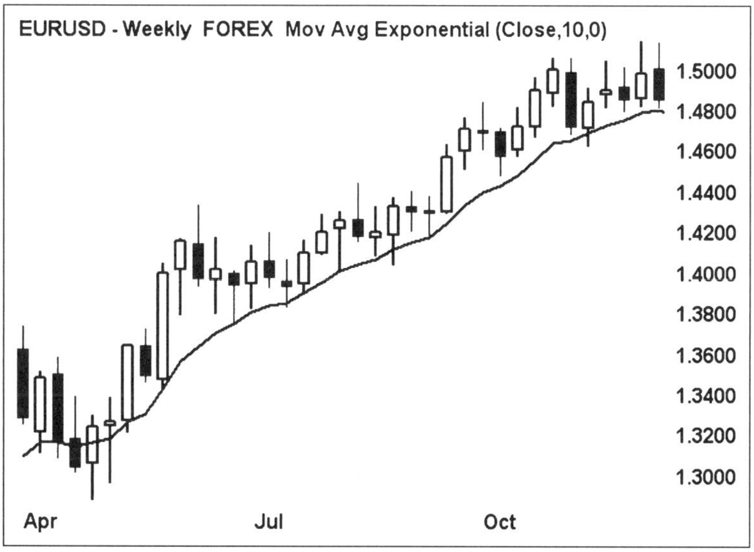

FIGURE 13.5 EUR/USD climbs its 10-week EMA in 2009.
Source: Created with TradeStation.

occurred in early May, and from there the pair sailed straight up the moving average for six months (see Figure 13.5).

During its 2009 rally, the ECB's minimum bid rate never fell beneath 1 percent. Meanwhile, the Fed Funds rate was officially listed as being in a range of between 0 percent and 0.25 percent for the entire year. So, while traders who were long EUR/USD were able to collect interest, it was never an overwhelming amount due to the narrow interest rate differential.

Perhaps in anticipation of a higher ECB rate, EUR/USD ran along its 10-week EMA for over six months during 2009 before finally breaking down in December due to a year-end USD rally. The euro was also weakened when ratings agency Fitch cut Greece's long-term debt from A– to BBB+ (see Figure 13.6).

S&P 500 1996–2007

This last example has nothing to do with currencies or carry trades, and it came to me as a something of a shock. Since the release of my first book, I've been contacted by numerous people who have adapted my techniques to various markets and time frames. One such individual pointed out that the S&P 500, when viewed on a monthly chart, shows very long stretches of using its 10- and 20-period EMAs as both support and resistance (see Figure 13.7).

Starting in 1995, the S&P 500 began a wicked uptrend on its monthly chart, which turned out to be the genesis of a huge bull market. Then in mid-1996, the index pulled back and found support on its 10-month EMA. It then bounced off the 10-month EMA

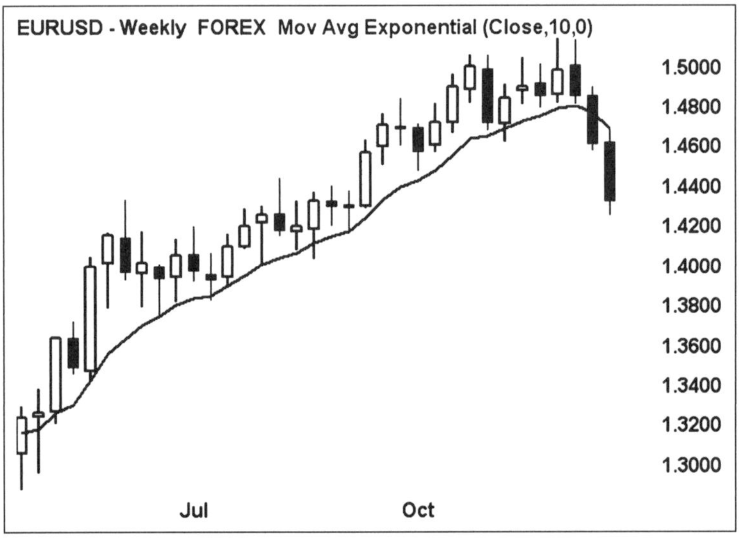

FIGURE 13.6 EUR/USD breaks its 10-week EMA in late 2009.
Source: Created with TradeStation.

several times in 1997 before finally breaking through in 1998, when it found support for three consecutive candles on its 20-month EMA (see Figure 13.8).

When a bear market finally took hold in 2001, the index found resistance numerous times on its 10-month EMA. This continued until mid-2003, when a double-bottom breakout ignited a new bull market rally (see Figure 13.9).

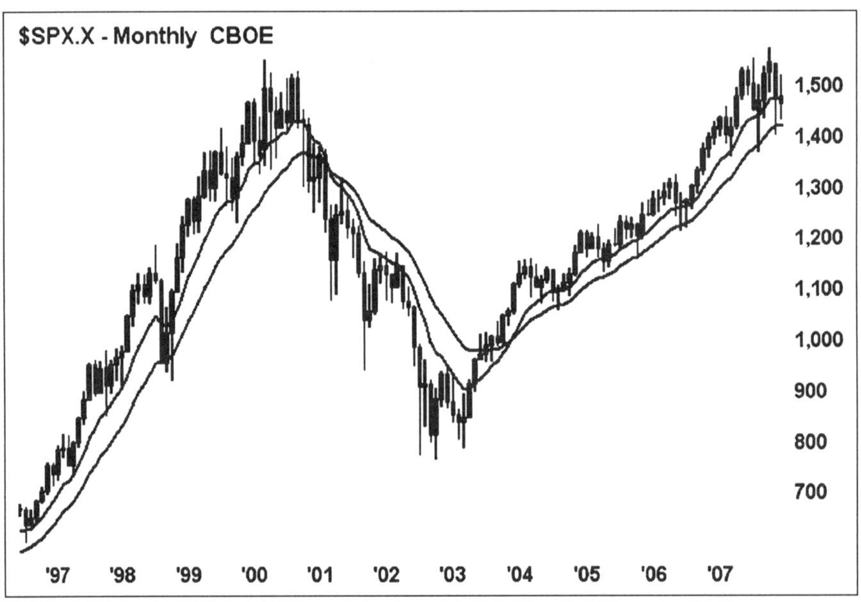

FIGURE 13.7 S&P 500 finds support/resistance on 10-month, 20-month EMAs.
Source: Created with TradeStation.

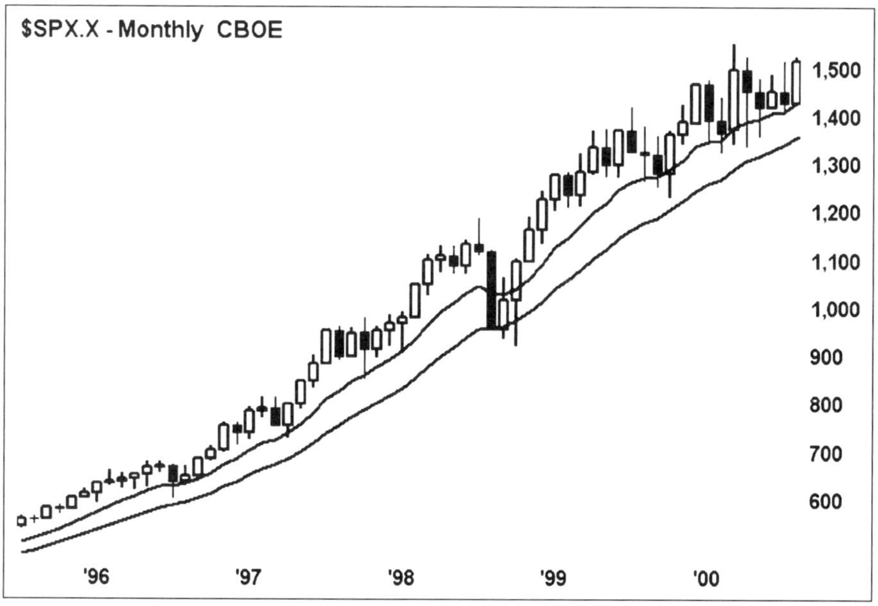

FIGURE 13.8 In a bull market, S&P 500 finds support on monthly EMAs.
Source: Created with TradeStation.

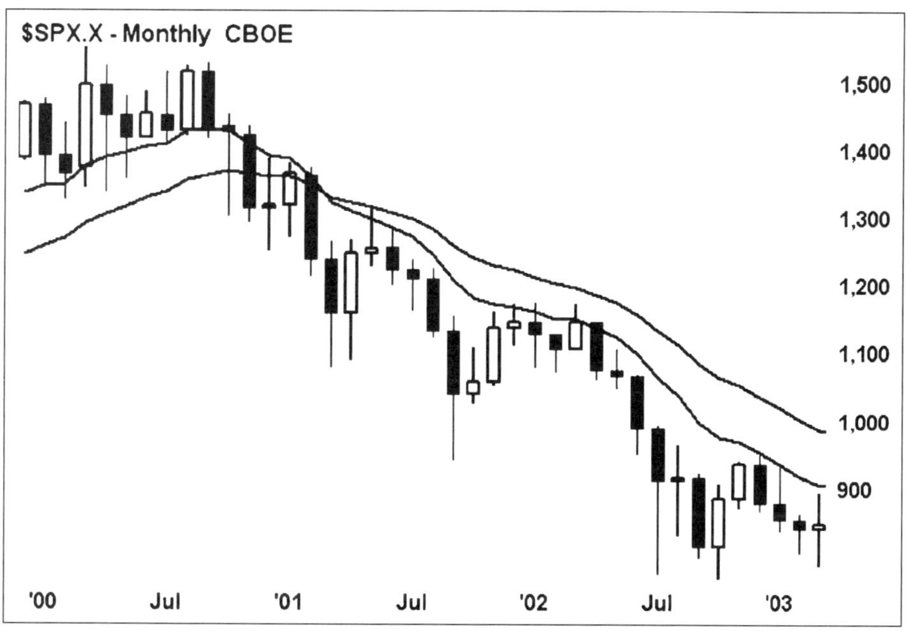

FIGURE 13.9 S&P 500 finds resistance on its 10-month EMA.
Source: Created with TradeStation.

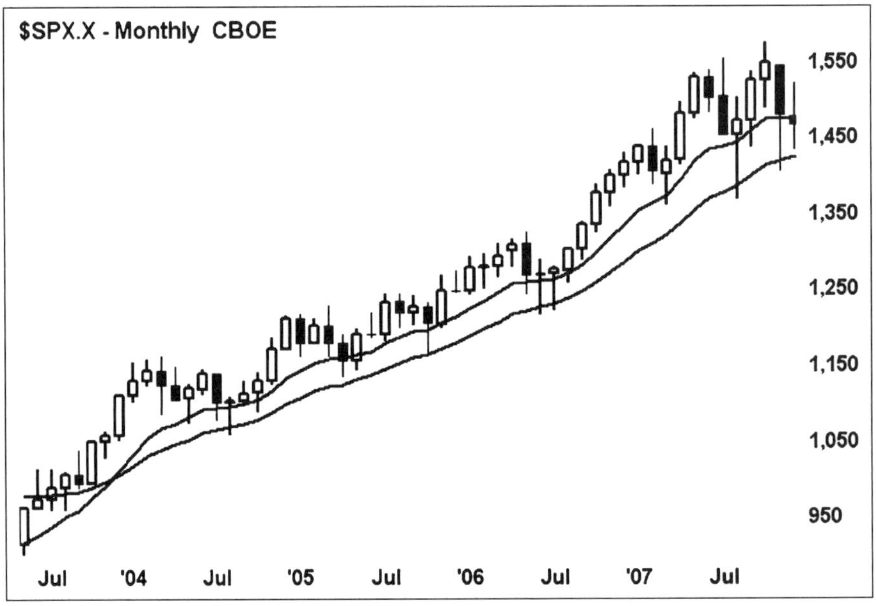

FIGURE 13.10 S&P 500 finds support on its 20-month EMA.

From mid-2004 until the end of 2007, the index found support on its 10-month EMA, and on occasions when the price broke through, support was often found on the 20-month EMA (see Figure 13.10).

Admittedly, this strategy doesn't work all the time, but why does it work so well on the occasions when it does? Perhaps we have identified an entry point for institutional traders. Or maybe it is just a coincidence. Whatever the reasons may be, consider this—if you catch just one of these big moves, just once in a great while, it could make a big difference in your account equity.

CHAPTER 14

SEEING INTO THE FUTURE

"The difference between a successful person and others is not a lack of strength, not a lack of knowledge, but rather a lack of will."

—Vince Lombardi, NFL Hall of Fame Coach

I've heard it said, and even read in other books about Forex trading, that when entering a carry trade, the trader captures the interest rate differential. In other words, if currency ABC has a yield of 6 percent, and currency XYZ yields 2 percent, the trader collects 4 percent interest. In Chapter 11 of this book, I described this as "the simple version" of the carry trade.

Now let's add another step to provide a more specific and accurate description. The idea that you would collect 4 percent interest isn't entirely accurate because ABC is a different currency and has a different value than XYZ. So, we could say that 4 percent interest collected on currency ABC is not the same as 4 percent interest collected on currency XYZ—it's an apples-to-oranges comparison. In order to calculate the interest more accurately, we need to make this into an apples-to-apples comparison.

To understand more clearly, consider this: 3 percent interest on one U.S. dollar is not the same amount as 3 percent interest on one British pound, unless the greenback and the pound are trading at parity. Since this is almost never the case, there must be a missing piece to the puzzle—some way to account for the difference in the relative values of the currencies.

The difference is this: In order to understand the amount of interest paid or received in terms of the second or "counter" currency in the pair, the interest rate differential must be multiplied by the exchange rate.

For example, imagine that you have a USD-based account. Now, suppose that currency AUD has a benchmark interest rate of 3.25 percent, and currency USD has an interest rate of 0.25 percent. Take the aussie rate of 3.25 percent and subtract the U.S.

Fed Funds rate of 0.25 percent, and the differential is 3 percent. So, the trader should collect approximately 3 percent interest, right?

Not exactly. In order to understand the interest in terms of the counter currency, in this case U.S. dollars, we must multiply that 3 percent by the exchange rate. So, if the exchange rate of AUD/USD were 0.7000, we would multiply 3 percent by 0.7 to get a result of 2.1 percent—the approximate rate of interest, in U.S. dollars, that we will collect on an annual basis.

PERPETUATING THE CYCLE

If the exchange rate of AUD/USD then rose to 0.8000, the actual interest rate, as calculated in U.S. dollar interest, would be 2.4 percent (3 percent times 0.8 = 2.4 percent). In this case, as the exchange rate rises, the AUD/USD carry trade becomes even more compelling because the real amount of interest collected in U.S. dollars increases. This perpetuates the cycle and gives the trade momentum, leading to some very long and dominant trends.

Let's take this one step further: What if the Reserve Bank of Australia were to raise rates to 3.5 percent? The differential would look like this:

$$3.5\% - 0.25\% = 3.25\%$$

So, 3.25 percent is the new differential. If we assume that the AUD/USD exchange rate were to then rise to 0.9000, we could estimate the interest rate on this trade for our USD-based account by multiplying the differential by the exchange rate:

$$3.25\% \times .9 = 2.925\%$$

And so it goes. It's interesting to note that although the differential has increased by only 25 basis points, the rate of interest collected by our carry trader increased from 2.1 percent to nearly 3 percent, due to movement in the exchange rate.

By the way, if you're wondering where the interest rates and exchange rates for this AUD/USD example came from, those were actual rates from 2009. From the chart, you can see how traders piled in to collect interest, and the more they piled in, the higher AUD/USD climbed. The process is self-reinforcing, so once it begins, it can continue for a very long time (see Figure 14.1).

THE REALLY, REALLY GOOD PART

The really beautiful part of this trade is the effect of leverage. For example, suppose that you are trading with leverage of 100 to 1; the trader must put up approximately $1,000 in order to control $100,000. When we participate in this carry trade, do we collect the interest on the $1,000 that we invested, or on the $100,000 that we now control?

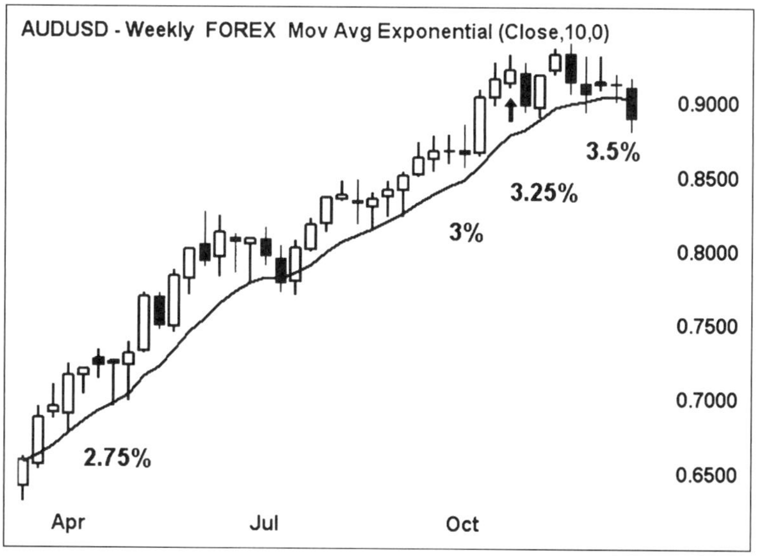

FIGURE 14.1 Interest rate differential between AUD and USD.
Source: Created with TradeStation.

After all, if I can collect 2 percent or 3 percent interest at an annual rate on the invested amount, that's okay, but it isn't going to rock my world. It would be hard to justify placing a trade in order to collect such a small amount of interest, and it is unlikely that many traders will enter the trade without a greater incentive to do so.

Well, I'm sure you've guessed the answer by now: We collect interest on the entire leveraged amount, in this case $100,000. This is what makes the carry trade such a fantastic opportunity.

Wouldn't you rather collect interest on $100,000? Isn't that better than collecting interest on $1,000? I'd say it's better—in fact, it's about a hundred times better!

Under the right circumstances, a trader can accumulate a tremendous amount of interest while holding this trade—just be certain not to hold it if it goes against you, as you could easily lose more on the trade than you collect in interest. Also, keep in mind that if you enter a trade in which you are long the lower-yielding of the two currencies, you will have to *pay* interest on the leveraged amount of the trade—and that amount could be quite substantial.

FUTURE PROJECTIONS

Hedge funds and other traders who take advantage of the carry trade aren't merely focused on current interest rate levels. Carry traders have projections of where they believe interest rates will be in the future—in fact, these projections may be influenced by the interest rate futures markets. These traders calculate the amount of interest they expect to receive based on an objective analysis of the policies of the central banks involved and the economies of the respective countries. This way, they can anticipate the amount of interest they will collect.

INTEREST RATE FUTURES

There are futures contracts specifically designed to predict future interest rates. They are useful because they are real contracts, backed by real traders placing real trades with real money. If the traders fail to place the correct trades, they will lose money.

This will weed out the inaccurate traders, theoretically making the predictions of the contracts more accurate. Therefore we assume that interest rate futures have a fair chance of being correct, because these traders are "putting their money where their mouth is."

Interest rate futures are certainly a better indicator than the opinion of an analyst who has "no skin in the game"—in other words, an analyst who has nothing to lose if he or she makes a wrong guess. Real money trumps talk every time.

FED FUNDS FUTURES

In the United States, the 30-Day Fed Funds futures (and options) contracts trade on the CME (Chicago Mercantile Exchange). There is a separate contract for each month. The contracts are easy to interpret: Simply subtract the contract price from 100 to determine the predicted average Fed Funds rate for that month.

For example, if the June 2012 contracts are trading at 97.00, the projected Fed Funds rate for that month would be 3 percent (100 – 97 = 3). If the August 2012 contracts trade at 96.75, then the projected Fed Funds rate for that month is 3.25 percent (100 – 96.75 = 3.25). The contract prices fluctuate as opinions about future interest rates can change from day to day, or even hour to hour (see Table 14.1).

In the preceding examples, interest rate hikes are "fully priced in." But what if the August 2011 contract is trading at 97.60? Does this mean that the Federal Reserve is going to set the Fed Funds target rate to 2.40 percent? That would be highly unlikely, because the Fed tends to make adjustments to interest rates in quarter-point increments.

TABLE 14.1 Hypothetical "Fully Priced-In" Fed Funds Scenarios

Month	Last Price	Implied FF Rate
Jun 2012	97.00	3.00%
Aug 2012	96.75	3.25%

THE WEATHER REPORT

I'm sure that at some point you've listened to a weather report. Depending on where you live, it might be normal for a meteorologist to predict a strong chance of rain tomorrow, with a slight chance of rain the following day.

Well, we would interpret a contract price of 97.60 in a similar way: It doesn't mean that the Fed is going to raise rates to 2.4 percent. It means that a Fed Funds rate of 2.25 percent is fully priced in *with a strong chance* of an increase to 2.5 percent.

When the contract price reached 97.75, a Fed Funds rate of 2.25 percent was fully priced in. In order to fully price in an increase to 2.5 percent, the contract price would have to fall to 97.50. By falling to only 97.60, the futures are telling us that while a rate of 2.25 percent is assured, a move to 2.5 percent is possible, but it's not a "done deal."

What if the same contract was priced at 97.70 instead of 97.60? Does this mean that the Fed will raise rates to 2.3 percent? No, we would interpret this to mean that a Fed Funds rate of 2.25 percent is fully priced in, *with a slight chance* of an increase to 2.5 percent. It's only a slight chance because 2.3 percent is much closer to 2.25 percent than it is to 2.5 percent.

Finally, always keep in mind that these figures project *future expectations* based on *current information* and are not infallible. Nobody knows for certain what the future might hold; we are simply using the information that we have now to estimate where future interest rates will be. That is one function of the Fed Funds futures (see Table 14.2).

TABLE 14.2 Actual Fed Funds Futures Contract Prices as of Dec. 31, 2009

Month	Last Price
Nov 2010	99.010
Dec 2010	98.905
Jan 2011	98.795
Feb 2011	98.620
Mar 2011	98.520
Apr 2011	98.390
May 2011	98.200
Jun 2011	98.140
Jul 2011	97.980
Aug 2011	97.850
Sep 2011	97.745
Oct 2011	97.640
Nov 2011	97.505

Source: Chicago Mercantile Exchange.

CAUSING A STIR

In addition to the Fed Funds futures, there are futures contracts for other key interest rates as well. For example, NYSE Euronext offers STIRs, an acronym for short-term interest rate contracts. These futures and options derivatives are based on short-term euro, sterling, and Japanese interest rates, and they can also be used to estimate future interest rates (see Figure 14.2).

As with the Fed Funds futures, a trader simply subtracts the contract price from 100 to determine the predicted future interest rate. Unlike the Fed Funds futures, which have a contract for every month, STIRs usually trade on a quarterly expiration cycle.

One of the most popular STIRs is the so-called "short sterling" contract. The March 2013 short sterling contract seems to predict a rate of approximately 4.50 percent (100 – 95.49 = 4.51) as of December 31, 2009 (see Table 14.3).

However, short sterling does not predict an overnight rate like the Bank of England's bank rate; it predicts a three-month interest rate instead. This is not the same as the Fed Funds rate, but it serves the same basic purpose.

So how is this useful? The bottom line is, if the short sterling contract indicates that three-month rates are going to rise by 25 basis points, traders often assume that the BoE's bank rate will also rise by 25 basis points. The correlation is not perfect, but it is usually reliable except during times when the markets are undergoing severe stress.

By monitoring these futures and options contracts and using them as indicators, you'll rarely find yourself caught by surprise when a central bank makes a change in interest rates. You'll also be able to project interest rate differentials into the future, in order to estimate the amount of income you'll receive on a carry trade.

Three Month Sterling (Short Sterling) Futures

Codes and Classification

Code	L	**Market**	NYSE Liffe London	**Vol**	144,726	31/12/09
		Currency	£	**O.I.**	2,129,235	30/12/09

Instrument - 31/12/09

Delivery	Open Interest (O.I.)	Day Volume
Dec 2010	281,844	15,313
Mar 2011	261,701	13,340
Jun 2011	154,528	13,239
Sep 2011	100,031	24,974
Dec 2011	93,077	16,411
Mar 2012	73,455	9,534
Jun 2012	45,406	5,345
Sep 2012	36,730	6,912
Dec 2012	23,580	2,062

FIGURE 14.2 Short-term interest rate contracts (STIRs) for the short sterling as of Dec. 31, 2009.
Source: NYSE Euronext.

TABLE 14.3 Short Sterling Contract for March 2013, as of Dec. 31, 2009

Market Data	31/12/09
Last (£)	95.49
QTY Last Trade	40
Change D/D − 1(%)	−0.03
Total Day Qty	309
Settlement (31/12/2009)	95.54
O.I (30/12/2009)	3,855

Source: NYSE Euronext.

PROJECTING INTEREST INCOME

Let's return to the AUD/USD example used earlier in this chapter. We'll assume that the current differential is 3 percent, and the exchange rate is 0.8000. According to our analysis, we believe the interest rate differential between AUD and USD will rise to 3.5 percent within three months and 4 percent in six months.

Although this increase in the differential is likely to have a positive effect on the exchange rate of AUD/USD (the "reward" for taking a long position is expected to increase, as is the "penalty" for entering a short position), we will take the conservative approach and base all of our assumptions on the hypothetical current exchange rate of 0.8000. In this example, the exchange rate will not move higher or lower; it will remain flat.

We'll assume that a 10-lot trade in a standard account has been entered: The trader has put up about $10,000 in order to control $1,000,000 (leverage of 100:1).

In this case, the initial amount of interest collected (in USD) would be 2.4 percent (3% × .8000) on $1,000,000, or $24,000. Divide this annual return by 12 months, and you can expect to receive $2,000 per month for the first three months.

After the first three months, the differential should rise to 3.5 percent, according to our projections. Assuming the same exchange rate of 0.8000, the trader will now receive interest at an annual rate of 2.8 percent (3.5 × 0.8000 = 2.8), or $28,000 on a position of 1,000,000. Again, divide this annual rate by 12 to get the monthly rate of $2,333. This is our projected monthly interest income for months 4, 5, and 6.

After month 6, we project the differential will widen to 4 percent and stay there. Even if the exchange rate remains flat at 0.8000, after six months we expect to receive an annual rate of 3.2 percent on one million dollars (4 × 0.8000 = 3.2). This comes to $32,000 annually, or $2,667 per month.

Now that our projections are in place, we can draw the following conclusions:

- If we hold the trade for 3 months, we expect to collect approximately $6,000 in interest (estimated $2,000 per month for months 1, 2, and 3).

- If we hold the trade for 6 months, we expect to collect about $13,000 in interest (estimated $2,000 per month for months 1, 2, and 3, and $2,333 per month for months 4, 5, and 6).
- If we hold the trade for 12 months, we expect to collect about $29,000 in interest (estimated $2,000 per month for months 1, 2, and 3; $2,333 per month for months 4, 5, and 6; and $2,667 per month for months 6 through 12).

Note that these projections do not assume that the exchange rate will move in our favor; all of the above calculations assume that AUD/USD's exchange rate will remain steady at 0.8000. As long as the trade doesn't go against us, we're going to come out ahead.

HOPE FOR THE BEST, PREPARE FOR THE WORST

But what if the trade does go against us? We are long 10 standard lots of AUD/USD, which means that every pip that this pair moves in the "wrong" direction will cost us $100. If we hold the trade for three months, what is our break-even point?

Well, we're assuming that we'll receive $6,000 in interest over the first three months, so at $100 per pip (10 lots × $10 per pip), we can afford to lose 60 pips on this trade and still break even—as long as we hold the trade for three months. Assuming that we entered the trade at 0.8000, this makes 0.7940 our break-even point.

If we hold the trade for six months, our anticipated break-even point is 0.7870. This is because we expect to receive $13,000 in interest over the next six months, which is equal to 130 pips at $100 per pip. If we hold on for a full year, we expect our break-even point to be 0.7710—the loss of 290 pips on 10 lots ($29,000) would be balanced by the anticipated gain of $29,000 in interest.

Remember that in all of the preceding examples, an entry point of 0.8000 is assumed, and we're also assuming that the exchange rate remains at that point. The trade could certainly go against us, so we need to have our stops in place. But isn't it nice to know that we can still break even on this trade, even if the exchange rate moves a few pips against us? Understanding and using this gives us a true advantage.

Of course, if the trade does move in our favor, that would be the best possible scenario. When this happens, some traders will pyramid into the gain—in other words, increase their position size as the exchange rate rises. I approve of this type of tactic, as long as the stop has been moved to the break-even point or higher. Pyramiding into gains is a great tactic for turning a good trade into an incredible gain. Talk about hitting it for six!

Unfortunately, most individuals will not pyramid into a gain—they are more likely to pyramid into a loss! They are not changing their lives for the better; they are using a tactic that will almost surely result in the end of their trading careers. Maybe it won't happen the first or second time, but sooner or later, this habit of adding to losses will catch up with them.

Another pyramiding tactic is to take the interest that we are collecting and use that to add to the size of the position; in other words, taking the interest from the AUD/USD trade and using it to buy more AUD/USD.

Yet another possibility is to take the interest and put it into a completely separate investment. That investment could be anything—another currency pair, U.S. Treasuries, shares of stock, or even commodities.

As traders, it is our duty to take any advantage, no matter how large or small, and make the most of it. That is exactly what traders are doing in the previous examples, and you could do it too.

A "COLUMBO" MOMENT

Now you know what to look for, both in terms of technical and fundamental analysis, in order to make money using this technique. Now that we've come this far, I want to add one more piece to this puzzle to make it complete.

There used to be an American television show called *Columbo*, in which a shoddy detective portrayed by Peter Falk would solve crimes. Every week, just when the criminal believed he'd gotten away with some dirty deed, Columbo, as he walked away, would turn to the smiling villain and say, "Just one more thing." Then he'd give his detailed analysis of the crime, which inevitably ended with the criminal in handcuffs.

Well, you're not a villain and I'm not a rumpled detective, but there is "just one more thing" that you need to know in order to really understand how the interest on this trade is calculated. You see, those interest rates set by central banks are not fixed rates. They are target rates.

A central bank can set a target for overnight lending rates (for example, the U.S. Fed Funds rate is an overnight target rate), but it cannot dictate to banks the exact rates at which they will lend and borrow money. The actual rates are determined by the supply of and demand for those loans, resulting in a constantly fluctuating overnight rate that is often slightly different from the central bank target rate.

While these differences may be slight—usually just a few basis points above or below the target rate—that difference could have an impact, either positive or negative, on the amount of interest you collect on a trade. This does not change the overall concept of the trade; it's just a fine point that deserved an explanation. Now you know!

A BAD HAIRCUT

A word of warning—when you receive interest payments from a broker, you might notice that in many cases, the size of the payment is a bit less than you imagined. In theory, the interest rollover should wash (the amount of interest collected should be the same as the amount paid by those on the other side of the trade). This discrepancy exists because there is a spread in the "swap" market, just as there is in every other financial instrument.

The bank charges your broker a spread on the interest, and the broker passes that charge on to you. Think of it as the price you pay in return for the bank's service of distributing the interest income from your carry trade.

It is also not unusual for your broker to take a little interest off the top; a "haircut," if you will. But is it a fair amount? Be careful—some brokers keep more of your interest than others.

Before you open your account, contact the broker and have them clearly explain how they intend to calculate rollover interest on your trades. It makes little sense to deal with a broker who plans to keep a lion's share of your interest. This should be a key factor in deciding which Forex broker you ultimately end up using, especially if you plan to make carry trades a big part of your overall trading plan.

SO WHY AREN'T YOU DOING IT?

The most amazing thing to me about the carry trade is that more people don't take advantage of it. Think about it: You can enter a trade and even if it doesn't go in your favor, you'll still make money as long as it doesn't move against you. The fact that you are collecting interest on the trade really stacks the odds in your favor. This is almost like cheating! But if it's so great, then why doesn't everyone do it?

That's a good question. I have heard every excuse you can imagine, but the truth is, most individuals simply don't want to trade this way. Most people assume that trading consists of pushing lots of buttons and entering lots of trades, of being glued to your screens like an air traffic controller and monitoring every tiny fluctuation in the markets. Trading can take this form, but that is not the only definition of trading, so please try to keep an open mind. You can certainly pursue an active trading style and participate in carry trades at the same time. If you can make money both ways, why wouldn't you?

In the final analysis, the carry trade requires knowledge, research, and patience. But remember, you are not going to be rewarded in this business based on the *quantity* of trades you place; you will be rewarded based on the *quality* of trades you place. One good trade will earn you more money than dozens of mediocre trades, so choose your battles carefully.

PART IV

COMMITMENT TO EXCELLENCE

CHAPTER 15

PURCHASING POWER PARITY AND THE BIG MAC INDEX

"Luck is a dividend of sweat. The more you sweat, the luckier you get."
—Ray Kroc, Founder, McDonald's Corporation

Now I'd like to introduce the concept of purchasing power parity, or PPP. Purchasing power parity can be best described as a valuation model for currencies. It is used by economists and long-term Forex traders to help determine if a currency is either undervalued or overvalued based on the prices of comparable goods. Purchasing power parity assumes that exchange rates will move to cause prices that are out of line to revert to a more "fair" valuation.

This concept is a little tricky, so let me begin with an example that is easy to digest. Imagine that you can purchase a hamburger in the United States for $2 USD. Okay, it is probably not a very good hamburger at that price, but I digress. The theory of purchasing power parity, or PPP, states that the same hamburger, purchased in a different country, should also have a value of $2 U.S. dollars, once the exchange rate is taken into consideration.

So, if one U.S. dollar is equal to 10 Mexican pesos (if USD/MXN exchange rate = 10.00), then the burger should be priced at 20 pesos in Mexico ($2 × 10 = 20 pesos). Or, if one British pound is equal to 2 U.S. dollars (GBP/USD currency pair is trading at 2.0000), this means that the same hamburger should cost about 1 British pound in the United Kingdom ($2 divided by 2.0000 = 1 GBP). Under these exchange rate scenarios, the burger would have the same value (2 USD) in Great Britain, Mexico, and the United States.

STRANGE BUT TRUE

I realize that this sounds completely insane, but there is an actual index, called the Big Mac Index, which has been featured in respected financial magazines like

TABLE 15.1 Price of a Big Mac in a Variety of Countries (Jan. 30, 2009)

	In Local Currency	In USD	Exchange Rate Jan 30, 2009	Under(−)/Over(+) Valuation vs. USD, %
United States*	$3.54	3.54	–	–
Argentina	Peso 11.50	3.30	3.49	−7
Australia	A$3.45	2.19	1.57	−38
Brazil	Real 8.02	3.45	2.32	−2
Britain	£ 2.29	3.30	1.44	−7
Canada	C$4.16	3.36	1.24	−5
Chile	Peso 1,550	2.51	617	−29
China	Yuan 12.5	1.83	6.84	−48

*Average of New York, Chicago, San Francisco, and Atlanta
Data source: Economist.com.

The Economist. The Big Mac Index compares the price of the popular McDonald's confection in a variety of countries and tries to determine which currencies are undervalued or overvalued based on this information (see Table 15.1).

Here's an example of the Big Mac Index at work: Based on the statistics in Table 15.1, a person buying a Big Mac in the United States can expect to pay $3.54. Meanwhile, a Big Mac purchased in China has a listed price of 12.5 Chinese yuan (CNY). The exchange rate at that time for USD/CNY at that time was 6.84.

According to the theory of purchasing power parity, that Big Mac from China should cost about 24.21 CNY ($3.54 × 6.84 = 24.21 CNY). This means that a Big Mac purchased in the United States costs nearly double the price of a big Mac purchased in China! Another way of looking at this would be to say that a Big Mac is undervalued in China by nearly 50 percent relative to its price in the United States.

GREASY TRANSACTION

Now let's extrapolate this greasy little transaction over two entire economies and make a broad assumption that other items sold in China are discounted to a similar degree. The theory of PPP states that the USD/CNY exchange rate should eventually move so that a Big Mac—and everything else that is easily obtainable in both the United States and China—will cost the same amount in both countries.

In the preceding example, the USD/CNY exchange rate would have to fall to 3.53 yuan per U.S. dollar in order for this to occur ($3.54 × 3.53 = 12.496). In order for the USD/CNY exchange rate to reach that level, the Chinese yuan would have to nearly double in value vs. the U.S. dollar, based on the given exchange rate of 6.84.

Now you know one reason why so many economists are calling for a huge increase in the value of the Chinese yuan relative to the U.S. dollar and other currencies, and why so many politicians and central bankers are screaming for China to allow their currency to float freely. By nearly every fundamental measure, including the Big Mac Index and purchasing power parity, China's currency is undervalued.

KING OF THE WORLD

Of course, the price of one hamburger tells us very little, and there are myriad reasons why an item may be priced differently in two countries. Maybe folks in China just don't care for the Big Mac or for McDonald's fare in general.

Anecdotally, I can tell you that in China, KFC and Pizza Hut seem to be the more popular choices for American fast food. Their parent company, Yum! Brands Inc., negotiated entry into China and gained a foothold prior to McDonald's, and as of this writing they have maintained that advantage.

In Shanghai, the visage of Colonel Sanders is omnipresent, peering down from the signage above ubiquitous KFCs with a tasty promise of Southern-fried greasiness. Huge advertisements bearing Sanders's likeness smile down at you from nearly every intersection. If I were a space alien and had just beamed down to Earth for the first time, I would think Colonel Sanders was the king of the world!

A RANDOM ITEM

So why is the Big Mac so much cheaper in China than in the United States? Perhaps it is a lack of demand that hinders the price of that sloppy burger in that country. Maybe people in China have a heightened awareness of the Big Mac's so-called "nutritional content," or perhaps they just have good taste. How can we account for all of the potential variables that might affect the price of a Big Mac, or of any other consumer item, for that matter?

The answer is simple: Economists don't really use a single random item such as a hamburger to determine the value of a currency. Instead, they apply the same valuation method as described above to a diversified basket of goods that covers everything from gas, fuel, and electricity to appliances, beverages, and tobacco.

Also factored into this equation are diverse elements such as rent, repair services, recreational equipment, and footwear. This gives economists a much wider sample of goods to work with, which has a tendency to smooth out the results. The basket of goods and services used to calculate PPP is actually similar to the goods and services used to determine gross domestic product, or GDP.

HELP IS ON THE WAY

Does all of this mean that you now have to calculate and compare the prices of a wide variety of goods in numerous countries around the world? If so, count me out. If that sounds like a lot of work, you're right, but luckily someone else is already doing the work for you. That someone else is the Organization for Economic Cooperation and Development (OECD), which calculates the PPP for a variety of currencies every month.

The results are published in a table format, which is meant to be read vertically. Each column shows the number of monetary units required to purchase the same basket

TABLE 15.2 Partial View of a Table of PPP Comparative Price Levels, Calculated Monthly by the OECD (March 2009)

Monetary Unit	CAD	MXN	USD	AUD	JPY	KRW	NZD
Canada	100	172	98	98	72	156	112
Mexico	58	100	57	57	42	91	65
United States	103	176	100	100	74	160	115
Australia	102	175	100	100	74	159	115
Japan	139	238	135	136	100	216	156
Korea	64	110	63	63	46	100	72
New Zealand*	89	153	87	87	64	139	100
Austria	117	201	114	115	85	183	132

*Secretariat estimates based on quarterly consumer prices.
Data source: Organization for Economic Cooperation and Development.

of goods and services, with parity represented by the figure 100. Currencies that are undervalued relative to the currency at the head of each vertical column will show a value below 100, and currencies that are overvalued will show a value greater than 100 (see Table 15.2).

In Table 15.2, we look to the currency at the top of the column and read down vertically. For example, under the column CAD we see the relative valuations for currencies vs. the Canadian dollar. In this column, Mexico receives a score of just 58, which is interpreted to mean that the peso is undervalued vs. the loonie. The score for New Zealand is 89, which could be interpreted to mean that the kiwi is also undervalued in comparison to the CAD, but to a much lesser extent than the Mexican peso.

The United States and Australia show values barely above 100, which are interpreted to mean that those currencies are fairly valued vs. the Canadian dollar. Finally, Japan's score of 139 means that the Japanese yen is most likely overvalued vs. the loonie and a good candidate to tumble vs. CAD in the near future.

The figures used in this table are from the OECD's calculations from March 2009. So how did CAD/JPY fare in the months that followed? Perhaps it's a coincidence, but the Canadian dollar rallied against the yen for several months, helping to push PPP closer to equilibrium (see Figure 15.1).

Note that in Table 15.2, the columns for MXN and KRW show high values virtually across the board, meaning that the Mexican peso and the South Korean won were undervalued against virtually all major currencies at this time. The low values across the board in the JPY column indicate that the yen was overvalued against virtually every major currency at the time this table was calculated.

Also sharing responsibility for these calculations is Eurostat, which keeps detailed statistics on European countries, including both members of the European Union and candidates for the EU. Roughly speaking, the OECD handles the PPP calculations for non-European countries, including Russia and Ukraine, and Eurostat covers the European nations. The end result is a joint calculation, fittingly called the Joint OECD-Eurostat Programme.

FIGURE 15.1 In spring 2009, CAD gains vs. JPY, which was overvalued according to PPP.
Source: Created with TradeStation.

GUSTAV CASSEL

So who came up with this brilliant idea in the first place? Credit is widely given to an influential Swedish economist named Gustav Cassel (1866–1945). Cassel believed that if purchasing power parity between two countries was in a state of disequilibrium, then the exchange rate or the purchasing power would adjust until equilibrium was eventually achieved. Cassel's theories go well beyond the scope of this book, but here is the simple, short version:

If the same refrigerator costs half as much to buy in Country A as it does in Country B, then folks in Country B will tend to buy refrigerators manufactured in Country A. This will drive up the price of refrigerators in Country A, due to high demand, and drives the price of a fridge down in Country B, where, sadly, the refrigerator merchants have been reduced to watching soap operas all day. This brings the prices of the two refrigerators closer to equilibrium.

This situation could also be described as *arbitrage*, and it assumes that the refrigerators are of similar quality. Arbitrage opportunities occur when the price of an item varies in different markets. The item could be a refrigerator, or an automobile, or even a stock or a commodity that trades on more than one exchange.

While the scenario might work well with refrigerators, it might not work as well with hamburgers, due to things like the cost of transportation—not to mention the fact that the hamburger might not be in very good condition by the time it arrived in Country B. Still, there is an undeniable logic to the overall concept of PPP.

NAKED IN A PARKING LOT

Finally, here's an interesting example of purchasing power parity at work. In late 2007, the Canadian dollar made huge, rapid gains against the U.S. dollar. The USD/CAD exchange rate shot from 1.0860 to 0.9050 in just under five months—a move of over 1,800 pips (see Figure 15.2).

As a result, the loonie achieved parity with the greenback for the first time in over 30 years—and then shot well beyond parity. Traders who were looking for support levels on USD/CAD had to dig out their disco boots, because the exchange rate reached levels that hadn't been seen since the mid-1970s (see Figure 15.3).

At about the same time, mysterious piles of used clothing began to materialize in the parking lots of U.S. cities near the U.S./Canadian border. What was going on? As the loonie grew stronger, items sold in the United States (which are valued in U.S. dollars) quickly became cheaper for Canadian citizens, so Canadians were crossing the border in droves to purchase new clothing from U.S. malls and shopping centers.

But what about the mysterious piles of used clothing? In order to evade duties and taxes that would be levied if they were caught bringing newly purchased goods back across the border from the United States, some Canadians were simply wearing their old clothes to the United States, ditching them in the parking lot, and wearing their new clothes home. Obviously, border officials are much more likely to search a package from a mall, as opposed to the clothing on one's back.

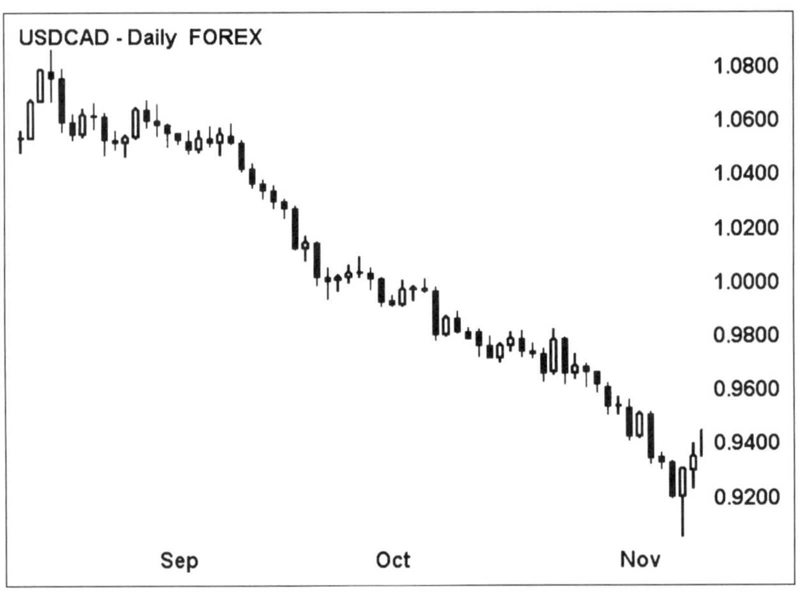

FIGURE 15.2 CAD gains sharply vs. USD, creating supply/demand imbalances.
Source: Created with TradeStation. © TradeStation Technologies, Inc. All rights reserved.

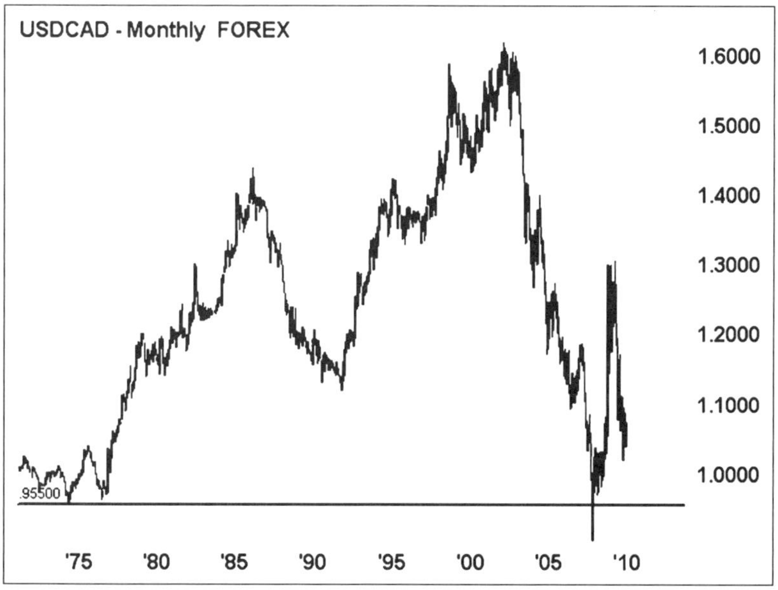

FIGURE 15.3 USD/CAD reaches parity for the first time since the 1970s.
Source: Created with TradeStation.

Meanwhile, clothing stores on the U.S. side of the border were selling out of merchandise, so to compensate, some of them raised prices to a level comparable to the real cost of similar goods on the Canadian side of the border, as measured from the perspective of a Canadian consumer. When the U.S. stores raised their prices, it brought the U.S. and Canada just a bit closer to equilibrium, at least where the cost of clothing is concerned.

TIME HORIZON

It's worth mentioning that purchasing power parity is a long-term valuation model, and these valuations tend to play out over a period measured in years, so it is not very helpful to day traders. Isn't it interesting that the longer term trader has so many tools at his or her disposal, while at the same time, many short-term traders have basically stacked the deck against themselves?

Remember, when using PPP it makes no sense to compare items that are not easily obtainable in a variety of places. For example, if a country has no McDonald's restaurants, then the price of a Big Mac in that location might be inflated due to the difficulty involved in obtaining one. Tariffs and taxes also can distort the equation, as they nearly did in the example of Canadians crossing the border to purchase U.S. clothing, so economists must account for any relevant transaction costs.

Now that you understand purchasing power parity and how to use it, it's time to move on to the next subject—but not before one last quote from McDonald's entrepreneur Ray Kroc, in honor of the Big Mac Index. Mr. Kroc wasn't known for trading, but he certainly had words of wisdom to share.

> "If you work just for money, you'll never make it, but if you love what you're doing and you always put the customer first, success will be yours."
>
> *—Ray Kroc, Founder, McDonald's Corporation*

CHAPTER 16

"SHOULD I GO LONG THE LOBSTER, OR THE FILET MIGNON?"

"The fate of the nation and the fate of the currency are one and the same."

—Dr. Franz Pick, Economist and Currency Analyst

When things are going badly, people often take extraordinary measures to try to set things right. Maybe you have encountered something similar in your own life. Sometimes these measures work, and sometimes they just make a bad situation worse.

Central banks also encounter this problem: When the economy goes into a tailspin, should we let markets sort themselves out, or should we take extraordinary measures to affect the markets directly? If the central bank does decide to take action, it has to weigh the pros and cons. Will the desire for a short-term gain inadvertently lead to long-term pain? Will their actions really help—and what will be the consequences of those actions?

QUANTITATIVE EASING

Quantitative easing is a way of pouring money into a cash-starved banking system. It is a "last resort" for central banks that have already cut interest rates to the bone and are still seeking ways to stimulate their economies.

In quantitative easing, which is sometimes referred to as "queasing," commercial banks receive cash from the central bank in exchange for government bonds and other investments, which helps the banks to build up their cash reserves. The central bank hopes that the commercial banks will then pass that money on in the form of loans to businesses and consumers, thus generating economic activity and stimulating the economy. Central banks buy their own government's bonds in an effort to drive down long-term interest rates, also in an effort to stimulate the economy.

Quantitative easing was practiced by Japan when it faced deflation—a period of falling prices—from 2001 until 2006. After the Japanese economic bubble burst during the 1990s, the Bank of Japan cut interest rates to zero. Still seeking further stimulus in 2001 and unable to reduce rates further, the BoJ introduced quantitative easing.

"QE" also has the effect of weakening the currency, which suited the Bank of Japan just fine. The tactic was also widely used by the United States, the United Kingdom, and other countries during the financial crisis of 2008 and 2009.

INVERSE RELATIONSHIP

When implementing this practice, a central bank purchases their own bonds, which pushes the price of those bonds higher. When bond prices rise, the yield of the bonds—the interest rate—is pushed lower. As we mentioned earlier, it can be said that when it comes to bonds, price and yield have an inverse relationship—when one goes up, the other goes down.

Central banks can target specific bond maturities in order to achieve a desired effect. For example, if a government buys 10-year or 30-year bonds, thus lowering the yields on those bonds, this may have the indirect effect of lowering mortgage rates (most of which are long-term loans, with their interest rates tied to long-term bond yields).

This indirect lowering of mortgage rates is intended to stimulate the housing market, which makes up a big portion of any developed economy. Construction workers, loan officers, carpet manufacturers, real estate agents, appliance makers, and people who work for hardware stores such as Lowe's or The Home Depot are some of the many who stand to benefit from a strong housing market.

THE DOWNSIDE OF QUANTITATIVE EASING

There is a downside to quantitative easing: First and foremost, where is the money to buy the bonds coming from? If central banks are simply printing money—literally creating money out of thin air—to buy the bonds, they run the risk of damaging and devaluing the currency. If the money to purchase the bonds is being borrowed, then future generations may be saddled with that debt.

By the way, although quantitative easing is often described as "printing money," often no new notes and coins are actually created. Instead, a central bank "creates" more money on its balance sheet (imagine if you could draw a few zeros on the end of your bank account balance) and then uses this money to buy the assets of commercial banks, such as home loans and government bonds, thereby pumping extra cash into the system.

The commercial banks have accounts with the central bank, and the new money will simply be credited to those accounts. In this scenario, you could say that the new funds are created electronically, as opposed to physically.

But will the money go to where it is needed, or will the banks hoard the cash to help deal with their own problems? The central bank has little control over what happens to that money after it enters the banking system.

HYPERINFLATION

What happens when you add too much money to the supply? When central banks print too much money, they turn the currency into worthless paper and create inflation, which can spin out of control into hyperinflation. This damages the quality of life in the country, as years of hard work and diligent saving can suddenly evaporate.

For example, in Zimbabwe, poor financial management by the Mugabe government at one point created an inflation rate of 98 percent *per day*! Try to imagine nearly 100 percent inflation per day: An item that costs $1 on Monday would cost $2 on Tuesday, $4 on Wednesday, and $8 by Thursday. By Friday, the item that cost $1 on Monday now costs $16! Zimbabwe's hyperinflation rate during November 2008 places it among the all-time worst cases, according to Professor Steve H. Hanke of Johns Hopkins University and the Cato Institute (see Table 16.1).

By the way, according to Professor's Hanke Hyperinflation Index for Zimbabwe (HHIZ), by November 2008, inflation reached a monthly rate of *79.6 billion percent*, and an annual rate of *89.7 sextillion percent*.

After that, he stopped compiling the figures. Perhaps he ran out of numbers!

HOW TO LOSE EVERYTHING

The Reserve Bank of Zimbabwe kept printing higher and higher denominations of currency in an attempt to keep up with runaway inflation. Eventually, a 100 trillion dollar

TABLE 16.1 Highest Monthly Inflation Rates in History

Country	Month with Highest Inflation Rate	Highest Monthly Inflation Rate	Equivalent Daily Inflation Rate	Time Required for Prices to Double
Hungary	Jul 1946	1.30×10^{16}%	195%	15.6 Hours
Zimbabwe	Mid-November 2008 (latest measurable)	79,600,000,000%	98.0%	24.7 Hours
Yugoslavia	Jan 1994	313,000,000%	64.6%	1.4 Days
Germany	Oct 1923	29,500%	20.9%	3.7 Days
Greece	Nov 1944	11,300%	17.1%	4.5 Days
China	May 1949	4,210%	13.4%	5.6 Days

Source: Professor Steve H. Hanke, February 5, 2009.

FIGURE 16.1 A 100 trillion Zimbabwe dollar note was issued in an attempt to keep up with runaway inflation.
Source: Reserve Bank of Zimbabwe.

note was introduced in an attempt to keep pace with the hyperinflation that they themselves created by printing too much money (see Figure 16.1).

Think for a minute about how it must feel to be a hardworking Zimbabwean who, through years of sweat and ingenuity, has managed to save up 25 million Zimbabwe dollars. You are considered wealthy, and you've earned every dollar.

Then, slowly at first but then at an escalating pace, your nest egg loses its value. You still have your 25 million Zimbabwe dollars; the problem is 25 million is not enough to buy a loaf of bread! You are now so poor that you can't afford to feed yourself. This is what can happen during periods of hyperinflation, and why it must be avoided at all costs.

YOUR MONEY'S NO GOOD HERE—LITERALLY

One night I was watching the international news, and they showed a merchant in Zimbabwe selling food from the back of a truck. Surrounding the truck were men waving white pieces of paper, which turned out to be gasoline coupons. The buyers were bidding with coupons because the merchant would not accept cash. Who could blame him?

Zimbabwe had collapsed into a barter system: Nobody wanted Zimbabwean currency, but at least a gasoline coupon held some value. Everywhere, people began to barter goods and services, because the currency had no value. Eventually, Zimbabwe scrapped its worthless currency and decided instead to use the U.S. dollar as its primary currency. Talk about jumping out of the frying pan and into the fire!

The phenomenon of a central bank or government destroying its own currency is nothing new; in fact, it has been going on for centuries. Usually, the collapse of a major

FIGURE 16.2 Hyperinflation in the Weimar Republic led to the introduction of a 500 million mark note.
Source: Goldinformant.com.

empire coincides with the debasement of its currency. For example, in the latter days of the Roman Empire, the silver content of coins was slowly decreased over time, reflecting increased inflation and empty tax coffers.

The waning days of the British Empire saw sharp losses and devaluations in the British pound, which was the world's most important currency in the years prior to World War I. The pound was soon to be supplanted as the world's reserve currency by the U.S. dollar.

In Germany in the early 1920s, during the days of the Weimar Republic, a currency collapse led to social unrest and created a climate that allowed the Nazi party to gain political control, with disastrous consequences. Unlike our earlier examples, this episode of hyperinflation was touched off in part by demands for German reparations after World War I. Just as in Zimbabwe, this episode of hyperinflation led to the introduction of larger denominations of currency, such as the 500 million mark note (see Figure 16.2).

You can read more about hyperinflation in the Weimar Republic in books like *The Black Obelisk* by Erich M. Remarque (Simon Publications, 2002).

YES, IT CAN HAPPEN HERE

I realize that I'm writing for an international audience, and I'm grateful for that opportunity. However, I'm alarmed by what is happening in my country, the United States. Despite all of history's warnings, just a few of which are listed in previous paragraphs, the United States has embarked on a huge campaign of printing and borrowing money. We seem to have convinced ourselves that we are going to "spend our way out of debt."

On several occasions, I have been told by certain economists and market observers that "it can't happen here"—in other words, if the Fed goes wild and prints too much money, somehow this will not have a negative impact on the quality of life in the United States. My response is that not only can it happen here, it already has.

In the years immediately following the American Revolution, the U.S. currency, then referred to as the continental, was debased and eventually became worthless. This occurred because there was nothing "behind" the fledgling currency—it was not backed by silver or gold. Essentially, it was an easily counterfeited IOU.

With all of the damage created throughout history via debased currencies and hyperinflation, why do governments and central banks still pursue this policy in the 21st century? Why would any country risk its very existence in this manner?

Perhaps they belong to a Keynesian school of economic thought. John Maynard Keynes, an influential twentieth century economist, believed that economies could be actively managed with positive effect.

Another possible reason for the debasement of a currency could be summed up in a single word—power. Think of the power that a government possesses when it can simply snap its fingers and make money appear out of thin air. The ruling government can then allocate those funds as it sees fit, both by pursuing its policies and by rewarding its supporters.

As the funds are selectively apportioned, the supporters of the ruling government become richer, and as the currency loses value, those who oppose the government become poorer. Obviously, the goal is not to make the currency worthless (essentially making everyone a pauper), but as we've seen, it's been known to happen.

That kind of power makes for a forceful aphrodisiac—especially to leaders who don't really care about the well-being of their populace—and those who possess it are not likely to loosen their grasp.

HERE'S HOW THEY GET YOU

When a government tries to sell the idea of a debasing the currency to the populace, they always rely on this old chestnut: A weak currency is good for exports. This is true: A country with a weak currency tends to sell more goods to its overseas customers. But what they don't tell you is this—because your currency is weak, you won't be able to afford those imported goods you love so dearly. As your currency falls, the prices of imported goods skyrocket.

So why don't we just buy things that are manufactured in our home country? Wouldn't that solve the problem of higher import prices? Unfortunately, it's not that simple when you live in a global economy.

For example, the United States can't simply decide to stop importing oil tomorrow. If the greenback collapses, the price of oil will scale untold new heights. The rally to $147 per barrel in 2008 will seem like the good old days if the dollar is allowed to collapse. High energy prices tend to have a ripple effect through an economy, as the cost of transporting any manufactured product, imported or domestic, rises.

SELF-DEFENSE

So how can you protect yourself? Many have turned to gold and other hard assets due to a lack of confidence in the U.S. dollar. Gold is considered a safe haven, but it is not immune to bubbles. I recently drove past a gasoline (petrol) station that had draped a huge banner down the side of the building. The banner featured three words in six-foot-high block letters: "WE BUY GOLD."

I've also noticed TV commercials in which '80s rap phenomenon M.C. Hammer implores viewers to sell their gold. This invites the following question: Should we really take investment advice from a formerly bankrupt rapper? Is he a contrarian indicator? In other words, if he says "sell," should we consider buying?

While the appreciation of the yellow metal may be justified on fundamental levels, such as central bank purchases, there is also an element of speculative froth around the edges, so be careful. That being said, every portfolio should contain at least some minor exposure to gold and other "hard goods" as a hedge against inflation and potential USD weakness.

In the end, your best defense against losing your wealth though the debasement of currency is knowledge. Now that you know about the Roman Empire, the British Empire, the Weimar Republic, and Zimbabwe, don't keep it a secret. Americans in particular need to learn more about this, because we have no collective memory of hyperinflation in our country. Let's not repeat the mistakes of the past.

Finally, I was speaking with a bond trader the other day. Several years ago, he and some colleagues were in Argentina on business. They were having lunch when they realized that the menu prices were increasing *as they ate.* As the trip wore on, this happened every day; in fact, it could happen several times during the course of a meal. I asked him how they responded.

"Well, being traders, everyone wanted to bet on which meal would increase the most in value," he said. "Should I go long the lobster, or the filet mignon?"

CHAPTER 17

SWAPS AND SPREADS

"The market can remain irrational longer than you can remain solvent."

—John Maynard Keynes, Noted Economist

Fear can be your friend. I don't mean that you should be afraid when you trade, because emotion, either positive or negative, is not your friend in the trading markets. But when the market itself shows a high degree of fear and panic, the results can be somewhat predictable.

If you can remain calm—and solvent—while everyone around you is losing their cool, you just might be able to use that fear in a constructive way. Let's look at how currencies behave under extreme conditions of stress—which currencies will benefit, which ones will fall, and why?

LIBOR PAINS

LIBOR is an acronym for London Interbank Offered Rate, the rate that banks charge each other for short-term, unsecured loans. It is a widely used benchmark for short-term interest rates, and it can be used as a general gauge of the health of the credit markets.

When banks are comfortable lending money to other banks, the LIBOR rates tend to fall; however, when money is tight and banks are less willing to lend, or if there is fear that a bank may default on a loan, the LIBOR rate rises. Nobody wants to be the person who loans money to a financial institution right before it goes under, so when banks are in crisis mode, LIBOR is on the rise.

Why would a bank need an overnight loan? They might need the money to meet reserve requirements—the amount of money that a bank is required to hold in cash or on deposit. When central banks want to restrict lending, they raise reserve requirements,

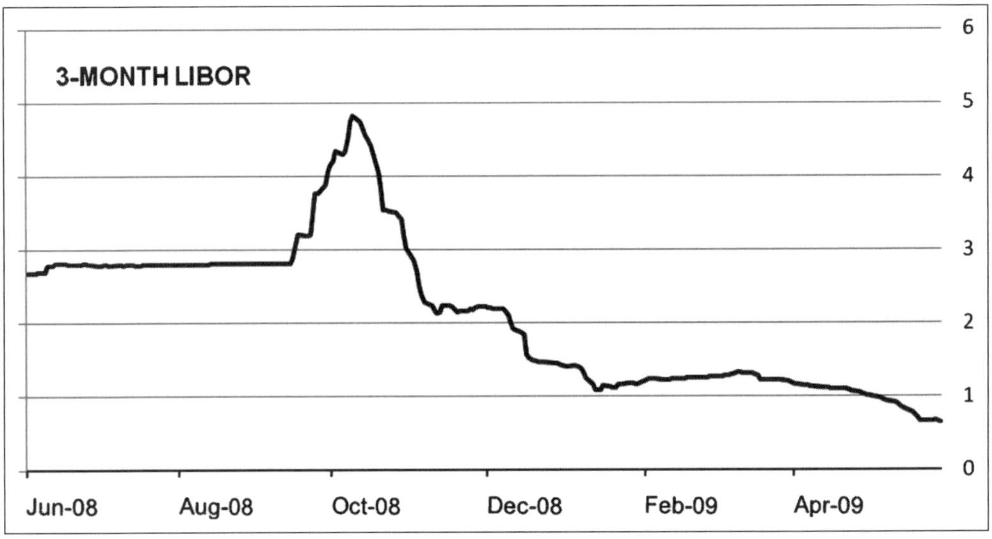

FIGURE 17.1 3-month LIBOR chart spikes in fall 2008.

forcing the banks to hold on to more capital. If banks have to keep more capital in-house, they will have less money available to lend. Sometimes, an overnight loan is needed to meet these reserve requirements (see Figure 17.1).

The spike on the LIBOR chart in the fall of 2008 coincided with the demise of Lehman Brothers, a huge U.S. investment bank. Because the U.S. government chose to allow Lehman to fail instead of providing a bailout, banks immediately raised the cost of overnight loans to other banks. At the time, the banks didn't know if other institutions would be allowed to fail—including banks to which they might be lending money. So, the banks demanded higher rates for overnight loans in return for the increased risk.

Soon afterward, the U.S. and other governments embarked on a series of bailouts of financial institutions, which in turn led to bailouts of companies in other industries. The bailouts effectively soothed the banks; eventually, there might be negative consequences related to creating and injecting huge sums of capital into the U.S. economy, but at least the banks knew that if they made an overnight loan to another bank, they would get their money back. As fear subsided, LIBOR fell dramatically.

GREASING THE WHEELS

Money is the grease that keeps the wheels of an economy turning, and when banks are afraid to lend money, there are negative consequences. The more concerned banks become about repayment, the more they will charge other banks for overnight loans. Banks can also become reluctant to lend money to businesses, which can hurt job creation and stifle economic growth. Sometimes, banks may hoard capital because of their own negative financial situation; more than just stinginess, it may be out of fear for their own survival.

Unlike interest rates set by central banks, LIBOR rates are determined by supply and demand. The British Bankers' Association (BBA) surveys 16 major banks, asking them what rates they are charging other banks for overnight loans. When the BBA receives the 16 different rates, they eliminate the four highest and the four lowest, and calculate the average of the remaining eight. The BBA conducts this survey every day.

Many adjustable-rate mortgages are tied to LIBOR. LIBOR comes in a variety of maturities, but the 3-month LIBOR is the most closely followed. Traders are less interested in the actual LIBOR rate itself than they are in comparing it to other rates, such as the Overnight Index Swap rate (OIS rate) and the 3-month T-bill rate.

THE DOLLAR AND THE YEN

How can we use this information to make money? When fear is high, traders rush to safe havens, such as the U.S. dollar. Frightened investors sell stocks on exchanges around the world; they often put the proceeds of these equity sales into U.S. Treasuries, and in order to do this, they need to obtain U.S. dollars.

Therefore, an increase in a fear gauge such as LIBOR is generally good news for the U.S. dollar. This is true even when that fear is the result of a negative event that occurred in the United States, such as the demise of Lehman Brothers (see Figure 17.2).

FIGURE 17.2 USD Index skyrockets in fall 2008 as Lehman Brothers collapses.
Source: Created with TradeStation. © TradeStation Technologies, Inc. All rights reserved.

But fear can benefit currencies other than the U.S. dollar. For example, if central banks slash rates in anticipation of a recession, currencies that traditionally offer a low yield, such as the Japanese yen, tend to benefit.

If rates around the world are falling, there is less incentive to place trades based on interest rate differentials. When traders perceive that rates will fall and differentials are going to tighten, they close carry trades. Since many carry trades feature a short position in JPY, falling rates can lead to a short-covering rally in the Japanese yen and other so-called "funding" currencies.

THE TED SPREAD

The TED spread is another one of the great "fear gauges" of the financial markets. A rising TED spread indicates growing concern among bankers and leads to tighter credit, while a falling TED spread indicates that credit is easing and banks are more willing to lend to other financial institutions.

The TED spread actually got its name from the two financial instruments it compares—the 3-month Treasury bill (T-bill) and the Eurodollar futures contract. Simply take the "T" from T-bill and combine it with the ticker symbol for the Eurodollar futures contract ("ED"), and the result is TED.

The Eurodollar futures contract simply reflects the 3-month LIBOR rate, so you could say that we are comparing a 3-month Treasury bill (which is considered a risk-free loan to the U.S. government) to the 3-month LIBOR, which is the going rate for lending money to another bank. But why would anyone want to make such a comparison?

Let's suppose that a bank has money to lend and has several options—the bank can either lend the money to another bank at the prevailing LIBOR rate, or it can make a risk-free loan to Uncle Sam by purchasing a short-term T-bill. Theoretically, a loan to a bank, which entails risk, should always net the lender a higher rate of return than a loan that is *guaranteed* by the U.S. government. Ah, but *how much* higher is the question!

The answer depends on fear. If credit is flowing freely and banks are stable, the lender will receive little "extra credit" for loaning money to the bank. However, if credit markets are in turmoil, banks will become reluctant to lend to other banks and will only do so at a hefty premium. This risk-averse attitude on the part of the lenders will cause the Eurodollar rate (3-month LIBOR) to climb.

Instead of making risky loans, banks may opt to simply put funds into U.S. Treasuries, a noted safe haven in troubled times. The more frightened investors become, the more capital they will stash away in U.S. Treasuries, including the 3-month Treasury bill.

This will drive the price of a 3-month T-bill higher, which at the same time causes the yield to move lower. As you know, in the fixed-income market, price and yield share an inverse relationship, meaning that when prices rise, yields fall. In times of extreme fear, the yield on a 3-month T-bill has been known to fall virtually to zero, as panicked traders rush to the safety of the U.S. government–backed investment.

To summarize, when fear is high, banks demand higher return for short-term loans to other banks. This causes the Eurodollar contract (3-month LIBOR) to rise. Meanwhile, scared investors tend to place more capital in safe Treasury bills, causing the yield on the 3-month T-bill to fall. As the yields on these two instruments move farther apart, the "spread"—in this case meaning the difference between the two interest rates—begins to rise. A rising TED spread is the hallmark of a fearful market.

Eventually, this fear will pass, and banks will become more willing to lend to one another. At that point, banks will begin to pull their money out of U.S. Treasuries (causing the 3-month T-bill's price to fall and its yield to rise) and lend it to other banks (causing the 3-month LIBOR to fall, and with it the Eurodollar futures contract). As the difference or "spread" between the 3-month T-bill and the 3-month LIBOR narrows, the TED spread falls, indicating that fear is easing and credit is easing along with it (see Figure 17.3).

In Figure 17.3, we see a great example of the TED spread at work. On the left side of the chart, the TED spread is approximately 1 percent (100 basis points), meaning that banks are getting an extra 1 percent return from lending to other banks than they would receive by simply buying 3-month T-bills.

Then, in late September 2008, fear spikes higher (along with the TED spread) as Lehman Brothers Holdings Inc., a major U.S. investment bank, is allowed to fail. This shocks the financial markets, because even though rumors of Lehman's impending demise had been circulating for months, markets had held out hope that a last-minute rescue would be engineered.

Suddenly, banks became very reluctant to lend money to other banks, as rumors swirled that more trouble was on the way. Fears of a widespread collapse abounded. The TED spread shot higher in response and stayed at astronomical levels (at one point

FIGURE 17.3 The TED spread spikes as lenders become fearful, and then falls as lenders regain confidence.

exceeding 450 basis points), until the U.S. and other world governments made it clear that they would stand behind the banks, offering financial backing and where necessary, bailouts. When this was made clear, the markets breathed a sigh of relief, and the TED spread returned to normal levels.

FLIGHT TO SAFETY

How can we put this information to good use? When investors are frightened and the TED spread is rising, the U.S. dollar tends to benefit (see Figure 17.4).

Why does the USD benefit? If investors are scared, they might sell stocks that are listed on exchanges all around the world. If they sell shares listed on the Barcelona Stock Exchange, they will receive euros in return, and if they sell stocks traded on the Sao Paulo Stock Exchange, they'll receive Brazilian Real. An international hedge fund manager who is bailing out of global equity markets may find his or her accounts flush with euros, Brazilian real, British pounds, and a dozen other currencies.

In order to invest these funds in U.S. Treasuries, these currencies must now be exchanged for U.S. dollars. If this behavior is repeated by other fund managers around the world, massive purchases of U.S. dollars will cause the greenback to rise sharply. This is one reason why the U.S. dollar performs well in troubled times.

What other currencies might benefit from a spike in the TED spread? Once again, consider the Japanese yen, a currency that tends to have a very low yield. The JPY is often used as a funding currency for the carry trade due to low interest rates in Japan. The success of the carry trade is dependent upon a significant differential between low- and high-yielding currencies.

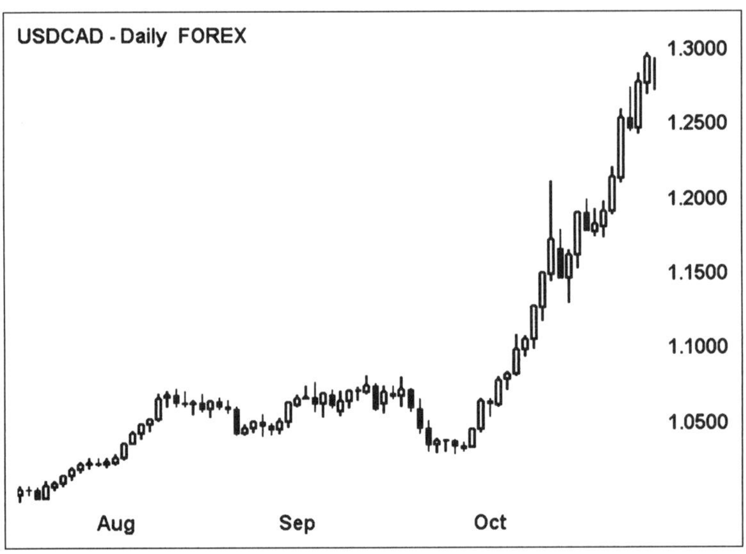

FIGURE 17.4 USD exhibits strength vs. CAD as the TED spread spikes in fall 2008.
Source: Created with TradeStation.

FIGURE 17.5 As the RBNZ slashed interest rates, traders closed long positions in NZD/JPY.
Source: Created with TradeStation.

Well, if the world's financial markets descend into panic, what type of reaction should we expect from central banks? Certainly lower interest rates would be expected. When faced with dire economic circumstances, the type of which may lead to a recession (or worse), it's normal for a central bank to cut rates—sometimes deeply.

For example, in 2008–2009, when New Zealand's central bank, the RBNZ, slashed its benchmark rate from a high of 8.25 percent all the way down to 2.5 percent, NZD/JPY took a hard tumble. The pair fell because the kiwi no longer possessed an attractive differential vs. the yen (see Figure 17.5).

A closer look at New Zealand's benchmark rate history reveals the speed and decisiveness that the RBNZ wielded in reducing its OCR yield from 8.25 percent to 2.5 percent (see Table 17.1).

As global rates fell and interest rate differentials grew narrow, the Japanese yen put in a strong performance vs. other currencies as well—even against the surging U.S. dollar, as indicated by the futures chart in Figure 17.6.

SOMEWHAT PREDICTABLE

However, the tide must turn eventually; fear is never a permanent state, it is always temporary. At some point, the equity markets will bottom out and start to look good again. Just as the behavior of frightened traders is somewhat predictable, so is their behavior as the markets transition back to "normal."

Subsiding fear will lead to an embracement of risk. Investors seeking better returns will sell their low-yielding, safe-haven investments and use the proceeds to dive back

TABLE 17.1 RBNZ Slashes Rates in 2008–2009

Date	OCR Rate
Dec 2009	2.50
Apr 2009	2.50
Mar 2009	3.00
Jan 2009	3.50
Dec 2008	5.00
Oct 2008	6.50
Sep 2008	7.50
Jul 2008	8.00
Jul 2007	8.25
Jun 2007	8.00
Apr 2007	7.75

Source: Reserve Bank of New Zealand.

into the equity markets. Eventually, traders will sell their U.S. Treasuries and invest the proceeds into dozens of markets, both in the United States and around the world.

When this happens, it causes money to flow out of the United States, in order to embrace risk and seek high returns. It will flow to places like the BRIC nations (Brazil, Russian, India, and China). Simply follow the money: When money is flowing out of the United States, it becomes very likely that the U.S. dollar will fall. If global interest rates

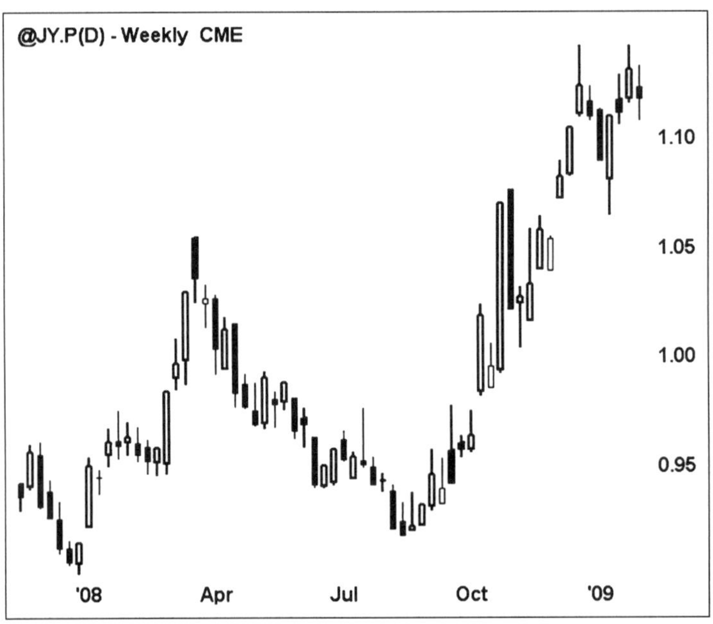

FIGURE 17.6 JPY futures chart indicates a strong yen vs. USD during the Lehman Brothers crisis.
Source: Created with TradeStation.

rise, it becomes very likely that the Japanese yen will fall as interest rate differentials grow fatter, igniting interest in the carry trade.

OVERNIGHT INDEX SWAP

Traders are less concerned with the absolute value of LIBOR than they are with LIBOR's comparison with the Overnight Index Swap (OIS). What is the OIS? If you've ever refinanced a mortgage loan, then understanding OIS—the Overnight Index Swap rate—should be a breeze.

Suppose you own a house with a variable-rate mortgage, and you fear that mortgage rates will be moving higher. You'd probably want to lock in a fixed-interest rate so that your mortgage payments will remain stable in the future.

But perhaps your neighbor feels differently, and he believes interest rates will be moving lower. He wants to trade in his fixed-rate mortgage for a variable-rate loan. What sorts of options are available to the two neighbors?

Each of them could drop by the local bank, pay a visit to the loan officer, and refinance their mortgages, but there will be fees for processing the new loans, and there may be penalties for terminating the existing loans. Perhaps the expenses involved in refinancing the properties would outweigh the benefits of the new loan terms.

A BRILLIANT IDEA

Suddenly, you and your neighbor hit upon a brilliant idea! Each of you will continue to make payments on your current loans, but you agree to swap the *terms* of the loans.

For instance, let's say you were correct in your assumption that interest rates would move higher; because you possess a variable-rate mortgage, your payments will increase. But that's no longer your problem, as your neighbor has assumed the terms of your loan. You will have to pay the higher rate on your loan, but your neighbor has agreed to pay the difference back to you.

So, if your monthly payment increases by $100, you must still make the payment, but your neighbor now owes you $100 per month. He has assumed the interest rate risk (remember, he thought rates would move lower). This effectively gives you a fixed-rate loan, even though you did not actually refinance your mortgage.

On the other hand, suppose your neighbor had been correct and rates fell. In this case, you would not have benefited from this drop in interest rates—even though you still possess a variable-rate loan. If your payments fall by $100, then you'll owe your neighbor $100—again, even though your loan has a variable rate, you have agreed to swap the terms.

From your perspective, you now have fixed-rate terms, even though your actual loan has a variable rate. Meanwhile, your neighbor enjoys the benefits of your lower rate, even though his actual rate is still fixed. If you understood the preceding paragraphs, congratulations! You now have a basic understanding of swaps.

LIBOR/OIS SPREAD

Although there may not be a large number of homeowners swapping their mortgage terms, there is a huge market for institutional swaps, especially for overnight loans. Similarly, in an OIS swap, two banks exchange the terms of their loans.

Let's suppose that two banks owe money on loans: Bank A pays interest on their loan at a fixed rate, while Bank B's loan varies based on fluctuations in an overnight rate. Perhaps Bank A believes that rates are headed lower and would prefer a variable rate, while Bank B takes the opposite view: They believe rates are headed higher and would prefer to lock in a fixed rate for their loan.

The banks could simply get new loans, but this isn't always feasible or cost effective. A better tactic might be for the two banks to trade, or swap, the terms of their respective loans. If the swap is made, Bank A effectively now has the variable loan it desired, while Bank B now enjoys the fixed loan terms formerly owned by Bank A.

In reality, each bank continues to service its current loan under its current terms, so Bank A is really still holding the fixed-rate loan, and Bank B still holds the variable-rate loan. Only the terms of the loans have been swapped, not the loans themselves.

If the interest rate on Bank B's variable-rate loan falls, it must pay the difference to Bank A. In this case, Bank A would benefit from its correct assumption that the overnight rate would fall. Bank B now holds the fixed-rate terms of Bank A's original loan, so Bank B cannot take advantage of the lower overnight rate; they are stuck with fixed-rate terms.

There are many players in this game, and all of them might be paying slightly different rates—in fact, the rates can vary on an intraday basis. In order to get a general idea of what banks are paying for overnight loans, the Overnight Index Swap rate is calculated daily. The OIS rate is based on the average interest rate paid during that day by institutions on overnight loans.

THE SPREAD

Now that we understand both LIBOR and the OIS, how do we use this information? We're not too concerned with either of these figures individually; traders and analysts are more concerned with the relationship between these two rates. Typically, LIBOR is higher than the Overnight Index Swap rate, and the spread between the two represents the price of risk.

When banks or institutions swap interest rates, one is not lending money to the other; they are simply exchanging the terms of their loans. LIBOR, on the other hand, represents

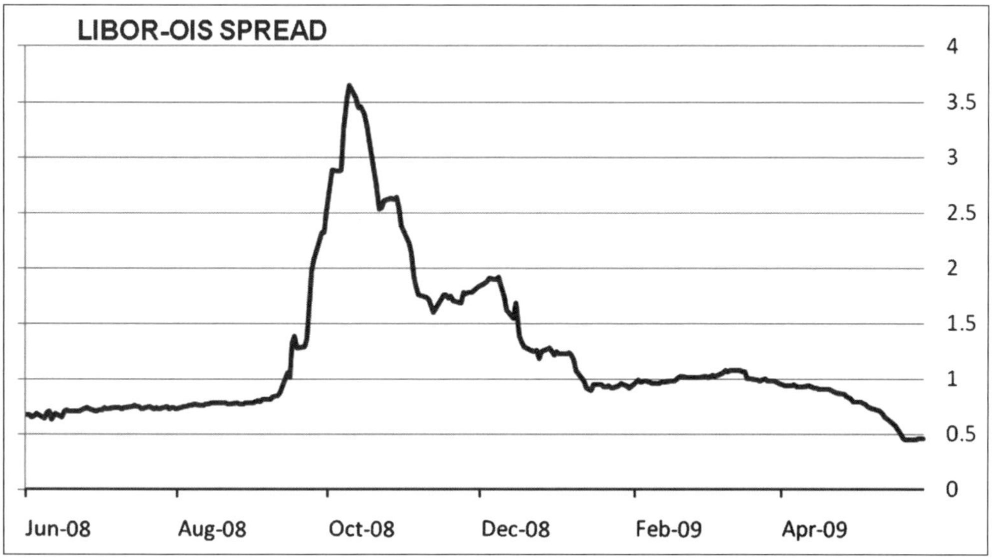

FIGURE 17.7 The LIBOR-OIS spread chart shows an increase and then a decrease in risk.

greater risk, as the money is changing hands from one bank to another. Because LIBOR represents the greater risk, it should also feature a higher rate.

So, the amount by which LIBOR exceeds the OIS is the LIBOR-OIS spread, which represents the price of risk. For example, if LIBOR equals 4.5 percent and the OIS equals 3.5 percent, then the LIBOR-OIS spread would be 1 percent. Figure 17.7 is a chart of the LIBOR-OIS spread.

When credit is tight, the spread between LIBOR and OIS widens. When the LIBOR-OIS spread is increasing, it tells us that banks believe the other banks they are lending to have a higher risk of defaulting on the loans, so they are charging a higher interest rate to offset this risk.

On the other hand, when credit is easy, the spread between LIBOR and OIS narrows. When the LIBOR-OIS spread is decreasing, it tells us that banks believe the other banks they are lending to have a lower risk of defaulting on the loans, so they are charging a lower rate to reflect this reduced risk.

The LIBOR-OIS spread is considered a better measure of credit risk in the interbank lending market than the LIBOR rate itself, because LIBOR is influenced by the rates set by central banks *and* by the credit risk in lending to other banks. Because the OIS rate is based only on the rates set by central banks (and has nothing to do with credit risk of lending to banks per se), subtracting OIS from LIBOR demonstrates the amount of the rate that is being charged in return for taking on risk.

CHAPTER 18

ALPHABET SOUP: THE BIS, THE IMF, AND THE OECD

"There is no room in your mind for negative thoughts. The busier you keep yourself with the particulars of shot assessment and execution, the less chance your mind has to dwell on the emotional. This is sheer intensity."

—Jack Nicklaus, Champion Golfer, Winner of 73 PGA Tour Events

When it comes to the appropriate mental attitude for trading, take the advice of Jack Nicklaus. The "Golden Bear" advises you to keep your mind on the game, not on emotion. Emotion, either positive or negative, is not your friend when it comes to trading. Keep your mind on your entries, stops, and exits, and tune out the noise of emotion. Focus on things that you can control, like the quality of your setups, and try not to worry about every little uptick and downtick. Don't focus on winning and losing; if you focus on learning all that you can and executing your plans correctly, winning will follow.

We're going to take a look at some of the major institutions in the world of finance. Each of these institutions provides useful information for the Forex trader, information that can help you to place winning trades.

BANK OF INTERNATIONAL SETTLEMENTS

Established in 1930 to monitor financial markets and regulate banks (and to help coordinate the payment of Germany's World War I reparations, in accordance with the Treaty of Versailles), the Bank of International Settlements (BIS) is one of the world's oldest international financial institutions. Based in Basel, Switzerland, with offices in Hong Kong and Mexico City, the BIS could be considered a sort of "bank for central banks."

For example, a central bank can intervene in the Forex markets through the BIS, in order to provide a layer of secrecy—in fact, it is widely suspected that the Swiss National

Bank has used the BIS in this exact manner in the past to weaken the Swiss franc vs. the euro.

The BIS has organized and/or provided emergency financing and support for countries such as Germany and Australia (1931 through 1933), France (1968), Mexico (1982), and Brazil (1998). It has acted as the agent for various European exchange rate arrangements, including the European Monetary System (EMS, 1979–94) which preceded the move to a single European currency. The bank does not accept deposits from, nor provide financial services to, private individuals or corporate entities (no, you can't open an account).

While individual central banks are free to create their own policies, one of the goals of the BIS is to make sure that banks are adequately capitalized. The BIS capital ratio requires that banks maintain a percentage of capital vs. their risk-weighted assets.

What does that really mean? Instead of requiring banks to keep a fixed percentage of capital vs. their assets, the capital requirement is determined by the riskiness of the assets. For example, an unsecured loan would be deemed riskier than a loan that is backed by collateral, so under BIS guidelines, banks that engage in risky lending are forced to maintain a higher percentage of capital than banks with more conservative lending policies.

CONTROVERSY AND CONSPIRACY

The BIS hosts monthly meetings for major central banks and publishes a widely influential annual review of the state of the global banking system. It has a colorful history and is often the centerpiece of elaborate conspiracy theories, usually involving an elaborate plot for world domination by a shadowy group of bankers.

While the merits of these theories are highly debatable, there is no question that some of the original board members had close ties to Adolf Hitler. In another controversy, the bank was nearly liquidated in 1944 after allegations that some members of the BIS assisted the Nazis in looting occupied countries during World War II.

The BIS also compiles a variety of statistics and surveys that are useful to currency traders. The most important of these is the *Triennial Central Bank Survey of Foreign Exchange and Derivatives Market Activity*, simply known to Forex traders as the *BIS survey*.

BIS SURVEY

You often hear about the extremely high volume and liquidity of the Forex market, but where do those statistics originate? Every three years, the BIS surveys the major participants in the Forex market. Central banks and other monetary authorities accumulate the data from their respective territories and provide it to the BIS.

Among other things, the collected information indicates the estimated volume in the spot and futures markets. The number is estimated because it would be incredibly difficult, if not impossible, to keep an accurate count of the actual volume in the FX markets.

The 2007 survey indicates daily turnover of $3.2 trillion USD, an increase of about 71 percent over the 2004 figure. The following statistics are taken from the 2007 BIS survey, which covered 54 central banks and 1,280 financial institutions. By the time you read this book, the 2010 figures will be available, which should serve as an interesting comparison to the earlier surveys.

Here are just a few of the things the survey is telling us:

1. EUR/USD accounts for the most activity by far, as 27 percent of all currency trades occur in that pair. This is why EUR/USD features the tightest spread on most currency trading platforms. USD/JPY is a distant second at 13 percent, and GBP/USD accounts for 12 percent of the action (see Table 18.1).
2. Great Britain clearly holds the title of heavyweight champion of Forex trading, with slightly more than one-third of all Forex trading activity emanating from the United Kingdom (34.1 percent). The United States comes in a distant second, providing 16.6 percent of all Forex trading activity. All of the other countries surveyed registered in single digits (see Table 18.2).
3. Far more transactions occur in the U.S. dollar than in any other currency (hence its status as the world's reserve currency). The euro is the second most actively traded currency, although it is steadily closing the gap on the USD. The statistics in Table 18.3 add up to 200 percent because there are two currencies in every Forex transaction.

TABLE 18.1 BIS Volume Statistics by Currency Pair

Pair	Share
EUR/USD	27%
USD/JPY	13%
GBP/USD	12%
AUD/USD	6%
USD/CHF	5%
USD/CAD	4%
EUR/JPY	2%
EUR/GBP	2%
EUR/CHF	2%
Other	27%
Total	100%

Source: BIS Triennial Survey 2007, www.bis.org.

TABLE 18.2 BIS Volume Statistics by Location

Country	Share
United Kingdom	34.1%
United States	16.6%
Switzerland	6.1%
Japan	6.0%
Singapore	5.8%
Hong Kong	4.4%
Australia	4.3%
France	3.0%
Germany	2.5%
Denmark	2.2%
Other	15.0%
Total	100.0%

Source: BIS Triennial Survey 2007, www.bis.org.

THE IMF AND THE WORLD BANK

The International Monetary Fund or IMF was originally formed in July 1944 in Bretton Woods, New Hampshire, with a stated mission to stabilize exchange rates and assist in the rebuilding of the world's economies in the aftermath of World War II. Like the BIS, the IMF puts out economic statistics and projections that may be helpful to currency traders.

TABLE 18.3 BIS Volume Statistics by Individual Currency

Currency	Share
USD	86.3%
EUR	37.0%
JPY	16.5%
GBP	15.0%
CHF	6.8%
AUD	6.7%
CAD	4.2%
SEK	2.8%
HKD	2.8%
NOK	2.2%
NZD	1.9%
OTHER	17.8%
Total	200%

Source: BIS Triennial Survey 2007, www.bis.org.

At the same time the IMF was formed, another entity called the World Bank was created. Together, these two entities are known as the Bretton Woods Institutions. So what is the difference between the IMF and the World Bank? Here is the explanation given on the IMF web site:

> *The fundamental difference is this: the Bank is primarily a development institution; the IMF is a cooperative institution that seeks to maintain an orderly system of payments and receipts between nations. Each has a different purpose, a distinct structure, receives its funding from different sources.*

Confused? You're not alone. Here's more from the IMF web site:

> *Even John Maynard Keynes, a founding father of the two institutions and considered by many the most brilliant economist of the twentieth century, admitted at the inaugural meeting of the International Monetary Fund that he was confused by the names: he thought the Fund should be called a bank, and the Bank should be called a fund. Confusion has reigned ever since.*

By now you're probably wondering, "How can an understanding of the IMF help a trader to make money?" While the IMF releases many statistics and projections, one that traders watch closely is the World Economic Outlook, or WEO.

Included in the WEO are projections for the rate of annual GDP growth in individual countries. For example, in October 2008, the IMF predicted that Canada would have the highest growth rate of the G7 countries for the year 2009, projected at an annual rate of 1.2 percent. In the same report, the IMF made its steepest reduction in the growth projections for the United Kingdom, which it predicted would contract at 0.1 percent during the year. Italy's growth was projected to be even lower at −0.2 percent, but it is counted as part of the euro area (see Table 18.4).

TABLE 18.4 IMF WEO Growth Projections for 2009, as of Oct. 2008

Country	Growth
Canada	1.2%
Japan	0.5%
Euro Area	0.2%
France	0.2%
United States	0.1%
Germany	0.0%
United Kingdom	−0.1%
Italy	−0.2%

Source: International Monetary Fund.

FIGURE 18.1 After the release of IMF growth projections, the GBP/CAD currency pair reverses course.
Source: Created with TradeStation.

Please keep in mind that the projections released by the IMF, the OECD, and other organizations can have an impact on market sentiment, which in turn can affect the performance of a currency. This impact can occur whether or not the projections are accurate. In this case, a trader who took heed of the IMF's projections and opened a short position in GBP/CAD (short the British pound, long the Canadian dollar) after the release of the report would have been rewarded handsomely (see Figure 18.1).

About one week after the release of the report, GBP/CAD, which had been trending higher, reached its peak near the 2.0700 figure. After meeting heavy resistance in that area for the next two weeks, GBP/CAD took a dive, falling to an area near 1.6700 by January 2009—a drop of about 4,000 pips in just over three months.

Could market sentiment, in part driven by the IMF report, have played a role? Or perhaps the IMF had simply assessed the economic prospects of the two countries correctly. One thing is certain: Those who paid heed to the IMF's World Economic Outlook report came out on top.

The IMF has been criticized at times for supporting oppressive dictatorships. For example, in January 2009, the IMF approved a $2.5 billion loan for the government of Belarus—one of the most oppressive regimes in Europe, and one that retains many Soviet-style economic policies. That same month, the Ethiopian government received a $50 million loan despite its brutal oppression of political opponents. Like the BIS, the IMF is often at the center of various conspiracy theories. It has also become a focal point for the antiglobalization movement.

ORGANIZATION FOR ECONOMIC COOPERATION AND DEVELOPMENT

Based in Paris, France, and formed in 1961, the Organization for Economic Cooperation and Development (OECD) has a stated goal of "bringing together the governments of countries committed to democracy and the market economy." In its original form, it began in 1948 as the Organization for European Economic Co-operation, formed to facilitate the reconstruction of Europe after World War II.

The OECD seeks to support sustainable economic growth and stability, but traders are more interested in the organization's economic growth projections, which are contained in a report called the *OECD Economic Outlook*.

For example, in the third quarter of 2008, the OECD made the projections for the G7 countries shown in Table 18.5.

The OECD projections indicated that Japan would have the strongest growth of the G7 countries during the second half of 2008, with growth of 2.4 percent in Q3 and 1.4 percent in Q4, while Great Britain would give the weakest performance and would likely slide into a recession.

But would the performance of the currencies mirror the OECD's projections? When the OECD updated its projections in early September 2008, the GBP/JPY currency pair was trading at 195.00, and during the months that followed, the Japanese yen mercilessly trounced the Great Britain pound (see Figure 18.2).

But does that necessarily mean that the OECD is a great predictor of future currency movement? Not at all: The descent of GBP/JPY was a result of deleveraging and plunging interest rates in the United Kingdom; as the interest rate differential between GBP and JPY disappeared, the pair lost literally thousands of pips.

TABLE 18.5 GDP Growth* in the G7 Countries

Country	2008 Q3	2008 Q4
Japan	2.4	1.4
United States	0.9	0.7
Canada	0.8	2
G7	0.8	0.7
Euro Area	0.4	0.8
France	0.2	0.6
Germany	0	0.1
Italy	0	0.6
United Kingdom	−0.3	−0.4

*Annualized quarter on quarter growth for the second half of 2008.

Source: Organization for Economic Cooperation and Development.

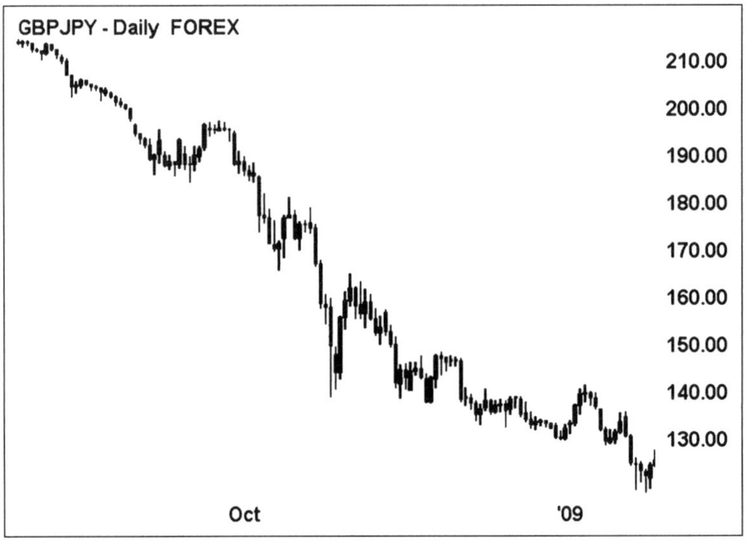

FIGURE 18.2 GBP/JPY falls hard after OECD growth projections favored the yen heavily over the pound.
Source: Created with TradeStation. © TradeStation Technologies, Inc. All rights reserved.

As it turned out, the OECD was way off target in its prediction for Japanese growth, in terms of both performance and ranking. Like most of the G7 countries, Japan experienced contraction in both Q3 and Q4 of 2008 (see Table 18.6).

Still, changes in projections by the OECD have the potential to create short-term market moves. That's why traders pay attention to the OECD, even though their predictions are not always accurate.

TABLE 18.6 OECD's Growth* Projections for Q3, Q4 2008 Prove Inaccurate

Country	2008 Q3	2008 Q4
United States	−2.7	−5.4
Japan	−3.9	−13.1
Euro Area	−1.5	−7.1
Germany	−1.3	−9.4
France	−0.9	−5.5
Italy	−3.1	−8.3
United Kingdom	−2.9	−7.0
Canada	0.4	−3.7
G7	−2.5	−7.3

*Annualized quarter-on-quarter growth.
Source: Organization for Economic Cooperation and Development.

One of the most valuable services provided by the OECD is the calculation of purchasing power parity, which is used by many traders to determine and predict exchange rate valuations. Under the Joint OECD-Eurostat Purchasing Power Parity (PPP) Programme, the OECD and Eurostat share responsibility for calculating PPPs (for more on this topic, please see Chapter 15, "Purchasing Power Parity and the Big Mac Index").

PART V

STAYING IN SHAPE

CHAPTER 19

FOR EVERY WINNER, A LOSER?

"It's easy to have faith in yourself and have discipline when you're a winner, when you're number one. What you got to have is faith and discipline when you're not a winner."

—Vince Lombardi, Pro Football Hall of Fame

In this book, we've explored numerous ways in which the world of sports and the world of trading intersect. The funny thing is, even though there are major similarities between those two worlds, there are some aspects that they do not share.

The parallels between sports and trading do not exist on every level, yet oddly, there is one similarity between sports and trading that does not exist, but that many traders believe exists. Maybe it's time to challenge that belief.

IS FOREX TRADING A ZERO-SUM GAME?

There is a misconception among some traders that every Forex trade must have a winner and a loser, thereby classifying Forex trading as a zero-sum game. So what is a zero-sum game? Any game that has a clear winner, a clear loser, and a finite ending could fall into the category of a zero-sum game.

The game must be finite in order to fit this description; in other words, it must reach a definite conclusion, like a game of football that ends in sudden death overtime, a hockey match that ends in a shootout, or a baseball game that concludes during extra innings.

For example, suppose you place a friendly bet with an acquaintance on the outcome of a football match. Each of you puts up an equal amount of money, let's say $100, and at the end of the game, one of you will walk away with $200 and the other will be $100 poorer.

That is a zero-sum game in its purest sense: Unless the game ends (and it *will end*, which is the key) in a tie, there will be one winner and one loser, and one team will win at the expense of the other. That's the end of the story. In purely competitive circumstances, virtually everything is zero-sum; a boxing match, a horse race, and a quiz show could all fall into this category.

A WINNER AND A LOSER

Now let's apply this concept to the currency market: Since currencies trade in pairs, it's a truism that when one currency wins, the other currency loses. For example, if the EUR/USD currency pair is rising, then the euro is gaining at the expense of the USD: One currency is winning, and the other is losing. This partially fits the description of a zero-sum game.

But that is *very, very different* from the statement that every currency trade has a winner and a loser. In order to challenge that statement, consider the following example.

Suppose you enter a long position in EUR/USD and at the same time, another trader takes a short position in the same currency pair. The broker simply matches the orders and collects the spread.

Does this mean that, just as in the previous scenario, one party has to win and one must lose? And is one trader's win dependent upon the other trader's loss?

Not at all. In fact, in this scenario both traders might win or lose; perhaps one has entered a short-term trade and the other has entered a long-term trade. Unlike the football match, these trades do not conclude after a specified amount of time.

Perhaps the first trader will take a profit quickly, but there is no rule that states the second trader must close his trade at the same time; in other words, there is no finite ending to the game. The result of one trade does not depend upon the result of the other. Later in the day, the price may reverse and the second trader may then take his profit as well.

In this scenario, the broker made money (on the spread) and both traders did too. This contradicts the oft-repeated statement that every Forex trade has a winner and a loser. It is simply not true.

OTHER TRADING SCENARIOS

By the way, stock trading is not a zero-sum game either. Suppose you buy 100 shares of XYZ at $40, and then sell it at $50. Another trader buys it from you at $50 and sells it at $60. Yet another trader buys it at $60 and sells it at $70. Which trader lost money? None of them did; they all made $10 per share.

What about any traders who may have been short XYZ? Although anyone who was short most likely lost money on XYZ in the previous scenario, there is no rule that states that anyone has to short XYZ stock, ever.

Also, it is highly unlikely that there are as many traders short XYZ as there are long, or more precisely, that there are as many shares sold short as there are purchased long, so we can't say that there is a loser for every winner in this scenario.

CLOSER TO ZERO-SUM

What type of trade can be accurately called a zero-sum game? Certain types of options trades come to mind. For example, suppose you purchase some XYZ call options. Where did they come from? In order for you to purchase those calls, someone else has to sell or "write" them.

If the price of XYZ stock reaches the strike price and beyond, the buyer wins, and if the price fails to do so, the seller wins. Also, the option has a definite point of expiration, thus giving us a finite end point for the trade.

While this more closely represents a true zero-sum game, it is clear that not every options trade falls into this category; in fact, either the purchaser or the seller of the calls (or both) could close this trade prior to the expiration date, so the result of one trade is not dependent upon the result of the other. But with the addition of a definitive end point, at least we are getting closer to the true definition of a zero-sum game.

What would be a good example of a zero-sum trade? If two banks enter into an agreement to create a one-touch option, and both sides agree to maintain their position until expiration, then clearly one of them will win and one will lose.

Either the price will or will not reach the strike price, so one bank must win. Whichever bank wins will do so at the expense of the other. You have a definite winner and a definite loser, and one will win at the other's expense. That, plus the fact that the option has an expiration date (representing a finite ending to the game), creates an actual zero-sum scenario.

MULTIPLAYER, INFINITE GAMES

Zero-sum games are games where a win by one player can only result in a loss by the other player; the term has little to no relevance when describing multiplayer infinite games, which is the category under which I would place Forex trading.

In trading, nothing is perfect for a variety of reasons. Certainly, the "game" never ends—it is continuous, thus defeating the specific of zero-sum that relies on calculable iterations for the sake of probability. Additionally, there are always players leaving the game and new money entering, again on a continuous basis.

One more thing to consider—the supply of money in nearly every country fluctuates; it is not fixed. Those who espouse the Forex zero-sum game theory need to explain how there must be a winner and a loser in every currency transaction in a world where an infinite supply of currency can be created from thin air.

I hope that this clears up any misconception of Forex trading as a zero-sum game; while it is true that one currency rises at the expense of another, that alone does not mean that every single Forex trade must have a winner and a loser. I realize that it sounds really cool to say that Forex trading is a zero-sum game, but that alone does not make it so.

CHAPTER 20

SCAM AVOIDANCE TECHNIQUES

"If you really want something in this life, you have to work for it. Now quiet, they're about to announce the lottery numbers!"

—Homer Simpson

It was a beautiful sunny afternoon in Acapulco; the birds were chirping as a tourist went parasailing effortlessly above the beautiful blue bay. I was enjoying the view from the terrace, sorting through e-mail, when I came across something that sounded a sour note on an otherwise perfect day—a letter from a person who had lost money in a scam. The sad part was, the scam was easily identifiable. Let's look at what happened to this trader; maybe from his experience, we can learn how we can avoid a similar fate:

> *Mr. Ponsi, I am very interested in the Forex market. I have some money that I would like to put into an active account but I can't get my demo account to make any money. I started with an automated trading company first. It was supposed to win more than lose. I didn't find that to be true. Then I read some stuff about financial calendars; they listed the times of the news conference but by the time I got to place my trade I had missed the spike. I really don't feel comfortable sinking my money in an account when I can't seem to make play money in the demo account. Can you help me?*

Yes, I can help you—don't do it! If you're not comfortable putting money into an account, then there is a good reason for that discomfort. In your case, the reason seems to be that you haven't learned how to trade yet—and that's the best reason imaginable to stay out of the currency market or any trading market.

Don't rely on automated systems or signal services: They almost always promise more than they deliver. Instead, learn how to make the right trading decisions on your own. You'll find that it is much more rewarding.

Automated trading systems like the one you mentioned tend to be more hype than substance. Because Forex is relatively new to the retail trading public, scammers who make unrealistic promises are becoming a constant nuisance. Here's a good rule of thumb, and it doesn't matter if you're trading stocks, futures, options, or Forex: If anyone promises outlandish returns, don't believe it; it's probably a scam.

For example, the web site for the automated trading program that you purchased claims returns of nearly 500 percent in 2005, nearly 700 percent in 2006, and nearly 1,000 percent in 2007. Just based on these so-called returns, this web site has scam written all over it. If this so-called trading robot were actually that profitable, it would be mentioned on the front page of the *Wall Street Journal* or the *Financial Times*. It would be a topic of discussion on CNBC, Bloomberg, and other financial news media outlets.

A quick glance at the disclaimer page yields yet another huge red flag, waving in the breeze: "No independent party has audited the hypothetical performance contained at this web site." The word "hypothetical" should set alarms ringing, because this means that those supposedly lofty returns from the years 2005, 2006, and 2007 never actually occurred—they are "hypothetical" returns.

This means that the system currently in use would have yielded those results back during those years, *if* it had been in use at that time. But it wasn't used, because if it had been, the returns would be listed as *actual* instead of *hypothetical.*

What the operators of this web site are doing is predicting the past. They have discovered a trading system that *would have* worked during the years in question, if it had been in use. The system probably will not work in the future, because markets are always changing, and the future will be different from the past.

Now, watch me predict the past with astonishing accuracy: I hereby predict that Barack Obama will be elected the 44th president of the United States. I predict that it rained last Tuesday. I predict that the Philadelphia Phillies will win Major League Baseball's 2008 World Series. I can even give you last week's winning lottery number!

If you were to grade me on my predictions of things that have already happened, you'd have to say that I'm very accurate. You'd also have to admit that the information is useless, unless you have somehow acquired the use of a time machine. *Hypothetical* returns are the backbone of many trading scams, so search every page of the web site, especially the disclaimer, for that word. The web site's operators are hoping that you will be so excited by your desire to receive big money without effort that you will be negligent in the performance of your due diligence.

Here is another red flag, in the form of a quote from the web site's home page: "Also you can be an absolute newbie to use our system—you don't have to know *anything* about trading and you don't have to have ANY experience." One thing stands out here: The promise of easy money with little or no effort.

Ask any real trader and he or she will tell you that trading is not an easy job, but the public can be easily led to believe that it's all very simple, and that no real effort is required. Even though deep down we should know that this is a false promise, much like fictional FBI agent Fox Mulder of the old television show *The X Files*, we *want to believe.*

This is what makes the scam so effective: Our desire for easy money is so strong that we are willing to suspend our disbelief. Scams of this nature are meant to appeal to the public's sense of greed. The promise of easy money is a hallmark of all scams, not just scams that are focused on trading.

DISHONEST FROM THE WORD "GO"

One day I was searching the web site of a popular financial news channel to check out my latest live TV appearance. I typed my name into the web site's search engine, and along with dozens of video clips I noticed several advertisements that mentioned my name. One of them read: "Ed Ponsi Recommended Forex Software! Proven Forex Software Doubles Money! 30K in 90 Days! See Video Here!"

I thought this was odd, since (1) I'd never heard of the company before, and (2) I have never recommended any Forex trading software.

Now think about this carefully, because so many of you have asked me about these "robots" and other forms of trading software. I firmly believe that the only people who make money with Forex robots are the people who create and sell them to an unsuspecting public. I don't recommend any Forex robots or any other automated trading system. They are the biggest scam in Forex today.

I hope that wasn't too ambiguous. Now that you know that I don't recommend them, what do you think of the people who claim that I do? When someone tells you they are selling Ed Ponsi Recommended Forex Software, they are lying. When you read the ad, their very first communication with you was a lie. If someone tells a lie to you right from the start, will you ever believe anything else that they tell you?

I've written about these scams numerous times in various articles, and it really upsets the scammers when I expose their methods for stealing people's hard-earned money. I'm sure this chapter will upset many of them as well. That's fine with me. People deserve to know the truth, and if some scammers get exposed in the process, well, that's too bad.

Besides, if by some chance their lousy robots actually worked, then they'd have plenty of money, so don't shed any tears on their behalf. Of course, if that were the case, they wouldn't have to lie about the robots, now would they? If they're telling the truth, then they're rich beyond their wildest dreams, just like the riches they are promising to you.

One day I received an e-mail from a person who seemed to be legitimate and seemed genuinely upset with something I had written. It began: "Ed, I think you are misleading people about these Forex robots."

The writer went on to say that he was making tons of money with his Forex robot, and it was the best thing that ever happened to him, and so on. I really felt bad about this: What if I really had given an unfair impression about Forex robots? What if there were actually good ones out there, and I had tarred them all with the same brush?

I consented to an e-mail dialogue with this person, and in subsequent e-mails, he kept extolling the virtues of this amazing, wonderful Forex robot. He also started to use an inordinate number of exclamation points in his writing: ". . . and I am making hundreds of pips every day!!! And I don't even understand how the Forex market works!!! I just let the robot do all the work!!!"

It all sounded so wonderful, so very easy, and so . . . familiar.

So I did a little background research on this person. It wasn't hard; I just entered his name into a search engine, which led me to a few business networking web sites. As it turns out, the gentleman was involved in computer programming and software development.

As I dug deeper, I learned that he was in fact the developer of not one, but several Forex robots. That's right—he was a developer of Forex robots, pretending to be an ordinary, concerned citizen. Not exactly a shocking surprise.

Let's focus on the part about multiple robots. It turns out that many of these scams consist of more than one robot product; the scammer is hoping that after you lose money on his first robot, you'll be willing to try another one. You might think that you're using a "different" robot, and perhaps you are, but often it is created by the same person who lost your money on the last robot. There will be no indication that the robots are related.

I also visited a web site at his insistence and learned that all of the wonderful returns—the returns that had inspired him to write so many exclamation points—had occurred in a demo account. In other words, the returns were hypothetical. Again, not a big shock.

He had even gone to the trouble of creating a Forex robot "review" web site. Of course, the web site did not present actual reviews; it was just an advertisement, masquerading as a place to learn about Forex robots. He had mimicked the style of other popular Forex review web sites, but in reality, it was nothing but an advertisement for his products.

Clearly he was trying to convince me that his robot was wonderful in the hopes that I would spread the word—a bit of free advertising for his business! Too bad that his business consists of taking money from people who "want to believe."

SUMMARY

Ralph Kramden. Homer Simpson. George Costanza. For decades, one of the staples of television entertainment has been the lovable loser, the person who always seems to be hatching some crazy get-rich-quick scheme. The result is always the same: Every episode ends with the scheme blowing up in our protagonist's face.

While we may find it entertaining to watch these fictional personalities in action, we don't want to *be* that person. It's been said that when opportunity knocks, it is often disguised as hard work. Well, when a scam comes knocking, it is often disguised as easy money. Real trading is hard work, but it can be enormously rewarding if you are willing to do what it takes to learn the business.

Why do I find these scams so irritating? Because innocent people who have a legitimate interest in learning how to trade are being taken advantage of, and because it sullies the reputation of the good guys that are out there. I hope this chapter has been helpful. Let's be careful out there!

CHAPTER 21

FIRE THE MANAGER!

"Even Napoleon had his Watergate."

—Danny Ozark, Former Philadelphia Phillies Manager

As mentioned earlier, the current U.S. Federal Reserve was created in 1913. Interestingly, this was not the first attempt to create a central bank in the United States. The early history of the United States featured several failed attempts, and the entire concept of a central bank was bitterly opposed by some of the U.S. founding fathers, especially Thomas Jefferson.

> "The central bank is an institution of the most deadly hostility existing against the Principles and form of our Constitution. I am an Enemy to all banks discounting bills or notes for anything but Coin. If the American People allow private banks to control the issuance of their currency, first by inflation and then by deflation, the banks and corporations that will grow up around them will deprive the People of all their Property until their Children will wake up homeless on the continent their Fathers conquered."
>
> *—Thomas Jefferson, 3rd President of the United States, Principal Author of the U.S. Declaration of Independence*

Baseball fans love to debate questions like the following: "Which was the greatest baseball team of all time?" Personally, I don't care for these types of discussions, because it's difficult to compare players who lived during different eras and played under different rules and against an uneven quality of opponents. For example, can you really compare a home run hitter during the steroid era to one who played during the dead-ball era? In situations like these, it's hard to make a fair comparison.

However, no matter which baseball team you believe to be the greatest of all time, there is one team that cannot be excluded from any such discussion—the 1927 New York Yankees. Boasting a win-loss record of 110–44, a team batting average of .307, and featuring all-time legendary players such as Babe Ruth and Lou Gehrig, the team is still popularly known by its nickname, the "Murderer's Row."

Six players on the team were eventually inducted into the Baseball Hall of Fame, along with manager Miller Huggins. In all, Huggins won six American League pennants and three World Series championships with the Yankees.

But the question remains, does this mean that Huggins was a great manager, or was he merely fortunate to manage some of the greatest players of all time? After all, even if Huggins was a truly great manager, there are still those who will ask the question: Did his teams win because of him, or did he win because he had such great players?

I'll leave the answer to that question to the pundits. But there is a point to this discussion: If the U.S. dollar is still the world's reserve currency, thereby making it the 1927 Yankees of the currency world, does the central bank of the United States, the Federal Reserve, deserve credit? Just as we can debate the importance of baseball manager Huggins to the dominance of the 1927 Yankees, is the "manager" of the currency responsible for the performance of the U.S. dollar?

Or is it possible that the dominance of the greenback is not enhanced, but actually threatened, by the Fed, in the same way that an incompetent manager can undermine a team of great players? To answer this question, let's take a very brief and hopefully somewhat amusing look at the recent history of the central bank of the United States, the U.S. Federal Reserve.

THE FED RIDES TO THE RESCUE!

The recent case against the Fed goes something like this: In 1999, due to the fear of a potential computer calamity that would lead to an economic meltdown (popularly known at the time as the "Y2K" phenomenon), the Fed charged to the rescue and pumped liquidity into the banking system.

The fears of a computer-based meltdown never materialized, but when you pump a banking system full of money, funny things can happen. This is due to the fact that once you inject money into the banks, it is difficult, if not impossible, to control where that money goes next.

Apparently, much of the money that was pumped into the banks found its way into speculative U.S. stocks, leading to a gain of about 85 percent of the NASDAQ index in

1999. That's right, the entire index nearly doubled in one year, and when the tech stock bubble finally burst in 2001, the U.S. economy went into a tailspin.

In an effort to clean up the ensuing economic mess, the Fed came charging to the rescue once again—this time, cutting the Fed Funds rate to 1 percent—which at the time was considered a historic low. The low rates endorsed by the Fed had the desired effect of stimulating the economy, but there was an unwanted side effect—a housing bubble was created.

Low mortgage rates caused home buyers to bid the prices of houses to unsustainable levels—exactly the same behavior that had driven the NASDAQ bubble just a few years earlier. When the housing market inevitably crashed, it took the U.S. economy down with it. You'll never guess who came riding to the rescue next!

HERE I COME TO SAVE THE DAY!

That's right, after wrecking the U.S. economy twice in less than a decade, the Fed was back to save us from ourselves once again, this time cutting rates to new historic lows. The Fed Funds rate was actually reduced to zero—well, not officially. Instead, the Fed designated that the new rate was a target of between zero and 0.25 percent. I'm guessing that the purpose of this new method of explaining the Fed Funds rate was enacted to create the illusion that the Fed still had room to cut the Fed Funds rate, if they really wanted to.

As of this writing, we still don't know what the consequences of this latest Fed rescue will be. Will the massive injections of liquidity and incredibly low rates lead to an explosion of inflation? Will the next bubble be in commodities prices? Will the U.S. dollar crash in a spectacular manner, similar to the German mark in the Weimar Republic during the 1920s or the Zimbabwe dollar in 2008?

I hope not. We're all waiting to find the answer, but in the meantime, as an American citizen I have just one humble request of the U.S. Federal Reserve: Please stop rescuing us!

ADDING INSULT TO INJURY

The credit crisis of 2008–2009 resulted in a dramatic expansion of the Fed's powers, its responsibilities, and its balance sheet. As if all of this weren't bad enough, the U.S. Federal Reserve then added insult to injury by requesting greater powers. The rationale for this naked power grab was that an enhanced Fed would have greater capability to rescue the U.S. economy should it once again spin out of control.

This conveniently ignores the fact that the Fed is in fact the source of, not the solution to, economic chaos in the United States. I have to stop writing now, as the effect of recounting all of this to you is somewhat deleterious. And by that I mean my head is about to explode.

A WORLD SERIES LESSON

> "Half this game is 90% mental."
>
> —*Yogi Berra, Baseball Hall of Fame, 3-time Most Valuable Player*

In 1979, the Philadelphia Phillies were riding high. Under the guidance of manager Danny Ozark, they had qualified for the playoffs for three consecutive years—each time falling just short of qualifying for Major League Baseball's World Series. During two of those seasons, the "Fightin' Phils" won over 100 games of their 162 games—a symbol of excellence in Major League Baseball.

The Phillies boasted one of the most formidable lineups in the league, featuring future Hall of Famers Mike Schmidt and Steve Carlton. Only a few years earlier, the team had been the doormat of the league, and now, under Ozark, the Phillies had achieved respectability.

The addition of superstar Pete Rose seemed to seal the deal, as the Phils were favored to win the division for a fourth consecutive season in 1979. But the team underperformed, and then Ozark was fired as manager. Perhaps Ozark himself put it best in the famous quote at the beginning of this chapter, a quote that is often incorrectly attributed to the great New York Yankee catcher and philosopher, Yogi Berra.

What were the Phillies thinking? Ozark had brought them from the dregs of the league to the edge of the Promised Land, and he was unceremoniously dumped in favor of Dallas Green, who was named interim manager for the final month of the season. Green was a blunt man, a former pitcher who had no previous experience as a manager in the big leagues. On the surface, the switch from Ozark to Green seemed perplexing at best.

And what was the result of this switch? During his first full season as manager, Green and the Phillies became Major League Baseball's 1980 World Series Champions. This was a goal that had eluded the Phils not just under Ozark, but for the team's entire history, dating back to 1883. Many observers believe that despite their accomplishments, Ozark's teams had underachieved, having failed to win championships despite the presence of Schmidt and Carlton.

The point is, even though Ozark had done a formidable job, the team needed to make the change in order to finally win the World Series. But if a baseball team can replace their manager and win a championship, can the American people replace the Fed and save their currency? That's an idea that probably hasn't occurred to most of us, yet it is plausible. In fact, there is some question as to whether the Fed, the central bank of the United States, should exist at all.

IS THE FED LEGAL?

There are those who believe that the U.S. Federal Reserve, which was created in 1913, is actually illegal according to the laws of the United States. The basis for this argument lies in Article 1, Section 8 of the U.S. Constitution, which states that only Congress has the authority to create and regulate the value of money.

There is also the issue of a 1935 Supreme Court ruling. That ruling states that Congress cannot constitutionally delegate this power to another group, and implies that Congress does not have the authority to create or bestow power upon a central bank.

Influential U.S. politicians like Ron Paul have argued for the abolishment of the Fed on constitutional grounds. On June 15, 2007, Paul (R–Texas) introduced HR 2755, the Federal Reserve Abolition Act. The stated purpose of this bill was "To abolish the Board of Governors of the Federal Reserve System and the Federal Reserve Banks, to repeal the Federal Reserve Act, and for other purposes."

But the bill never made it past the introductory phase and was never put to a vote in the U.S. Senate or the U.S. House of Representatives. Dr. Paul's book, succinctly titled *End the Fed* (Grand Central Publishing, 2009), makes a compelling argument for the dissolution of the U.S. Federal Reserve.

One thing is certain: The U.S Federal Reserve is one of the most powerful entities on earth, and as a result of its recent bumbling, it is likely to become even more powerful. It reminds me of a quote from one of the less-heralded presidents of the United States, James A. Garfield.

> "He who controls the money supply of a nation controls the nation."
>
> —*James A. Garfield, 20th President of the United States*

AFTERWORD

I awoke in Singapore, half a world from home. It was going to be a busy day, the second day of my sold-out seminar. I studied my notes and made my way to the TV studio for a live appearance that would be seen all over Asia.

I left the television studio after the 90-minute interview and hopped a taxi back to the hotel where a packed audience waited in the auditorium. As the speakers blasted "Rock You Like a Hurricane," I took the stage. The connection was immediate, the energy fantastic. The audience responded enthusiastically, granting several standing ovations.

Within the next 48 hours, I would make three more TV appearances and give one interview to a magazine. I wanted to sleep but went to a party instead, thrown by a good friend at one of the networks. As luck would have it, central bank officials from the United States and Europe were also there. I sipped a cold Heineken and shared a laugh with the U.S. central banker on the porch, while the European central banker ironically strummed "Brother, Can You Spare a Dime?" on the guitar in the parlor.

Could this really be my life?

The story of this book is literally a journey. I began working on it under the eerie pink skies of Mexico City, not far from Diego Rivera's studio, and on a balcony overlooking the beach in Acapulco. As I finish now, on the last day of 2009, I'm sitting on a rooftop deck on the side of a mountain in Brazil, in a small town just outside Rio de Janeiro. From my protected perch, I can see storms rolling toward me through a green valley, a surreal sight indeed. Tonight, it will be *picanha*, *cerveja*, and guitars.

Along the way, parts of this book were written in such far-flung locales as Dubai, Singapore, London, and even in the Tokyo airport during a particularly long flight delay. Countless hours were spent in coffee shops in and around New York City, sipping hot java and banging the keys.

I hope this book answered many of your questions. I do see your questions piling up in my e-mail, and I try to read most of them. I'm humbled by the fact that so many of you have sought my advice. Unfortunately, if I answered all of you individually, there would be literally no time to do anything else! So, please accept my apologies, as the growing volume of questions has made answering them difficult.

I hope you appreciate the fact that this book was not one long sales pitch, as so many books on trading seem to be these days. I realize there were several references to my first book, but that was out of necessity: I really want you to understand my trading tactics and philosophy, and the two books in combination should help clarify my position and solidify your knowledge.

I'd like to ask a favor of you—let me know what you want. How can my company, FXEducator.com, be of better service to you? For example, should we create a new DVD series? You've purchased thousands of copies of the FXEducator DVD series, and your feedback has been awesome. Or would you be more interested in live training events? We are considering a series of small (no more than 20 attendees) live training events, featuring personal instruction, in various locations. You can contact me through my web sites, www.fxeducator.com and www.edponsi.com, and let me know if that's something you'd like.

If you wish, you can also follow me on the social networking web sites Facebook and Twitter (http://twitter.com/edponsi). I'll be posting links to my TV appearances as well as keeping you informed on upcoming events and appearances.

In closing, I'd just like to say thanks. Your overwhelmingly positive response to my work is the reason why it continues.

ABOUT THE AUTHOR

Ed Ponsi is the president of FXEducator.com. As an experienced professional trader, he has advised hedge funds, institutional traders, and individuals of all levels of skill and experience. Ed has made numerous television appearances on CNBC, CNN, the BBC, Fox, Bloomberg, and ForexTV, and has been profiled in magazines such as *Technical Analysis of Stocks & Commodities* and *Trader's Journal.* His dynamic and humorous style sets him apart from the "suit and tie crowd." Ed is the author of *Forex Patterns and Probabilities*, a top-selling book on currency trading. Ed's popular DVD series, *FXEducator: Forex Trading with Ed Ponsi* is now available at www.fxeducator.com and www.edponsi.com.

INDEX